'MY DEAR MISS RANSOM...'

# 'My dear Miss Ransom...'

Letters between Caroline Ransom Williams
and James Henry Breasted, 1898-1935

edited by

Kathleen L. Sheppard

Archaeopress Publishing Ltd
Gordon House
276 Banbury Road
Oxford OX2 7ED
www.archaeopress.com

# Archaeological Lives

ISBN 978 1 78491 782 1
ISBN 978 1 78491 783 8 (e-Pdf)

Printed in England by Oxuniprint, Oxford

This book is available direct from Archaeopress or from our website www.archaeopress.com

To Dad, thank you for everything

CAROLINE RANSOM WILLIAMS, 1908. ORIGINALLY PUBLISHED IN THE
1908 BRYN MAWR COLLEGE YEARBOOK, SCANNED AND DISPLAYED
HTTP://WWW.BRYNMAWR.EDU/LIBRARY/EXHIBITS/BREAKINGGROUND/
DEPTHISTORY.HTML BREAKING GROUND, BREAKING TRADITION, BRYN
MAWR COLLEGE, PUBLIC DOMAIN

# Contents

# List of illustrations

Cover: Epigraphic Survey Staff Photo, 1926-1927, Courtesy of the Oriental Institute of the University of Chicago. Ransom Williams, second from left in the second row from top; Breasted seated in middle, third row from top.

Frontispiece: Caroline Ransom Williams, 1908, Originally published in the 1908 Bryn Mawr College Yearbook, scanned and displayed http://www.brynmawr.edu/library/exhibits/BreakingGround/depthistory.html Breaking Ground, Breaking Tradition, Bryn Mawr College, Public Domain

Figure 1: CRW to JHB, 10 June 1913, Letter 0043, Courtesy Oriental Institute Archives, University of Chicago. nsw, or king

Figure 2: CRW to JHB, 10 June 1913, Letter 0043, Courtesy Oriental Institute Archives, University of Chicago. qn or ḳn, meaning might or powerful

Figure 3: CRW to JHB, 23 November 1923, Letter 0140, Courtesy Oriental Institute Archives, University of Chicago. Harhotep

Figure 4: Bookplate from a book donated to the MMA's Egyptian Art Department by Ransom Williams. Courtesy Charles Jones, Ancient World Bloggers Group. http://ancientworldbloggers.blogspot.com/2008/08/bookplates-of-scholars-in-ancient.html

Figure 5: CRW to JHB, 17 April 1932, Letter 0207, Courtesy Oriental Institute Archives, University of Chicago.

Figure 6: CRW to JHB, 17 April 1932, Letter 0207, Courtesy Oriental Institute Archives, University of Chicago.

Figure 7: CRW to JHB, 25 November 1934, Letter 0231, Courtesy Oriental Institute Archives, University of Chicago.

Figure 8: CRW to JHB, 25 November 1934, Letter 0231, Courtesy Oriental Institute Archives, University of Chicago.

Figure 9: CRW to JHB, 25 November 1934, Letter 0231, Courtesy Oriental Institute Archives, University of Chicago.

# Acknowledgements

I would like to thank the Department of History and Political Science at Missouri S&T for generous funding and support during this project. I had to travel to Chicago on multiple occasions to complete the data gathering part of this book and my home department provided the financial and professional support for that. The University of Missouri Research Board generously funded part of this research, as well. While I relied on countless people for their support and expertise, any mistakes are my own.

Thank you to everyone who has answered the seemingly endless barrage of questions I have asked about Ransom Williams, Breasted, the Oriental Institute, the Metropolitan Museum, and more. When I look for someone who is difficult to find, I lean on people at various institutions: librarians at Bryn Mawr and Mount Holyoke who were just as baffled about some citations as I was; JoAnn Creviston at the at the Registrar's Office at the University of Chicago; the wonderful editors of the John Tyndall Correspondence Project for allowing me to use and follow the conventions they have developed; the Curatorial staff, especially Dr. Catharine Roehrig, in the Egyptian Art department at the MMA allowed me to search through their archives for two weeks on short notice; the librarians at my home university, Missouri S&T, have never failed to be helpful and cheerful while I consistently bring books back late while asking for more and more interlibrary loans.

Thank you also to the kind librarians and support staff at the Oriental Institute at the University of Chicago. They are always welcoming when I arrive for however long or short I stay. Anne Flannery and Foy Scalf helped with the finishing details of the work contained here and I am grateful they are so kind. To John Larson, the previous archivist at the Oriental Institute, thanks go to you especially for your generous aid in finding documents, your deep and broad knowledge of the institution and people who have worked there, and for encouraging and supporting this volume; this volume would not have been possible without your work and support.

Thanks to Sarah Ketchley, Director of the Emma Andrews Diary Project, for sharing research tips and tricks; Leila McNeill and Anna Reser, the editors of *Lady Science*, for allowing me my first publication about Ransom Williams and for writing about women who have been, but should not be, left out of the narrative; Julia Roberts, Ulf Hansson, James Snead, and Jonathan Trigg of HARN who have been an amazing support network and lovely to work with; Julie Jonsson, a friend who has an impact on my work always; Lynnette Regouby who asks all the questions I never think of; and, as always, my former PhD adviser and current mentor, Katherine Pandora, who continues to give me the confidence to keep working and writing.

Dan McDonald has given me love, encouragement, support, and time to write; and Miles, our son, who has given us so much joy throughout each day, thank you for being you and being mine.

My father, Lawrence Sheppard, passed away during the final stages of this book, and it is to him, his enthusiastic support, and his memory that I dedicate this book.

# Editorial principles

This volume contains 239 letters between James Henry Breasted and Caroline Ransom Williams kept at the Oriental Institute Archives at the University of Chicago. My aim was to transcribe all of correspondence between them in order to introduce Ransom Williams' scientific life. I have lightly edited the text and heavily noted the content.

Ransom Williams wrote letters to other staff at the Oriental Institute during times when Breasted was in the field. She wrote to Charles Breasted, T. George Allen, Harold Nelson, and others, but I chose not to include those letters. Instead, this volume presents all of the existing letters between Breasted and Ransom Williams in order to preserve their narrative and demonstrate their relationship. There are two letters (0007 and 0010) from Ransom Williams to Frances Hart Breasted, James' wife, included here as it is assumed he would have read those letters. There are two letters to Charles Breasted concerning the death of James (0241 and 0242). I also included nine letters in the appendix, as they dealt with a publication issue for which Ransom Williams went to Breasted for advice.

## Organization and Structure of Letters

The letters are presented in chronological order. There are a few letters that were written on the same day, so I tried to put those in the correct order; there are other letters where the date on the original letter is a typo, and I have noted those instances in the text. Some letters are long, spanning 5 pages in the original. Others are one-line telegrams. I have artificially formatted each letter for uniformity and ease of reading. Datelines and letterheads as well as closings and signatures have been formatted to save space. All new paragraphs have been indented.

Each letter has its own header, which includes a standardized date format and a number, starting at 0001. The letterhead, date, and other information about where the letter came from is included in the letter's own dateline. In general, I have not included the addressee's information, because the letters are only between Breasted and Ransom Williams, so the addressee's information is implied.

## Spelling and Abbreviations

All of Breasted's letters to Ransom Williams were typed, in order to provide a carbon copy for his files. Most of Ransom Williams' letters were handwritten in the early years, then typed later on. While I have not noted which ones were written in which format, I have kept spelling and grammatical errors in the hand-written letters, marked with [sic], but I have silently fixed those errors in the typed letters. Since Breasted's letters were typed, his signature is implied but missing or rubber stamped, therefore I have included his initials: JHB. As much as I could, I kept the original spelling of their words. For example, in the early twentieth century, many words beginning with an I or an E such as inclose or enclose were transposable; I have maintained the original spellings throughout. In a few, but not many, letters, Breasted's secretary made notes about what he did with Ransom Williams' letters— where the letters should be filed, when letters were answered, and more. I did not include this information because it was more administrative during the time the letters were being handled and did not add to the narrative.

When hieroglyphics are included, I have included the original image of the symbol in the letter, to maintain the integrity of the meaning.

Words or letters missing because they have been destroyed or are not recoverable due to holes or glue attaching pages will be noted, e.g. *<words missing>*. This notation is used by the John Tyndall Correspondence Project and the Darwin Correspondence Project.[1] Words that are missing or difficult to read in the original text, but that I have been able to decipher to the best of my ability, are noted with italicized brackets, e.g. *[come together]*.

## Notes

Part of the point of collections of correspondence is not only to tell the story of a career through letters, but also to include the social, political,

---

[1]  See, for example, James Elwick, Bernard Lightman, and Michael S. Reidy (eds), *The Correspondence of John Tyndall* (London: Pickering & Chatto, 2014; Pittsburgh: University of Pittsburgh Press, forthcoming volumes).

and scientific context within which these people were operating. I tried to be as thorough as possible, detailing Ransom Williams' life and work in the footnotes included with the letters. Because both Ransom Williams and Breasted were top scholars in their field, they knew many of the same people and a lot of scholars from around the world made their appearance, however briefly, in their written discussions. I tried to find and introduce as many as I could. Any biographical information presented in the notes is from the 4th Revised Edition of *Who Was Who in Egyptology*, unless otherwise stated.[2]

I call Ransom Williams by her married name throughout the notes, even in the notes attached to her letters before she was married. This is for uniformity. However, in her citations, I use her name as she originally published. That is, she published under Caroline L. Ransom before she got married and Caroline Ransom Williams after. When discussing Ransom Williams and Breasted in the notes, including citations of their work, many times I have abbreviated their names: CLR or CRW and JHB, respectively.

I also abbreviate a few organizations:
EES: Egypt Exploration Society
MMA: Metropolitan Museum of Art
NYHS: New York Historical Society
OI: Oriental Institute (University of Chicago)

I used the original transliteration of Egyptian words in the original letters, but corrected them to present consensus in notes, where possible.

When information is gathered from websites, I have generally not included those citations in the Works Cited information in the back matter. A few exceptions are biographies from *Breaking Ground: Women in Old World Archaeology* and some of the Oriental Institute Museum Publications.

---

[2] Morris L. Bierbrier, *Who was Who in Egyptology*, 4th Revised Edition (London: The Egypt Exploration Society, 2012).

# Preface

It is easy to get lost, especially when your letters and stories are unbound and buried in an archive. Unless someone is willing to discover and make discoverable the correspondence and bits of text that make up part of a life, then this information, though safe, Is temporarily struck from the record. One of the reasons that this collection of Caroline Ransom Williams' correspondence with James Henry Breasted is so poignant, is that it makes readable an intellectual relationship that is not widely known.

The letters that Dr. Kathleen Sheppard has assembled here present many points of interest to the reader. Much could be written about Caroline Ransom Williams' singularity as a woman and a scholar of her time, but what is striking about her letters with Breasted—unearthed from the Oriental Institute's Museum Archives—is how deftly they intertwine intellectual curiosity with charismatic observations and inquiries into everyday life. Her life was restricted in many ways by circumstance, but she was unstoppable in her scientific pursuits. These letters reveal a personality that grounds her scholarship, friendships, and domestic life in an intelligent and heartfelt devotion.

The enthusiasm and relative consistency with which Breasted and Ransom Williams write to each other creates a rhythm both formal and familiar. The reader notices this rhythm in the progression of her salutations, which begin with "Sir" and move through several incarnations before settling on the jovial "Professor Breasted." Their friendship of 37 years is apparent in their mutual commiseration on publications, the complexities of epigraphy, among other questions of the day. And yet, nowhere is its emotional resonance felt more acutely than when Ransom Williams writes to Charles Breasted upon learning of her friend's death in 1935:

I am grieving with you and all the members of Dr. Breasted's family. To me, too, the loss is irreparable and I feel it keenly. I never had a truer, kinder, more helpful friend than your father had always been to me from the time in 1898 when I first became his pupil.

The publication of these letters is significant for the Oriental Institute's Museum Archives in that it sheds more light on the history of scholarship in the field of Egyptology, as well as the history of the Oriental Institute. Without biographic studies and transcription projects such as this one, people and places that contributed in no small part to the work of the Institute would remain hidden safely away. A collection such as this is a step toward making the historical record legible, a task at the heart of the Oriental Institute's mission.

Anne Flannery
The Oriental Institute Museum Archives
Chicago, IL

# Biographical introduction

This volume tells one small part of a scientific life in the history of archaeology. Caroline Louise Ransom Williams was a central figure in the history of American Egyptology, archaeology, and women's education. Her mentor was James Henry Breasted, well-known as the first American Egyptologist and founder of the Oriental Institute at the University of Chicago. There have been a number of scholarly and popular works about Breasted, the Oriental Institute, and the continuing important work it does in Egypt and the Near East.[1] Breasted is usually included in disciplinary histories as well. Conversely, Ransom Williams is little more than a footnote in the published history of archaeology.[2] She is also hard to find in archives, which is unfortunate because her life and work bring an important perspective to the early days of Egyptology and Egyptian archaeology in the US. The aim of this volume is to introduce Ransom Williams, to begin to tell her story, and to demonstrate the impact she had on the discipline by presenting all of the letters between her and Breasted that are kept in the archives at the Oriental Institute at the University of Chicago. The Oriental Institute holds Breasted's correspondence with scholars from around the

---

[1] A few examples: Charles Breasted, *Pioneer to the Past: The Story of James Henry Breasted, Archaeologist, Told by His Son Charles Breasted* (New York: Charles Scribner's Sons, 1943; Reprint edition, Chicago: University of Chicago Press, 2009); Jeffrey Abt, *American Egyptologist: The Life of James Henry Breasted and The Creation of His Oriental Institute* (Chicago: University of Chicago Press, 2012); and Geoff Emberling (ed.), *Pioneers to the Past: American Archaeologists in the Middle East, 1919-1920*, Oriental Institute Museum Publications, 30 (Chicago: The Oriental Institute, 2010).

[2] C. Breasted, *Pioneer to the Past*, 321n; Abt, *American Egyptologist*, 292, 365, 391; and Jason Thompson, *Wonderful Things: A History of Egyptology, Volume 2: The Golden Age: 1881-1914* (Cairo: The American University in Cairo Press, 2015), 240-42. The only biographical account available is Barbara S. Lesko, 'Caroline Louis Ransom Williams, 1872-1952,' in *Breaking Ground: Women in Old World Archaeology*, ed. Martha Sharp Joukowsky and Barbara Lesko, http://www.brown.edu/Research/Breaking_Ground/bios/Ransom%20Williams_Caroline%20Louise.pdf (accessed 22 December 2016).

world from the early 1880s until his death in 1935. The 239 letters between Breasted and Ransom Williams' can be found within the folders of collected correspondence during these years, among correspondents from around the world.

In the history of archaeology, it was the men who went out into the heroic, exciting, exotic field to dig in the dirt and make fascinating discoveries while women usually stayed back in institutions—museums, universities, archives, professional societies—to do the administrative duties for the men while they were far away. Because of this, men usually get credit for much of the scientific work while women get left out of the story. It is by telling the stories of the women in the domesticated spaces that we learn the whole story of a discipline. These points are not new, but they are important to repeat here.[3] Women worked in archaeology and they were important to maintaining the stability of the discipline as well as using innovative methods and theories to make important strides in understanding the ancient world. Ransom Williams was part of a larger cohort of scientific women whose lives may not have left a record like hers did. Her story is therefore central to studying the development of the discipline of Egyptology and archaeology in the United States, and it is through the letters in this volume that we glimpse a life that is unique while at the same time analogous to the lives of other professional women in the period.

Caroline Louise Ransom was born in Toledo, Ohio, on February 24, 1872. Her parents, Agnes (Ella) Randolph and John Ransom, were

---

[3] For women in archaeology, see Getzel M. Cohen and Martha Sharp Joukowsky's pivotal volume *Breaking Ground: Pioneering Women Archaeologists* (Ann Arbor: University of Michigan Press, 2004). It has a number of short biographies of women who worked in the field, but tend not to discuss women in home institutions. The project continues on the website, *Breaking Ground: Women in Old World Archaeology,* and includes short biographies of many women in the discipline, including the one biography of CRW. See http://www.brown.edu/Research/ Breaking_Ground/introduction.php (accessed 22 December 2016). There are many good volumes to choose from that discuss women in domesticated spaces, but important works in the history of American women in science are, especially, Margaret Rossiter, *Women Scientists in America: Struggles and Strategies to 1940* (Baltimore: Johns Hopkins University Press, 1982); *Women Scientists in America: Before Affirmative Action, 1940-1972* (Baltimore: Johns Hopkins University Press, 1995); *Women Scientists in America: Forging a New World Since 1972* (Baltimore: Johns Hopkins University Press, 2012).

prominent in their community and relatively comfortable financially. As a young girl living in late-nineteenth century America, in a larger city like Toledo, she probably went to a coeducational primary and secondary school.[4] In 1890 she attended Lake Erie Seminary (now Lake Erie College), a women's college in Painesville, Ohio, not far from home, for one semester. From 1890-92 she joined her aunt, Louise Fitz-Randolph, who was an art history professor at Mount Holyoke Seminary (College as of 1893), on a European Grand Tour trip. This type of trip was a popular rite-of-passage for well-to-do Europeans and Americans to take in the late-nineteenth and early-twentieth century, usually before they entered university. Itineraries typically included London, Paris, Venice, and Rome, but sometimes the trips would extend into Egypt; Ransom's did.[5] I have not been able to find many details about her trip, except what she mentioned in the following letters, but it is clear that she was inspired by her time in Europe and Egypt to study the ancient world and its art.

Upon their return home, Ransom went to study at Mount Holyoke. It was likely that her aunt's presence there was a deciding factor for her parents allowing her to go to school so far away. She graduated with a Bachelor's degree in Art History (Phi Beta Kappa) from Mount Holyoke in 1896, and then went home to Ohio to teach at Lake Erie Seminary for a year. Using her art history training, she made what she called 'a very exhaustive study of all works upon Egypt within my reach' in order to give lectures at evening classes.[6] She continued to study on her own time, and in August of 1897 gave a lecture on 'The Egyptian Doctrine of the Future Life as influencing the Architecture of the Tombs' at 'the Museum' in Chautauqua, New York.[7] This work made her realize, she wrote to Breasted in 1898, 'that to study in a scientific manner this earlier national art, I need a more intimate acquaintance with other aspects of the ancient Egyptian

---

[4]  Cf. David Tyack and Elisabeth Hansot, *Learning Together: A History of Coeducation in American Public Schools* (New Haven, Conn.: Yale University Press, 1990).

[5]  See Lisa Coletta (ed), *The Legacy of the Grand Tour: New Essays on Travel, Literature, and Culture* (Lanham, Md.: Rowman & Littlefield: 2015), especially Elisabetta Marino, 'Three British Women Travelers in Egypt: Sophia Lane Poole, Lucie Duff Gordon, and Emmeline Lott,' 51-70.

[6]  See letter 0001 in this volume.

[7]  Ibid.

civilisation and above all a knowledge of the hieroglyphic language.'[8] So she undertook to find a graduate program that would help her pursue this goal.

As was common for aspiring post-graduate students at the time, she wrote to the leading scholars in the field she wanted to pursue, asking for advice, applying to their programs, and even asking for scholarships within the same letter. We do not know how many people she wrote to, but one of them was Breasted at the University of Chicago, who just three years earlier had started the first university department for Egyptology in the US. She wrote asking for his support in coming to Chicago for a Master's degree, and told him that she was interested in either Classical archaeology or Egyptian archaeology, whichever department had a fellowship for her.[9] He and Professor Frank Tarbell in Classical Archaeology were supportive, and she arrived at Chicago in the autumn of 1898. She received her MA in 1900 in Classical Archaeology and Egyptology. During these two years, there is little to no written correspondence between Breasted and Ransom, likely because they could communicate in person. But it is clear that Breasted and others at Chicago regarded her highly. Upon the completion of her Master's degree, Breasted encouraged her to study in Berlin with well-known language expert, and Breasted's former professor, Adolf Erman. She may have been Erman's first female student, and was among the first women to study Egyptology on the Continent—the very first being Mary Broderick who studied under Gaston Maspero at the College de France in 1888, just 12 years earlier.[10] Ransom was in Berlin for three years, and was awarded an assistantship in the Egyptian department at the Berlin Museum. In 1903, she returned to Chicago to finish her PhD in History of Art and Egyptology in 1905 with a dissertation entitled 'Studies in Ancient Furniture.'[11] She was the first woman to receive her PhD in the field in the United States. From 1900 to 1908 there are no extant letters between the two scholars in this archive. Until 1905, she saw Breasted regularly in her

[8] Ibid.

[9] Ibid.

[10] Lesko, 'Caroline Ransom Williams,' 2.

[11] CLR, *Studies in Ancient Furniture: Couches and Beds of the Greeks, Etruscans, and Romans* (Chicago: University of Chicago Press, 1905). Degree information from JoAnn Creviston in the Office of the University of Chicago Registrar, pers. comm. 3 January 2017.

doctoral studies, but from 1906-08 there is no obvious reason why there are no letters. It is possible they did not write, but more probable that the letters simply do not survive in the archive.

In 1905, she accepted a position as an Assistant Professor in the Department of the History of Art and of Classical Archaeology at Bryn Mawr College, in Pennsylvania. From 1905-1910, she taught Egyptian Art and Art History courses.[12] Even though she taught at least five classes per year and had heavy administrative duties, Ransom continued to research and visited the Oriental Institute at least once in 1908 for research and preparation for a trip to Egypt while on sabbatical the following year.[13] In 1909, she traveled with her mother and her aunt to Egypt, and detailed the trip in a letter to Frances Breasted.[14] Ransom also began research for a book on Egyptian Art at this time—a project which did not come to fruition because her career changed drastically in 1910. By this point she had become the chair of her department at Bryn Mawr, but she suddenly changed her plans and accepted a position as the Assistant Curator in the new Department of Egyptian Art at the Metropolitan Museum of Art (MMA) in New York City. According to a letter she wrote to Albert Lythgoe, the Curator of Egyptian Art at the MMA, she wished to specialize her research but did not think she could do it while balancing a heavy administrative and teaching load. She asked Lythgoe if he could use help in the 'endless amount of cataloging and writing of handbooks' that the museum was doing at that time, and he brought her on immediately as Assistant Curator.[15]

This position put Ransom in charge of one of the fastest growing and leading collections of Egyptian art and artifacts in the United States, if not the world. She was clearly at the top of her field, but she rarely got to go into the field. Lythgoe and his excavating crew were often in Egypt during the winter months, so she was tasked with a number of administrative duties in his absence, often acting as the Curator when decisions needed to be

---

[12] See the *Annual Report of the President of Bryn Mawr College* (Philadelphia: John C. Winston, Co., 1908-11).

[13] Letter 0006.

[14] Letter 0007.

[15] CRW to Albert Lythgoe, not dated, likely 30 March 1910, Caroline Ransom Williams Papers, Carolyn [sic] L. Ransom Williams 1909-1917, Metropolitan Museum of Art, Department of Egyptian Art Archives; also in Thompson, *Wonderful Things,* 241.

made, letters written, and exhibits organized. In this, she was not unlike a number of other administrative women who stayed behind in the domestic museum spaces while the male archaeologists were out in the field. She often had to postpone her own work, publications, and personal time in order to take care of museum curatorial duties. Although her mother was living with her in New York the entire time, she thrived in this work and published a number of short articles and handbooks for the museum, as well as one of her best known works, *The Tomb of Per-neb*.[16] She and Breasted continued writing to each other, asking for professional advice, asking about personal lives and issues, and keeping each other updated on their general well-being.[17]

In 1916, her life changed again when the Great War forced the MMA to make some staff and budget cutbacks. It is not clear whether Ransom left of her own accord or if she was let go, but at this point she decided to marry a long-time suitor from her hometown of Toledo, Ohio. Dr. Caroline L. Ransom became Mrs. Grant Williams on June 28, 1916 in Mercer, Pennsylvania. She was 44 and he was 52. It is not clear when Grant, a real-estate developer, first proposed marriage to Caroline, but it seemed to have been early on in her career and he continued to pursue her, especially upon the completion of her PhD.[18] Instead of marrying him right away, she chose to follow her career goals and not give up her work. In the early days of her marriage, however, she encountered a new set of issues. She had new domestic concerns with her aging mother and her new husband.

---

[16] *A Handbook of the Egyptian Rooms, Metropolitan Museum of Art* (New York: MMA, 1911); 'The Value of Photographs and Transparencies as Adjuncts to Museum Exhibits,' *MMAB* 7:7 (July 1912): 132-34; *The Stela of Menthu-Weser* (New York: MMA, 1913); 'Egyptian Furniture and Musical Instruments,' *MMAB* 8:4 (April 1913): 72-79; 'A Model of the Mastaba-Tomb of Userkaf-Ankh,' *MMAB* 8:6 (June 1913): 125-130; 'Nubian Objects Acquired by the Egyptian Department' *MMAB* 8:9 (September 1913): 200-208; 'The Stela of Menthu-Weser,' *MMAB* 8:10 (October 1913): 213, 216-18; 'A Late Egyptian Sarcophagus,' *MMAB* 9:5 (May 1914): 112-120; 'Pots with Hieratic Inscriptions,' *MMAB* 9:11 (November 1914): 236-243; 'A Commemorative Scarab of Thutmose III,' *MMAB* 10:3 (March 1915): 46-47; 'Heart Scarab of Queen Amenardis,' *MMAB* 10:6 (June 1915): 116-117; 'Three Sets of Egyptian Gold Pendants,' *MMAB* 10:6 (June 1915): 117-120; *The Tomb of Perneb: With Illustrations* (New York: MMA, 1916).

[17] There are a few letters in the MMA's archives between CRW and JHB. Since JHB saved carbon copies of most of his letters, they are presented here. For example, letter 0025 in this volume is also in the MMA archives.

[18] Lesko, 'Caroline Ransom Williams,' 3.

They hired help, but caring for household issues fell largely on Ransom Williams' shoulders. Further, although her desire to work and her ability to do so did not seem to change very much, she was isolated from many of her professional pursuits. Because Toledo was on a main train line, she was able to continue working in New York, both for the MMA and for the New York Historical Society, curating the Abbott Collection of Egyptian Antiquities, by commuting several times a year between 1917 and 1924. She also did some piecework at the Cleveland Museum of Art, the Minneapolis Institute of Arts, and the Toledo Museum of Art. Ransom Williams found the back and forth of commuting tiring, and with the growing unpredictability of her mother's health she decided to give up her work in New York for a little while. She found some steady work in Toledo at the museum and continued to research at the Haskell Library at the University of Chicago. In 1926-27, she went to Egypt with Breasted's Epigraphic Survey to work on Medinet Habu and Breasted encouraged her to bring her mother along. When she returned to the US, she continued her research projects and taught for one year at the University of Michigan, but interestingly continued to turn down Breasted's requests for her to teach at Chicago citing domestic responsibilities. In 1935 she took one final trip to Egypt, working with the MMA's Egyptian Expedition and with the Oriental Institute on the Coffin Texts project in Cairo. She was there for a few months and it was in this time she learned of Breasted's death, in December of 1935.

Breasted's story is well-known and well-told, so details of his career are not included explicitly here. Their joint story ends with her reaction to the news of his death, but her story continues until her death in 1952 and what is known about her in those years is detailed in the Epilogue to this volume.

As a woman at a new university and in a new field, she was in a unique position in the early twentieth century. There were certain paths open to her, but at the same time she had to forge new ones. Her professional trajectory was not unlike those of her male colleagues at the time: she came from an upper middle-class family, got a university education, went on a Grand Tour while at university, and then decided to get an advanced degree. She pursued her education as any of her male colleagues did and followed in the footsteps of her mentors, training with the experts in Berlin and finishing her PhD. She took faculty and museum positions and did the foundational disciplinary work that should have made her a well-known name in the field. In short, she did everything she was supposed to do. She was a scholar, author, and well-respected instructor. She was not a groundbreaking institution founder, although she gave aid to Breasted, who was. She was not a best-selling author, although sometimes she happily prepared the materials for best-selling books, edited, proofread, and indexed them for Breasted and others. She was not a professor who trained a whole generation of scholars who went on to take over the discipline, but she helped start the archaeology department at Bryn Mawr, whose faculty did do that in the end. The work she did was not what many would call glamorous, but it was worthwhile, foundational, discipline-building scholarship. She did the research, wrote the books, gave the talks, wrote the reviews, and went into the field. Unlike her male colleagues, however, domestic concerns took over her professional life so she was unable to make the professional leap that she was poised to make in 1916.

The life of Caroline Ransom Williams is in these letters. I present them here with notes explaining a few broader historical contexts, introducing characters that come into the story, and citing some of the scholarship mentioned throughout. I have not done a complete contextualization or analysis of her life, as that is work for another volume.

# The correspondence

31 January 1898                                                    0001

Dear Sir:
It is my earnest desire to pursue during the year of 1898-9, in the University of Chicago such studies as will best fit me for original investigation in regard to the development of Ancient Art. I am today sending to the President of the University an application for a fellowship in either the Department of Classical Archaeology or the Department of Egyptology. If I were granted a fellowship in the first-named department I should wish, with Dr. Tarbell's[1] approval, to take my minor work in Egyptology, and if there is no opening for me in Classical Archaeology, I very much hope there may be one in Egyptology.

My interest in Egyptian Art began with a general course in Art History, taken in the Spring of 1890.[2] I then went abroad for two years and besides study of the collections of Egyptian antiquities in the British Museum, the Louvre, the Museums of Berlin and Turin, I had the great privilege and pleasure of journeying to the First Cataract in Egypt and of spending several weeks in Cairo. In 1896, during my senior year in college,[3] I again gave particular attention to Art History, beginning with Egyptian Art. Last winter (1897), I made a very exhaustive study of all works upon Egypt within my reach, in preparation for four lectures upon Egyptian

---

[1]  Dr. Frank Bigelow Tarbell, Professor of Classical Archaeology, who was with the University of Chicago from the beginning (*The University of Chicago Magazine*, Vol. XIV, No. 1, [November 1921], 54).
[2]  At Lake Erie Seminary, where she was a student for one semester.
[3]  At Mount Holyoke College, South Hadley, Massachusetts. 1893 was the first year that it was a College, after the school phased out their seminary curriculum—which included religious and domestic training—and changed their name from Mount Holyoke Seminary to Mount Holyoke College.

Art, which I gave before large afternoon and evening classes in this city.[4] I inclose with this letter the syllabi of my lectures,[5] which were illustrated with photographs, plates from Dr. Binion's Mizraïm[6] and from publications of the Egypt Exploration Fund and maps and drawings enlarged from various books. I also spoke in August '97 in the Museum in Chautauqua, N. Y. upon 'The Egyptian Doctrine of the Future Life as influencing the Architecture of the Tombs.' I succeeded in making the subject of Egyptian Art attractive to others, but, for myself, learned that to study in a scientific manner this earlier national art, I need a more intimate acquaintance with other aspects of the ancient Egyptian civilisation and above all a knowledge of the hieroglyphic language.

I venture to write to you, hoping that you may be interested to say any good word that you can to further my cause.

Very respectfully | Caroline Louise Ransom | Toledo, Ohio | January 31, 1898

**17 March 1898**                                                      0002

March 17, 1898 | Lake Erie Seminary |
Painesville, Ohio

Dear Sir,

Allow me first to express my appreciation of your kind letter of February ninth, and then if I may, to ask a favor.

A question has been raised by one of the teachers here as to the pronunciation of the Egyptian words 'Ra', 'ka' and 'ba'. I have given the long sound of the vowel because in books on Egyptology I have occasionally noticed the words written thus, Rā, kā, Amen-Rā. My critic claims that she has always heard the vowel pronounced as 'a' in 'father.' Will you kindly tell me the correct usage in regard to these words and also in regard to compounds, such as 'Ra-hotep', 'Ra-emka'? I have found the pronunciation

---

[4] She returned to Lake Erie Seminary in Painesville by this time.
[5] Not included in file.
[6] Samuel Augustus Binion, *Ancient Egypt or Mizraïm. Profusely illustrated with fine engravings and colored plates by the best artists, from the works of* L'Expedition de l'Egypte, *Lepsius, Prisse d'Avennes, &c., &c.* (New York: Henry G. Allen, 1887).

of Egyptian and Assyrian names very troublesome and have really been obliged to be a law to myself, as I am not acquainted with any works that give any assistance in this matter. I send under separate cover a copy of the topics which I am using in a two weeks [sic] study of Egyptian Art. The references are to such works as are in the library here. The topics fit into the adjustable note-books used by the students. I have a fine class of eighteen students who are taking up the subject of Egyptology with great enthusiasm. Next term they are to study briefly Assyrian, Greek and Roman Art, Early Christian, Romanesque and Gothic Architecture (for which I have topics in preparation) as well as listen to weekly lectures which I shall give on the history of painting.

I was very much troubled to learn last Saturday, through Dr. Tarbell, that the application which I had so carefully prepared, as well as all my letters of recommendation had never reached the President of the University. Thus Evans, Principal of this institution has very kindly written to President Harper which was sent yesterday noon. I very earnestly hope that it will actually come to the President's notice, as Miss Evans is well acquainted with my work. It will be a great disappointment to me if I cannot study hieroglyphic next year.

Very respectfully | Caroline L. Ransom

**6 April 1898**                                                    0003

Dear Dr. Breasted,
Just a word to thank you very sincerely for the kind interest you have shown in the matter of a fellowship for me. I am very much rejoiced at the result and eager for the opportunities of next year. I expect to spend the summer in Berlin and to report for duty in Chicago the first of October. I thank you also for the explanation in regard to vowel sounds in Egyptian names.

Very respectfully | Caroline L. Ransom | Toledo, Ohio | April 6, 1898

**28 March 1899**                                                                 0004

Dear Dr. Breasted,
Unavoidable interruptions prevented my answering at once the examination questions, which you so kindly mailed to me last week.[7] I send the exercises under separate cover today.[8]

I hope that this week is bringing you some hours of leisure and recreation.

With kind greetings to yourself and Mrs. Breasted,

Sincerely | Caroline Ransom | Tuesday, March the twenty-eighth, eighteen hundred ninety-nine


**6 May 1900**                                                                   0005

Eichstrasse 11, Hannover | May 6, 1900

Dear Dr. and Mrs. Breasted,
One of my anticipated pleasures all the winter has been to see you soon in Berlin.

But now I am a month later in reaching Germany than I had expected to be and I have decided not to go to Berlin to live until next October. So I fear there is a small chance of our meeting unless your plans are changed. Even now you may be far away. If I remember rightly you expected to leave Berlin some time in June. My room looks out into a stretch of gardens with peach trees in bloom and many flowers.

I arrived only last Thursday after a thirteen days [sic] voyage from New York on the Rhein of the N. G. Lloyd line. Perhaps you wonder why I have given up Berlin for the present. It is simply that I have decided that it is not best for me to do any close work this summer so I am keeping out of temptation. Here I shall live out of doors and incidentally make some progress in the language. One of my Lake Erie friends who lived three years in Hannover is to be here this summer again. It as through her that I came to the Kettlers. In the house there are three others besides myself,

---

[7] Ransom Williams may have been home in Ohio during a break in classes, because she was still studying at Chicago at this time.

[8] Not included in file.

all of whom talk German readily – I am the only beginner. One of them is, I believe, an acquaintance of yours – Miss Edwina Ewing of St. Louis. She is to be married here in June to a Dutchman, von Haaek is his name. It is fun to hear her talk of 'my Dutchman.'

Your letters written from the steamer last August I greatly enjoyed. I hope that the winter has brought all and more than you anticipated of pleasure and profit.

May I not hear from you again sometime?

Very cordially yours | Caroline L. Ransom

**17 June 1908**                                                    **0006**

Low Buildings | Bryn Mawr, Penn. | June 17, 1908

My dear Professor Breasted,

I feel quite sure that you are in this country for someone wrote of having travelled from Naples to Gibraltar with you who were bound for New York – not to mention the summer announcements which aren't always reliable.

I am writing especially to ask whether you will be at the University in the month of August. If so, so far as my plans are shaping themselves now, I should like to spend a few weeks there and use the library and bother you with an occasional question. I have received my leave of absence for the second semester of next year and expect to go to Egypt. I should like to do as much work, preparatory to that opportunity, this summer, as my strength permits. Year after next I give a two-hour course in Egyptian Art and I want to give it with slides, so that as well as some private work, I have in mind. Have you any negatives you would be willing I should have slides made from just for class-room use here, of course? This all sounds as if I were going to very troublesome, but I will try not to be, if you will let me come.

I am staying on here to get rested and to put college material in order. I wish I had known earlier of your return voyage and I should have begged you and Mrs. Breasted to stop here. I do hope you will visit me here some day. Please give my warm greetings to Mrs. Breasted.

With kind regards, | Sincerely, | Caroline L. Ransom

**18 June 1909**                                             **0007**

Norddeutscher Lloyd Bremen |
Damper 'Schleswig' | June 18, 1909

My dear Mrs. Breasted,[9]
We are enroute to Naples, my mother and I, after more than four months in Egypt. So often I have thought of you and Mr Breasted and wished to send you some word. But you, who know the life there, can well understand how difficult it was to settle to writing, and will pardon that neglect, as well, I hope, as the less excusable one of not writing to you after my delightful visit with you in Chicago.

I have heard from Miss Kimball what an altogether delightful baby your little son[10] is. Won't you tell me more about him, his name, and how he fares? I wonder if I shall see him first when he is about as old as Charles[11] was when I first made <u>his</u> acquaintance. Perhaps not until still later, for I see no prospect of visiting Chicago again very soon.

I did not get away until January 21st. Some private affairs of ours necessitated our staying in the United States until after the 1st of January, so I did not even ask Miss Thomas to let me off before Christmas. We landed in Alexandria February 8th, and as you see, have stayed on into the summer heat. We went south to the II. cataract, but, alas! no further. It did not seem worth while merely to take the train journey to Khartoum when we should miss everything of interest to me by the way. We were several weeks in Luxor and through Mr. Lythgoe's[12] kindness were able to go to the oasis of Kharga, where we were entertained at the Metropolitan Museum camp.

---

[9]  This letter to Frances Breasted is included as it is assumed that Breasted himself read it. Much of it deals with things that Breasted would have interest in.

[10]  James Henry Breasted, Jr. (1908-1983), became an art historian and studied ancient Egypt. He was the director of the Los Angeles County Museum from 1946-51 ('James Breasted Jr., Art Historian, Dies; Led Coast Museum,' *The New York Times: Obituaries* [6 May 1983]).

[11]  Charles Breasted (1897-1980), who became an archaeologist at the urging of his father. He wrote his father's biography, *Pioneer to the Past: The Story of James Henry Breasted,* (1943). He also directed, *The Human Adventure*, a film produced by the Oriental Institute in 1935.

[12]  Albert Morton Lythgoe (1868-1934) was an American Egyptologist. He studied at Harvard and became the first Curator of Egyptian art at the Museum of Fine Arts in Boston, from 1902-1906. He then became the Curator in the Egyptian Art Department of the Metropolitan Museum of Art from 1906-1929 (Emeritus until 1933).

We went into the Faioum too. After the Congress closed, I stayed on to take photographs and otherwise to work in the museum. I have 150 subjects with my 5x7 camera from the museum and about 75 from the vicinity of Cairo. I did not attempt to work with the larger camera in Upper Egypt, as conditions in our rapid travelling unfavorable, but of kodaks [sic] such as the few duplicates enclosed, I have about 400. It was a great satisfaction to me to traverse the pyramid field from Abu Roash to Lisht. This we managed by detachments. We stayed at a small hotel the 'Sphinx,' which started this season at the pyramids and from there visited Abu Roash, Fauriyet el Aryan, Abu Gurob, and Abusir, as well as the Gizeh group and we went repeatedly to Bedrashein for days at Sakkara or Dashur and twice I paid visits at Lisht, when I first reached Egypt and the end of May. Mr. Lythgoe has the whole of the temple and the upper part of the causeway at the southern Lisht pyramid laid bare and it is clear that the O[ld].E[gyptian].[13] style of funerary temple as simplified at Abusir was continued in the M[iddle].E[gyptian].[14] Dr. and Mrs. Borchardt[15] were very kind to us. What a charming home they have on the Gizereh![16] Life in Cairo must be quite endurable under such conditions. But, it general, it seems to be one a dreadful place. We lived at the Villa Victoria and were very well satisfied. We went first to the Hotel Continental, but it seemed too big and full of commotion! The food at the Villa Victoria is <u>excellent</u>, but there was so much building in progress in the neighborhood that the noise of the workmen was very disturbing. For the last fortnight partly on that account and partly to economize we moved to the Pension Simon, which we found good for the price charged. The last few weeks the mosquitoes drove us nearly distracted. Of course we slept under nettings, but in the daytime they tormented us continually. One of my old fellow-students in Berlin, Dr. Roeder,[17] who is on the <u>Service des</u>

---

[13] Probably meaning Old Kingdom period (c. 2649-2150 BCE).

[14] Probably meaning Middle Kingdom period (c. 2030-1640 BCE).

[15] Ludwig Borchardt (1863-1948), founder of the German Institute for Ancient Egyptian Archaeology in 1907 in Cairo. He was the archaeologist who excavated Tell el-Amarna and found the famous sculptor's workshop with the bust of Nefertiti, now in the Neues Museum in Berlin.

[16] Island in the Nile River in Cairo.

[17] Ernst Günther Roeder (1881-1966) was a German Egyptologist who studied under Erman at Berlin. He got his PhD in 1904, so knew CRW when they were in Berlin together. He helped with the Dictionary and joined the Antiquities Service from 1907-11. He was the Director of

Antiquités turned up in Kharga, when we were there. He was on a private quest at that time at the Hibis temple. Since then I have seen a good deal of him in Cairo. I just missed Professor Schäfer[18] to my sorrow in Cairo. He left for Germany about the time we arrived in Cairo. Herr Dittrich,[19] of whom Professor Breasted told me, did all my developing and printing and made me nearly 800 lantern slides from his negatives and mine and those I was able to borrow! I expect to get other slides from Stoudter and Mr. Petrie,[20] as well as to have some made at home from publications. I think I shall have a good collection. It has certainly been labor enough thus far!

We have stayed so long in Egypt I have given up going to Germany. We shall make a considerable stay in Rome and then go for a little time each to London and Paris. We sail September 11th. Miss Randolph[21] was with us until recently and with our little party it was possible to do many things which I could not possibly have accomplished alone, such as long desert rides and excursions to unfrequented places. It was an ideal arrangement for me. My aunt and mother were very good about letting me run away from them for brief visits in Lisht and Sakkara, but nearly everything we did together my mother even taking the long day's excursions via Bedrashein with six hours or so on donkey-back as when we went to Dashur.

the Hildesheim Museum from 1915-1945 and then of the Berlin Museum from 1940-1945, until he was dismissed from his positions because he was a Nazi supporter.

[18] Heinrich Schäfer (1868-1957) was a German Egyptologist, and studied with Erman c. 1887. He was the director of the Egyptian Museum in Berlin, 1914-35, and a Professor at Berlin University. He catalogued much of the collection at the Museum.

[19] It is not clear who this is, but he must have been a photograph developer.

[20] William Matthew Flinders Petrie (1853-1942) was a British Egyptologist. He occupied the first Edwards Chair of Egyptology at University College, London and founded the program there (1892-1935). Much more could be said about him, and more has been. See, for example, Margaret Drower, *Flinders Petrie: A Life in Archaeology* (Madison, Wisc: University of Wisconsin Press, 1985).

[21] CRW's aunt, Louise Fitz-Randolph. She was an important influence in CRW's life. She attended Mount Holyoke seminary, graduating in 1872. She went on to study at Harvard, and in London, Zurich, Berlin, Rome, Athens, and Paris. She earned her MA from Mount Holyoke in 1904 and became a distinguished professor there, teaching from 1892-1912, being emerita from 1912 until her death in 1932. She taught at Lake Erie Seminary when CRW was a student there, and brought her to Mount Holyoke after their time together in Europe and Egypt. See Mary C. J. Higley, ed. *One Hundred Year Biographical Dictionary of Mount Holyoke College, 1837-1937. Bulletin Series 30, No. 5* (South Hadley, Mass.: Alumnae Association of Mount Holyoke College, 1937), 131.

How I hope that you are both very well this summer and that in the Autumn you will find time to write to me.

With the very kindest regards, also from my mother, | Very sincerely yours, | Caroline L. Ransom

I mustn't forget to announce that my department at Bryn Mawr has been awarded a resident fellowship. I have been pleading for one, ever since I went there and you can imagine how glad I am. The first incumbent is an extremely good student who has already two years of graduate study.

**5 January 1910**                                                    **0008**

Chicago | January 5, 1910

My dear Miss Ransom:

I was very much interested to receive your letter of December 31st and also much disappointed that I had missed seeing you in Baltimore. I attended the session in Toronto last year but was unable to read my paper this time.

I am glad to hear of your project. In the first place, I am selfishly pleased because I attempt to give a survey course in the history of art in the University and find it very burdensome without a text book as a basis. I have full confidence that you could produce a useful, well arranged, and trustworthy book and shall be very glad to write Professor Kelsey to this effect.

I have been looking over the outline and it seems to me to cover the ground. I have been constantly troubled by the same difficulty which you mention, namely, whether or not to trace each department of art from the beginning to the end, period by period, or to complete each period in all departments before taking up the next. I have finally adopted the plan which you have yourself used. As it seems important that each period should be complete rather than that we should have a series of fragments from each period. The interruption involved in this <words missing> think, preferable to the other difficulty. An introduction such as you suggest in Modern Research in Egypt would be very useful, but I fear you would meet some difficulty in discussing it briefly. Would you begin with the decipherment or deal only with material, that is, uninscribed documents? I do not think that any rustiness you may feel regarding the language will be a serious handicap in the production of this book, and I wish you every success. If I can, in any way, be of assistance, please call upon me. If you desire it I shall be glad to look it over in manuscript or in proof, or any portion of it about which you care for advice.

Mrs. Breasted has long been indebted to you, I believe, for a letter and is now writing you.

With best wishes from us both for the New Year, I am, | Very sincerely yours, | JHB

JHB:M

**25 January 1910**                                                0009

Bryn Mawr College, Bryn Mawr, Penna. | Department of the History of Art and of Classical Archaeology | January 25, 1910

My dear Mr Breasted,

I was most cheering to have you respond so cordially about my wish to write a book on Egyptian Art.[22] Thank you so much both for your letter to me and for writing to Professor Kelsey. It the thing goes through, I shall no doubt be very grateful to avail myself of your kind offer to look the book through in the manuscript. Certainly, if you can find something for me to do as a slight return—such as proof-reading for you or making out some indexes. For I realize what an in road on your time, your generous offer means. However, I'm trying not to fix my mind on the plan too intently, lest it fall through. At present I am waiting for a verdict having submitted a plan and some of the illustrative material. Did I tell you that I have over 800 negatives from Egypt? It was such a pleasure to hear from Mrs Breasted the other day.

With Kindest regards, and warm appreciation of your kindness, | Sincerely yours, | Caroline L. Ransom

---

[22] This book never came to fruition, as her career changed paths not long after this letter.

19 February 1910                                         0010

Bryn Mawr College | Bryn Mawr, Penna. |
Department of the History of Art and of
Classical Archaeology | February 19, 1910

My Dear Mrs Breasted,[23]
It was a great pleasure to receive your card this morning[24], and I was very
glad to know that Professor Meyer[25] is with you, for I wished to write to
him.

I heard his lectures in Berlin the last semester I was there, until I gave
up all university work to serve as a voluntärin in the Egyptian department
in the Museum – and I met both Professor Meyer and Frau Meyer more
than once at the Ermans[26].

I have ventured to write Professor and Mrs Meyer here. I thought
perhaps they would be interested to see something of one of our women's
colleges. Of course I know nothing of their plans and how fully their time
is bespoken, but if they could manage it, I hope we could give them a
pleasant time. Miss Thomas[27] said some weeks ago, if she were home (she
is away working for the endowment very frequently), she would wish
them to stay in the 'prophet's chamber' at the Deanery. Miss Thomas and
Miss Garrett[28] have a beautiful home and entertain charmingly. But if Miss

---

[23] This letter to Frances Breasted is included as it is assumed that Breasted himself read it.
Much of it deals with issues that Breasted would have interest in.

[24] Not in archive.

[25] Eduard Meyer (1855-1930) was a German Egyptologist and chronologer. He worked with
Adolf Erman in Berlin, and was close friends with Breasted after his time there.

[26] Adolf Erman (1854-1937) was a German Egyptologist and linguist. Erman was responsible
for much of the development of the study of Egyptian philology. He taught Breasted, Ransom
Williams, and many others in these pages. Many of those who studied with Erman in Berlin
from the 1890s-1910s remained friends. Erman appears a lot in the following letters, so
more will be said about him there.

[27] Martha Carey Thomas (1857-1935) became Dean of Bryn Mawr in 1884 and President in
1894 until 1922 (http://msa.maryland.gov/msa/educ/exhibits/womenshall/html/thomas.
html [accessed 22 December 2016]).

[28] Mary Garrett (1854-1915) was a founder of Bryn Mawr and donated annually to their
endowment. She was wealthy American suffragist and fought, with Thomas, to open Johns
Hopkins Medical School to women (*The Johns Hopkins University School of Medicine*: http://

Thomas should be away, I am sure I could make them very comfortable at the Lord Buildings. I also ventured to ask Professor Meyer to address our advanced students in classics and semitics [sic]. This would be in the Art Seminary room sitting about a table a company of twenty to thirty people. Our undergraduates would be less interested and if the whole college were involved a date would have to be fixed long in advance. But for an informal address to the advanced students an audience could be gathered on a few hours notice. This will leave Professor Meyer free, in case he is willing to consider it at all, to fit the visit in here just when it suits his convenience. The graduate students went to hear Professor Meyer's open lecture at the University of Pennsylvania and enjoyed it so much. They would greatly appreciate the privilege of hearing him here. A number of them, of their own accord, have come to ask if the college were not going to invite him here. When I took the matter to President Thomas, she said she had had it in mind but the year is one of such financial distress here, on account of efforts to clear the debt and raise the endowment in order to meet the conditions of the General Board, that she was not authorized to make even so small an extra expenditure as the amount a public lecture would be. I could offer Professor Meyer thirty dollars for the informal address to the smaller company, but hesitate to do so—the sum isn't perhaps to be despised if he could come here at the time he is in the neighborhood (he told me he was coming to Philadelphia again). On the other hand, I think a man of his distinction often prefers to make an address as a favor to receiving a small sum for it. Dear Mrs Breasted, would you mind advising me? You know the Meyers so well. In the letter sent in Mr Breasted's care, I merely asked whether they could come, and whether Professor Meyer would address the advanced students, without saying anything one way or the other about compensation.

I am bothering you—just in a busy week—with my long letter! Do forgive me. I am so much interested in the news about Doris. I am going up to New York next week to see if I can get her some Tiffany's glass candlesticks and shade. I think she would like something distinctively American, don't you? The photograph hasn't reached me yet, but of course it will in a mail or two. I am so eager to see it and thank you many times.

www.medicalarchives.jhmi.edu/garrett/biography.htm [accessed 28 October 2016]).

Please do persuade Professor and Mrs. Meyer that it would be worth while to visit Bryn Mawr. I should so love to have them tell the Ermans about the place. With warmest greetings to you all.
Sincerely yours, | Caroline R.

The first time I heard Professor Meyer was in Halle. I went there to visit his classes and those of Professor Blan; it must have been 1901.
My undergraduate course in Egyptian Art has increased from 17 students in the first semester to 30 students in this. We are just beginning the Middle Empire.

**12 May 1910**                                                                                                         **0011**

Hotel Irving | 26 Gramercy Park | 
New York | May 12, 1910

My dear Mr Breasted,
Mr Tarbell has already told you of my change of plans, so he says.[29] I wrote to him immediately because I hoped he would have some suggestion about filling my place at Bryn Mawr. I wished so much I could have a good talk with you before accepting the position, but writing is so unsatisfactory and conditions made it necessary for me to decide so promptly, that I did not attempt to consult with you. I hope you will approve and will not think it impossible, now that I shall have the opportunity to devote all my strength to <words missing> for me to do good work in the Egyptian field. Mr Lythgoe is to stay in this country another year, so there is still so much to do in installing material in the new wing and then he expects to be absent quite indefinitely, excavating in Egypt, and in the summer months writing up

---

[29] She was referring to her decision to go to work as assistant curator in the Egyptian Art Department at the Metropolitan Museum of Art (MMA). She went to work to catalogue and assess the materials coming in from the MMA's expeditions in Egypt. She 'also performed essential administrative tasks for the department during Lythgoe's absences. Her contract allowed at least two months abroad each year, most of which she spent in Germany, benefiting from renewed contact with Erman and study in European museums while keeping up with the latest in Egyptological scholarship' (Jason Thompson, *Wonderful Things: A History of Egyptology, Volume 2: The Golden Age: 1881-1914* [Cairo: The AUC Press, 2015], 240-42.)

results, and I shall have a position of great responsibility and opportunity in charge of the collections here. I am very happy over the change because in Bryn Mawr my work was of such variety, it was impossible to master any one thing; then, too, there were such financial worries; the Metropolitan has means to look after its work without straits. I do not go on duty here until the first of October, so I am going abroad and shall spend July and August in Berlin. I shall take up the language again at once and shall be so delighted to do so.

Professor and Mrs. Meyer spent a part of the day at Bryn Mawr. It was such a privilege to have them with us. Professor Meyer spoke informally to a small audience the hour before luncheon. Then a luncheon was given for them at the Deanery (President Thomas's house) and after luncheon they saw the college buildings, then had tea in my rooms before going to the train. They were so appreciative of the little I could do for them and such charming guests, altogether I enjoyed every moment of their stay and they made me feel that they enjoyed seeing the college.

I must tell you that my Egyptian art book is in abeyance for the present. Mr Brett decided that it would not pay financially. But it doesn't matter now, I shall have more than enough to do at the Metropolitan of work that will lead to publication.

One of my students is going abroad this summer to remain a year and she has started a thesis on the Corinthian Capital.[30] So many important examples are in situ that I have suggested to her the use of the telephotographic apparatus. If it isn't asking too much, a post-card in reply will do – I should very much like your opinion as to the relative desirability of the Goerz and the Bausch & Lomb attachments. The student cannot afford to buy an expensive foreign lense [sic]. Do you think it feasible for her to get good results with these American telephotographic attachments? I have excellent photographs from my work in Egypt with the comparatively inexpensive instrument I bought in Chicago in 1908, but of course I was not attempting the long distance pictures. I should be grateful for just a word of reply soon, because the student has decided to sail a fortnight from Saturday and is thinking of getting an American camera before she goes. I go back to Bryn Mawr Sunday. I am here tonight to meet Miss Randolph.

---

[30] Mary H. Swindler (1884-1967), who was one of Ransom Williams' students at Bryn Mawr around this time.

Tomorrow we attend the meeting of the Managing Committee of the American School of Classical Studies in Athens. I am going through the throes of finding an abiding place in New York! It is far from easy to get air, sunshine and space, not to mention good food, within the limits of a modest income!

Please give my warm remembrances to Mrs Breasted and share this letter with her. I am grateful for what she did to persuade the Meyers to go to Bryn Mawr.

With kind regards | Sincerely yours | Caroline L. Ransom

**16 May 1910**                                                    0012

Chicago | May 16, 1910

My Dear Miss Ransom:

I sent you at once by postal card a hasty reply to your question regarding cameras, which I hope you received.

I was very much pleased indeed to hear of your call to the Metropolitan and that you had accepted, for I know it enables you to do what you had so long wanted to accomplish. I have no question that you will do excellent work in the Egyptian field. I think it will be a satisfaction to you to resume the work on the language, but as soon as I heard of your call I found myself hoping that you would be able to go on with the history of art, - I mean the book. Your position in the Museum, though, of course, an arduous one, ought to contribute much to the work on the volume.

I find it difficult for me to speak of Mr. Brett's financial caution with patience. I find him throwing cold water in so many directions.

I have this spring been trying to use Maspero's[31] manual for assigned readings, but the more I use it, the more hopeless does the hodge-podge seem. There is absolutely nothing of a general nature in the way of a small volume to which one can refer a student of Egyptian art. There would be

---

[31] Gaston Maspero (1846-1916) was a French Egyptologist, professor, linguist. From 1881-86 and 1899-1914 he was Director of the Antiquities Service in Cairo. More on him below. Here, JHB is referring to Maspero's *Manual of Egyptian Archaeology: Guide to the Study of Antiquities in Egypt. For the Use of Students and Travellers,* New Edition. Transl. Amelia Edwards (New York: G. P. Putnam, 1895).

enough sale for such a book in Cairo alone, in my judgement, to carry it financially. If you say so, I would be very glad to lay the matter before the Scribners as a feasible project. They are accepting my judgement in a number of important matters and I think they might accept it in this. They are much more anticipative than our conservative friend Mr. Brett.

I'm very glad that you are again to have a season abroad. Do not overwork but come back with renewed energy to put into that history of art.

Mrs. Breasted would join me in kindest regards if she knew I were writing,

Wishing you a very pleasant stay abroad, I am, | Very sincerely yours, | JHB

**18 May 1910**                                                    0013

Bryn Mawr College | Bryn Mawr, Penna. | Department of the History of Art and of Classical Archaeology | May 18, 1910

My dear Professor Breasted,
Your letter of May 16th has just reached me. Thank you very much for it as well as for the card.

My plans have had another upheaval, this time with reference to the summer. My mother was taken suddenly and acutely ill the other day. She is almost in usual health again, but the physician tells us that she will be liable to sudden attacks and advises me not to separate myself from her. Then she so clings to me, I could not put the ocean between us, and at present an ocean voyage would not be good for her. So the European journey and study in Berlin are given up.

It may be best for us to spend the summer just here, inasmuch as I have great confidence in the physician who has her case in charge. On the other hand, that may not seem necessary. I am writing especially to inquire whether you are to be in residence at the University any part of the summer. If so, we might find it possible to go to Chicago.

It is very encouraging and comforting to have your approval with regard to the Egyptian Art book. I believe that Scribners handle in this country the 'Apollo' series and that a volume in that series is to be devoted to Egyptian and Assyrian Art and is to be written by Professor Maspero. I am afraid therefore they would not be willing to push another volume on Egyptian Art, though I doubt whether Maspero's plan, in the limited space at his disposal, would fill the need. Of course I should be delighted if Scribners would take it up, but I am afraid the volume planned in the 'Apollo' series will kill any chance I might have with them. Possibly I could get the Metropolitan to bring it out as a 'Handbook' of the Museum, similar to the Berlin handbooks. If despite the 'Apollo' volume, it seems to you advisable to broach the matter with the Scribners firm, I should be very grateful indeed to have you do so. I think I shall divide my working time about equally between language and study along the lines of the proposed volume, for the last will all be to the good in museum work, in the introductory paragraphs in the general catalog, even if I do not publish a history of art. I should be glad if it should turn out feasible on both sides for me to be in consultation with you and to work in Chicago.

With kind regards, | Sincerely yours, | Caroline L. Ransom

What would you think of my trying to get in connection with Dr. W. Max Müller,[32] perhaps reading some texts with him, if I find that I must remain here? I have a slight acquaintance with him through the Philadelphia Oriental Society of which I am a member.

**23 May 1910**                                                                    **0014**

Chicago | May 23, 1910

My dear Miss Ransom,

I was very much pained to hear from your letter of the 15th that your mother has been seriously ill. I sincerely hope that there may be no recurrence and that she may regain her full health. I can understand your disappointment in changing your plans for your summer's study. I very much regret that I am not to be here this summer. It is the first summer vacation in America

---

[32] Wilhelm Max Müller (1862-1919) was a German Egyptologist and linguist. He was a student of Erman's in Berlin, and held professorial posts in Pennsylvania from 1890-1919. CRW worked with him throughout her career until his death.

that I have taken. We are to go to Michigan to spend the hot months instead of either teaching or crossing the water as we have always done. I wish I knew what to say about your undertaking work with W. Max Müller. He is undoubtedly an able man and his instruction would be valuable. He is troubled with a chronic skepticism towards everything and everybody. As to his character, I would rather tell you about it than write what I have to say.

Regarding the history of Egyptian art, I am glad that you are willing that I should take up the matter with Scribners, which I shall endeavor to do just as soon as the questions we are now discussing are settled. I hope I can explain to Scribners that their prospects of ever securing Maspero's volume in the Apollo series are very slim. Maspero's name is in a number of such series, like that of Kent's 'Library of Ancient Inscriptions' and the probability that he will ever furnish these volumes is exceedingly remote. This last volume of Maspero's is also promised to Scribner. So this makes two of Maspero's volumes expected by Scribner. The one in the Kent series has been announced for seven or eight years. I hope therefore a mere paper plan will not deter them from undertaking your volume.

If I am able in any way to advise you regarding your summer work please let me know.

With kindest regards I am, | Sincerely yours, | JHB


**16 October 1910**                                                    0015

The Beresford | 1 West Eighty-first Street |
[New York] | October 16, 1910

My dear Mr Breasted,
You were so kind last June as to tell me to write to you if I needed any advice about my work through the summer. I gave the greatest part of my time to reviewing the grammar and various texts I had read with you and in Berlin, then to working through the first volume of Sethe's Urkunden[33] with the

---

[33] Linguist Kurt Sethe's *Urkunden der 18. Dynastie. Abteilung IV, Band IV, Heft 13-16: Historisch-biographische Urkunden.* (Leipzig, 1909). This is part of a larger collection of hieroglyphic texts that were hand-copied and translated. Sethe (1869-1934) trained at Berlin under Erman, like JHB and CRW; he succeeded Erman at Berlin and is considered one of the greatest figures in

help of the translations in your <u>Records</u>[34] – a work I am now so happy as to possess. But now with the beginning of my museum work I find myself in trouble. I have been set to prepare labels for the 'Coffin Room', containing late coffins and stelae, mostly XXVI. dynasty and Ptolemaic. There are phrases and even signs which baffle me. Then the latter part of the summer I collated the text of the Philadelphia mastaba as given in Mariette with the original and translated it so far as I could, but there are passages there I am not sure of. I find that any museum work does not begin until ten and I can easily get in one hour and a half study in the morning, just when I am freshest. I want to devote this for the present to the languages until I can read readily enough to glean archaeological material from the texts along the lines of work I have so often talked over with you. But I so much wish I could have some help until I can get on my feet again after this long interruption of my Egyptian studies. I am writing to you in the hope that possibly you are not so busy but that you could give me some help by correspondence. I should wish, of course, and I am now perfectly able to do so, to give compensation for the time it cost you, so far as it is expressible in monetary values. I'm hoping that you want some Egyptian books badly that you don't feel quite like affording and will let me get them for you in return for assistance. What I should like to do is to send you occasionally a batch of sheets with text and transliteration and translation so far as I can give them to be corrected, much as I used to hand in papers when a student in Chicago. If this would be a burden or for any reason you do not wish to do it, you will say so, will you not? What would you suggest if it is not feasible for you? I might try to make some arrangement with Dr. Müller or even with someone in Germany. Or I can work along alone. I have already ferreted out some things, but you know what round about method one has to use if a word or phrase is neither in Erman's <u>Glossar</u>[35] or in one's head. Your <u>Records</u> have been invaluable to me and will be still more so when I get the principal publications of texts to use with them. The later volumes

---

Egyptian philology in the 20th century.

[34] JHB, *Ancient Records of Egypt: Historical Documents from the Earliest Times to the Persian Conquest, Collected, Edited, and Translated with Commentary*, 5 vol. (Chicago: University of Chicago Press, 1906).

[35] Adolf Erman's *Aegyptisches Glossar: Die Häufigeren Worte der Aegyptischen Sprache* (Berlin: Verlag von Reuther & Reichard, 1904).

of the Urkunden have just reached me and are being bound. The new work is opening very pleasantly and I am happy in all the opportunities it offers. Mr Lythgoe is an ideal person to work with. At present I have no executive work or care of any kind, but put in all my hours studying. Of course when Mr Lythgoe returns to the field, considerable responsibility and routine work will fall to me, but I am reveling in this year given wholly to work that counts intellectually.

We have found a pleasant place to live, my mother and I, across the park from the museum.[36] I am able to return to luncheon with my mother and am not dependent on surface cars or subway which is a great blessing. I hope that we may see you here, and if Mrs Breasted can come too we shall be so glad.

The Philadelphia mastaba is the one which was in St. Louis and was considered for the Field Columbian Museum, is it not? I noticed, to my great surprise, a piece of it in the Boston Museum, when I was there, a fortnight ago. In the last week of September I paid a visit in the Newport home of Mr Theodore M. Davis.[37] It was such a treat to see his art treasures. Besides valuable Egyptian objects he has paintings by all masters, mediaeval

---

[36] The two women moved into the Beresford—an apartment hotel built in 1889 at 81st street and Central Park West. There were no kitchens in the apartments, which rented for $100-$150 per month (around $2500 today), and meals could be eaten in the dining room for $7 per person, per week (Christopher Gray, 'Streetscapes: The Beresford, the San Remo, the Majestic, the El Dorado, the Century; Namesake Precursors of Central Park West's Towers,' *New York Times* Sept. 14, 1997). Apartment hotels were popular in the early 20th century, as Gray noted in his article, so people—especially single women—could 'avoid the cares of housekeeping.' The Beresford especially had 'sweeping views of Central Park' so that residents could 'dine under such conditions [that] must surely aid both appetite and digestion.'

[37] Theodore M. Davis (1838-1915) was an American lawyer and businessman who became wealthy through investments and banking work in New York City in the late 19th and early 20th centuries. He was associated with Boss Tweed and other Gilded Age robber barons (e.g. Charles Wilbour). He made 18 trips to Egypt from 1887-1914, in which he opened a number of tombs in the Valley of the Kings. Much of his private collection is now in the MMA. A new biography from John M. Adams, *The Millionaire and the Mummies: Theodore Davis's Gilded Age in the Valley of the Kings* (New York: St. Martin's Press, 2013) brings to light new issues not covered in *WWWIE*. Diaries of the trips, recorded by his companion, Emma B. Andrews, exist in the archives at the Egyptian Art Department of the MMA and are currently being transcribed by the Emma Andrews Diary project: http://www.emmabandrews.org/project/ (accessed November 1, 2016).

ivories, XV. century Florentine and Sienese reliefs in marble, more lovely things than I can communicate.

With kindest regards, also to Mrs Breasted, very sincerely yours |
Caroline L. Ransom

**19 October 1910**                                                         **0016**

October 19, 1910

My dear Miss Ransom,

I was very glad indeed to receive your letter reporting the progress of your work in the Metropolitan Museum. Your report quite makes me envious, it is so suggestive of academic ease and opportunity to work. Here there is of course the usual rush.

Now with regard to the help which you are needing. I cannot possibly resist a call of this character, and I am ready to do all in my power, but I am unwilling to discuss the matter of remuneration. We will just let virtue be its own reward.

Let me confess in the beginning however that I may not always command the information which you desire. The Ptolemaic texts and documents of late date in hieroglyphic are often very difficult indeed. There are many local methods of writing, and dialects which I am far from claiming to command. For instance the method of writing and the grammar at Dendera are so highly specialized and so peculiar to the place, that Junker[38] has recently issued a special grammar of the Dendera texts which I have not yet been able to work through. This will give you an idea of the situation, but so far as I am able, I shall be glad to serve. I will only ask that a very clear and practical plan for connecting your translations with your copies of the original texts be adopted. It would be best to use a blue pencil and to number paragraphs and lines of original and translation in blue pencil with corresponding numbers. I shall then be able to find my

---

[38] Hermann J. B. Junker (1877-1962) was a German Egyptologist who studied at Berlin under Erman, earning his PhD in 1904. Started his career with the *Grammatik der Denderatexte* (Leipzig: J. C. Hinrichs'sche Buchhandlung, 1906). While he began as an epigrapher, he continued as a field archaeologist and was responsible for clearing and recording many of the Giza mastabas.

way through your notes and make the comparisons without loss of time in bringing the two together.

I hope you have a list of corrections for my Records – a piece of work which I was obliged to do altogether too rapidly, even after they were in proof.

I am very much pleased to hear that you are able to spend so much time on the language, and I hope that it may all contribute to your work in the art in which you are chiefly interested, I infer. I may be visiting New York in February and it will be a great pleasure to accept your invitation and to see something of your work. Mrs. Breasted joins me in kindest regards.

Very sincerely yours | JHB

P.S. I went to the St. Louis Exposition myself, especially to inspect the Philadelphia mastaba. I recommended its purchase to the Field Museum, for it was very cheap, but they were so slow in moving that Mr. Wanamaker stepped in first and secured it for Philadelphia, much to my regret. We now have two mastabas here however at the Field Museum but they are not to be unpacked or mounted until the new building is available. The Philadelphia mastaba is not very good work as you of course saw.

**29 October 1910**                                              **0017**

Metropolitan Museum of Art |
New York | October 29, 1910

Dear Mr Breasted,

I am availing myself of your great kindness first by sending the inscriptions of a XXVI. dynasty sarcophagus. I send them under separate covers, a photograph of the main inscription in our package and my copies and work in another. If you would care to keep the photograph, I should be very glad to have you do so, as I can easily get another copy.

The main inscription has cost me a good deal of time, in the first place to identify it at all! – it is the 72nd chapter of the Book of the Dead. I started to write it out in vertical columns, with variant readings from the Turin papyrus and the New Empire versions published by Naville[39] in other parallel vertical columns, but I had to give this up for the present for lack of time. But I have gone over the text pretty carefully with Naville's book on my right and the Lepsius[40] Totenbuch[41] on my left! The thing that interests me particularly is to know just how definitely the text was fixed in the Saitic[42] recension. I should like now to compare this text with other late versions, but thus far have not found any available here except the Turin papyrus.

I have written out a few definite questions in blue pencil with references to page of my copy and line of text, hoping this would save your time. I should be very sorry to impose on you any task of comparing versions or of reading my penciled notes. So please understand that in sending my full material, it is not with any thought that you can look it over in detail, but merely to have it in your hands if at any point you wished to see the variant reading. I have enclosed a directed envelope which can be used in returning the material. If any way occurs to you in which I can arrange material more conveniently, please be sure to tell me. I should like again in a few days to ask light on various small parts, but there will be nothing long again for some time to come. I cannot thank you enough for your generous

---

[39] Edouard Naville (1844-1926) was an Egyptologist and Biblical scholar. He was the first to excavate for the Egypt Exploration Fund (EEF) officially in 1882. His publication of his excavations at Tell el-Mashkuta in 1883 became the format for publications of this type in the future. He preferred large temples and monuments, unlike Petrie and others.

[40] Richard Lepsius (1810-1884) was an early German Egyptologist who studied ancient languages. He wrote a now-famous letter to Ippolito Rosellini in which he accepted, expanded and corrected on Champollion's decipherment of hieroglyphics; this 'marked the turning-point' for the study of ancient hieroglyphs.

[41] *Das Todtenbuch der Ägypter nach dem Hieroglyphischen Papyrus in Turin* (Leipzig: bei Georg Wigand, 1842) is the book CRW refers to. In it, he transcribed and translated the Book of the Dead Papyrus Turin 1791, which came from the Ptolemaic period; this was the model for all other translations and transcriptions of Book of the Dead papyri and the basis of the numbering of the spells. See http://archiv.ub.uni-heidelberg.de/propylaeumdok/467/ for more explanation and a pdf copy of the text (accessed 1 November 2016).

[42] Refers to the Saite Period, a late period in Ancient Egypt denoted by the 26th and 28th dynasties, whose pharaohs ruled from Sais in the Western Delta from c. 664-525 BC and c. 404-378 BC. 525-404 BC comprise the First Persian Period (27th dynasty). For an excellent history of this period, see Alan B. Lloyd, 'The Late Period,' in *Ancient Egypt: A Social History*, ed. B. G. Trigger, B. J. Kemp, D. O'Connor and A. B. Lloyd (Cambridge: Cambridge University Press, 1999), 279-348.

kindness to me. I shall live in hope that the opportunity may come to me some day to serve you. This department has a great future before it I am sure. The work of excavation and purchase is to go on indefinitely and we hope to build up a single strong collection. I think you would be surprised to know how much is here already.

With best greetings to you and Mrs Breasted | and again my warmest thanks for your kindness | Sincerely yours | Caroline L. Ransom.

Please tell me whether you prefer to have me address you at the University or at your house.

**25 November 1910**                                                    **0018**

Metropolitan Museum of Art |
New York | November 25, 1910

My dear Mr Breasted,

I have too long delayed in telling you that my material on the Saite sarcophagus arrived safely. I thank you many, many times for all your helpful corrections and suggestions.

I shall not get at any further study of the Saitic rescension immediately, but I should like to later if I ever am prepared to handle it. Yet I must struggle along even now with these late incorrect texts of our sort and another because there are so many inscribed coffins, stelae etc of XXVI. dyn. or later in the collection. Just at present I have been diverted from them to take care of newly acquired Coptic material of which I have made an inventory this month and about which I want now write a Bulletin article. It is interesting yet I feel restless when the Museum work doesn't involve some work with the texts, because I am so anxious to make progress in the language. I shall be able to go back to the coffins when I have disposed of the Coptic Shrines I hope. I've been roped into addressing the Classical Club of Barnard College[43] this week, so November hasn't afforded as much

---

[43] Barnard College was (and is) a women's college in New York City. It was founded in 1889 with the aim of giving women the same rigorous education as men; in 1900 it joined with then-all-male Columbia University and remained a women's college when Columbia finally allowed women in 1983. www.Barnard.edu (accessed 1 November 2016) CRW's association with them points to their early successes in their mission.

time of the language as I had hoped. I shall surely do better next month. With sincere regards and thanks | C.L.Ransom

**19 November 1911**                                                              **0019**

Norddeutscher Lloyd, Bremen |
Dampfer 'Kronprinzessin Cecilie' |
November 19, 1911

My dear Professor Breasted:

You will have received an invitation to the opening of the Egyptian Department of the Metropolitan Museum and thus know that the long task of installation is at an end.[44] As I did not have a holiday last summer I am getting away now for two months. I shall go first to Berlin and tell Professor Erman what I want to accomplish and abide by his advice as to where to work.

I was intending to send you a copy of the Handbook of the Egyptian Rooms[45] which we brought out on the evening of the opening. But just before I left it was decided to send out a certain number of honorary copies and of course your name was placed on the list. The book was put through a great rush and I fear this is all too evident. Of course nobody could expect uniformity of literary style in a book written by four people, but we ought, in my opinion, to have [come together] on matters of spelling, the use of hyphens etc, and to have criticized one another's sections. But for all that there was no time. The book was not even thought of five weeks before the date of the opening; up to that time we were expecting to issue a new brief special number of the <u>Bulletin</u>. We all wrote our several sections at home in the evening, for there was work to do at the Museum to keep us busy during the day. I lay to overweariness at the time of writing some of my own slips. I notice now that I have said that the Pyramid Texts occur in various fifth dynasty pyramids instead of fifth and sixth dynasty. But

---

[44] According to the History of the Egyptian Art Department at the MMA, the department was established in 1906 to manage the growing collection of Egyptian art and artifacts at the MMA. It seems in this letter that the department did not open to the public until November 1911.

[45] Metropolitan Museum of Art, *A Handbook of the Egyptian Rooms* (New York: MMA, 1911).

the special purpose of this letter is to explain that I was not unmindful in writing of the help you had given me on the sarcophagus of Har-Khebit.[46] The reasons why I did not acknowledge it in the Handbook are that in the first place I made only partial use of the material, as you will see, and, in the second place, it did not seem to me quite the suitable place. If, when we get our museum publication, I publish it with text and discussion, I shall then make acknowledgement of your kindness.

I read a long time ago in the Chicago Record that you were to give some lectures in New York in March of 1912. I hope this is true. It will be such a pleasure to see you.

We have had a very good voyage for a wintry one. But I shall be glad to land on Tuesday – I am not very fond of the sea! Mrs Harkness[47] writes of the great interest and pleasure of a course she is taking with you – I quite envy her the privilege.

Berlin will not seem the same to me without Professor Kelsale who died last winter, but I shall be glad to see the Ermans again.

With kindest regards, also to Mrs Breasted | Sincerely yours | Caroline L. Ransom

**25 February 1912**                                                    **0020**

The Beresford | 1 West Eighty-first Street |
February 25, 1912

My dear Mr Breasted:-
Through my aunt, Miss Randolph, I have heard definitely of your engagements in the East and I cannot tell you how much I am anticipating seeing you in New York. Mother and I so much wish to have you come to see

---

[46] Early 26th dynasty sarcophagus on display at the MMA. Albert M. Lythgoe, 'Recent Egyptian Acquisitions,' *The Metropolitan Museum of Art Bulletin* 2:12 (December 1907): 193-194.
[47] Mary Emma Harkness, née Stillman (1874-1950), married to Edward S. Harkness (1874-1940) who was a philanthropist and collector. He was a friend of Lythgoe's and was appointed a trustee of the MMA in 1912, chairman of the MMA Egyptian Committee in 1914. Thanks to his wealth and generosity, he made numerous gifts to the Egyptian Deparment, which funded expeditions to Saqqara (allowing the excavation and retrieval of the tomb of Perneb, see below).

us here at the Beresford.[48] I know you will be very much fêted but won't you please dine with us at least once? You shall set the date just when you can best fit it in to your other engagements. I am just back from Berlin, having seen many of your good friends there, so perhaps you will be glad to have news of them.

Dr Burchardt[49] asked me if I would intercede with you for a copy of the Marriage Stela of Ramses II. He said you had promised it to him. I can imagine it possible that you have reasons for not wishing to put the inscription into his hands yet, but if it is merely a question of time in which to copy your copy for him, may I venture to offer my services as copyist. If you could bring your copy with you, it need be out of your hands only a little time at the museum, where it would be quite safe. It would be good exercise for me, for I have never taken any pains to write hieroglyphs well until the question came up in Berlin of my making the Zettel of our inscriptions for the dictionary[50] and I set to work to learn to copy better.

I haven't heard whether your lectures at Union Theological Seminary are open to the public, but I am hoping that they are. I shall write soon to the secretary and find out.

Of our department at the museum, Mr Lythgoe and Mr Winlock[51] are in Egypt, Mr Mace[52] is about but is giving his entire time to publications

---

[48] CRW and her mother lived in the Beresford for about four years.

[49] Max Burchardt (1885-1914) was a German Egyptologist who studied with Erman and got his PhD in 1908; he had been an assistant at the Berlin Museum in 1904, likely overlapping with CRW which is why she knew him. He died while serving Germany in the First World War.

[50] This and all further references to 'the Egyptian dictionary' or 'the dictionary' when mentioning Erman have to do with arguably his greatest work, the *Wörterbuch der ägyptischen Sprache*, which was published in 5 volumes in Leipzig from 1926-31 and two more volumes from 1957-63. The dictionary was the concentrated work of Erman and Hermann Grapow (see note 68), with contributions from leading Egyptologists at the time, including JHB, CRW and many of the scholars they discuss in their letters.

[51] Herbert E. Winlock (1884-1950) was an American Egyptologist who trained with the MMA but never received a PhD. He was Director of the Egyptian Expedition of the MMA from 1928-32; Curator of the Egyptian Department of the MMA from 1929-39; Director of the MMA from 1932-39. He was a high-quality excavator who trained under Lythgoe and others.

[52] Arthur C. Mace (1874-1928) was an Egyptologist trained by Petrie in the field. In 1906 he joined the MMA excavations at Lisht, and from 1909 he was assistant Curator in the Egyptian Department at the MMA. CRW would have worked closely with him (except for the War

and I have the responsibility of the department. I have an assistant who is to work chiefly on the inventory and we are just starting in on that. Then our labels are still very incomplete, so that it will be many months before I can get at any very satisfactory piece of work. Still the writing of labels is most informing and I am well content. I am working at hieratic by myself along lines suggested by Dr Müller who gave me private lessons during my stay in Berlin.

I am so sorry that Mrs Breasted is not to be with you. I should like so much to see her again. Please give her my best greetings.

Mother joins me in kind regards to you and in hoping that we may have the pleasure of welcoming you here.

Sincerely yours | Caroline L. Ransom

**15 March 1912**                                                    **0021**

The Beresford | 1 West Eighty-first Street |
March 15, 1912

My dear Mr Breasted:-

Just a word to make sure that you have our address and to say that the Broadway car to 81st and then to walk east to Central Park West (we are just on the corner) is your easiest way to reach us, if you are living near Union Theological Seminary. I hope you will be well enough to come on Sunday for we so much anticipate seeing you soon.

We greatly enjoyed the lecture this afternoon.[53] It is kind of Union Theological Seminary to open the lectures to the public and to place them at an hour when busy people can attend. There would have been a much larger delegation from the museum and from the Beresford, but for the storm.

---

years). In 1919 he returned to the MMA and was made Associate Curator in 1922. He assisted Howard Carter in clearing the tomb of Tutankhamun from 1922-24.

[53] He gave a total of 8 (possibly 10) lectures in March at the Union Theological Seminary in the Morse Series. He published them later in 1912 as *Development in Religion and Thought in Ancient Egypt: Lectures Delivered on the Morse Foundation at Union Theological Seminary* (New York: Charles Scribner's Sons, 1912). He dedicated the book 'To Adolf Erman, in gratitude and affection.'

Sincerely yours | Caroline L. Ransom
I forgot to say that we dine at seven.


**29 April 1912**                                                    **0022**

Metropolitan Museum of Art |
New York | April 29, 1912

My dear Professor Breasted:

It has given me the greatest pleasure to read through the 256 page proofs which have thus far reached me. I don't feel, however, that I can have helped you much, the pages are already so nearly perfect that I have found almost no printer's errors. I enclose a list of pages to facilitate the transfer to the proof you intend to return to the printer of any corrections I may have found which had escaped your attention. I have been puzzled, as I always am, by the titles of French books. The <u>Style-Book</u> of the University of Chicago, ed. 3, p. 19 lays down the law: 'In <u>French</u>, Italian, Spanish, and Scandinavian titles, capitalize proper nouns but not adjectives derived from them.' French books themselves differ in practice but more often follow this rule than not. I find in a French book in our library, for instance, 'Mémoires Mission français,' 'Mission' evidently being considered a proper noun here, and the adjective being uncapitalized. On the other hand, De Vinne, <u>Correct Composition</u> p. 435 quotes a number of French titles capitalizing all the important words in the titles. At least you will want to apply one method throughout your footnotes and insert the accents.

I have the prints from my negatives ready and will send them today with the proof. I am not satisfied with all the prints. Any which you find that you can use and want a better print of, I can have done over. With the kindest regards, also to Mrs Breasted, and so many thanks for the pleasure the proofs have given me,

Sincerely yours | Caroline L. Ransom

**14 May 1912**                                                    **0023**

The Beresford | 1 West Eighty-first Street |
May 14, 1912

My dear Professor Breasted:-

You have given me far too generous acknowledgment both by letter and in your book for the little I was able to do on your proofs![54] It was such a pleasure and privilege to try to help a bit with the proof. I only hope you will let me do the same on the Nile book—only without preface acknowledgment, for your kind mention of me in this book is reward enough for two times!

When you decide what photographs of mine you can use, let me lend you the negatives, for I am afraid only a few of those prints I sent you are usable. Then you can have prints made just to your liking. Mr Lythgoe returns about July 1st and soon after I hope he will take up the matter of the prints from his negatives which you would like.

I am expecting daily now a consignment of eighteen cases from Egypt containing a great deal of valuable material. This year will see much added to our collections as a second consignment is to follow this one. I am to have the responsibility of unpacking these first cases alone. Among the objects is a XII dynasty stela with 19 inscribed lines – dated in the 17th year of Sesostris I. Below the inscription Menthuweser sits before a table of offerings with various children ranged before him.[55] The inscription, so far as I have thus far made it out from a small photograph, does not seem to contain historical facts but only to relate what a good man the deceased was. Nevertheless it is a notable piece. It is a comfort to have an inscription of a good period to try, I have had to struggle with so many Saitic and Ptolemaic[56] ones since I came here.

---

[54] JHB, *Development of Religion and Thought in Ancient Egypt.* The acknowledgement she writes about states: '…it is a pleasant duty to express my indebtedness to my friend and one-time pupil, Dr. Caroline Ransom, of the Metropolitan Museum, for her kindness in reading the entire page-proof…' (xii; see letter 0022).

[55] The stela of Mentuwoser is from the 12th dynasty, in the Middle Kingdom, found at Abydos. It shows Mentuwoser at his funeral banquet. The MMA was given the piece in 1912 by Edward S. Harkness as a gift after he bought it from Dikran G. Kelekian. It is on display at the MMA in Gallery 110. (http://www.metmuseum.org/collection/the-collection-online/search/544320 , accessed 10 November 2016)

[56] Refers to the Ptolemaic period, which essentially began in Egypt with the death of

I wish Chicago were not so far away and we could hope to see you oftener here! We shall do our best to attract you by making the Metropolitan collection as good as it can be made. Then it is the place to gather archives as fast as possible. There was no chance to show you all the Davies paintings and the architectural plans and drawings already assembled, also the Koch photographs of the inscriptions of the Itibis temple. We are to have 100 feet in the basement of the new wing for storage and student material, also a student room and four exhibition rooms above. So what you saw here is just the beginning of the development.

I am eager now for the appearance of the book on religion. I do so wish we could have the translation of the entire Pyramid Texts. My kind regards please to Mrs Breasted. How much we should enjoy occupying the guestroom, it is very good of you to want us. Only we don't go west very often. Please both of you come soon to New York.

With kindest greeting from us both | Caroline L. Ransom


**31 July 1912**                                                   **0024**

Wildmere House | Minnewaska,
Ulster Co., N. Y. | July 31, 1912

My dear Professor Breasted:-

On Saturday last I mailed to you from New York the prints from Mr Lythgoe's negatives which you desired. The positives and print from which you selected were all enlargements, but I trust that the prints mailed to you are sufficiently clear, though from such small negatives, to serve as copy for your book, so far as you care to use them. Mr Lythgoe was entirely cordial about letting you have them and I only hope they have reached you in time. Mr Lythgoe had so much to do about expedition publications when he reached home on July 1st, that I could not take up the matter at once.

You will see that I am having a _real_ vacation. I wonder if you and Mrs Breasted know Minnewaska. It is only eight miles from the better

---

Alexander the Great in 332 BC; it was officially begun in 305 BC with Ptolemy I Soter declaring himself pharaoh. An interesting history of this period is Michel Chauveau's _Egypt in the Age of Cleopatra: History and Society under the Ptolemies_ (Ithaca: Cornell University Press, 2000).

known Lake Mohawk where the Peace Conferences are held. The Mohawk hotel and the two hotels here are all under the management of the Smiley brothers. Miss Randolph and my mother are here with me and we are enjoying the place very much. There are wonderful drives, rugged trails to follow and a little gem of a lake. We go back to New York next week and I shall have another eight days in the museum. Then on August 20th I sail from Boston on the Cunarder Laconia, and go directly from Liverpool to London for a few days and from there without stop to Berlin. I have to be back the middle of October, so shall have only four weeks of solid work, but even that little time will be worth much to me. There are a few things I wish to look up in London and by going by way of England, I have the pleasure of sailing with a friend and the voyage instead of being something to endure, merely, will be a real recreation. This friend is a biologist and is going out to Constantinople for two years to take charge of the biological department of the woman's college there; Dr Patrick,[57] the president of the college, sails on the same steamer with us. If you care for any of my negatives, or there is anything I can do for you in the museum, please let me know. I can be reached there between the 6th and 19th of August. Before coming away I unpacked seventeen cases of antiquities; now our basement storage place is filled up with seventy-two cases, the second and third shipments from Egypt, which were awaiting customs inspection when I left. There is some excellent new material. You will want to see it sometime. I should like so much to help about the proofs of the Nile book if they do not appear before October 15th when I get back. Will you please share this letter with Mrs Breasted to whom I owe a letter I believe.

I trust the new house is progressing to your satisfaction. Mother and Miss Randolph add their greetings to mine.

With kindest regards to you both | Sincerely yours | Caroline L. Ransom

---

[57] Mary Mills Patrick, who was president of the Constantinople Women's College from 1890-1924. She wrote an autobiography called *Under Five Sultans* (New York: The Century Co., 1929) which detailed her time at the College. See http://www.oac.cdlib.org/findaid/ark:/13030/kt3489r737/ for information about her collected papers.

18 February 1913                                    0025

Metropolitan Museum of Art |
New York | February 18, 1913

My dear Professor Breasted:-

A few days ago I received a letter from the President of the Archaeological Institute of America asking me to take charge of the section on Egypt in the <u>Bulletin</u> of the Institute, about to be issued monthly.[58] He said that you had suggested me for this post. As I felt obliged to decline, I wish to tell you briefly my reasons. We are simply overwhelmed with work here, new material is being added so rapidly to the department. Seventy cases of expedition material are now on the way from Egypt, and there will be other shipments of purchase material later in the year. The brunt of the work in unpacking, accessioning etc of this material falls on me and one office assistant. Then we have elaborate plans for department publications in the near future and I am already obliged to write for the Museum <u>Bulletin</u> about as many popular articles as I care to write. Furthermore, as all the Egyptologists whom I know have their hands more than full I should dread the editor's task of trying to elicit articles from them. For all these reasons and still others I felt obliged to declined [sic], which doesn't mean of course that I was not very pleased and grateful to you for suggesting my name.

Now that I am writing I should like to say that I hope if you review Maspero's <u>Egyptian Art</u>[59] for the <u>Nation</u> that you will call attention to the erroneous legend accompanying Fig 40, p. 25. This is unmistakably the ivory comb owned by Theodore M. Davis which the greater part of the time is on loan in the Metropolitan Museum. We have it at the present moment!

I trust that 'all the Breasteds, large and small' are well this winter and enjoying their new house! I was very pleased to receive their Christmas greeting. My best regards, please, to Mrs Breasted. My mother and I often refer with pleasure to the glimpses we had of you last Spring and hope that you will come again ere long. A recent letter from Miss McCurdy[60] of

---

[58] This would have been a formidable administrative task for Ransom Williams (or any other scholar) at this time. It would also have made her name widely- and well-known in the field.

[59] Gaston Maspero, *Art in Egypt* (New York: Charles Scribner's Sons, 1912).

[60] Grace Harriet McCurdy received her PhD in 1903 from Columbia and taught at Vassar from 1893-1937. See more about here at http://greekandromanstudies.vassar.edu/about/

the Greek Department, Vassar College, spoke of how much your lecture given there last autumn was enjoyed. Then Dr. Patrick, President of the Constantinople College for Women wrote the other day to thank me for a copy of 'Religion and Thought in Ancient Egypt' and was warm in her expression of how interesting she found the book. She is a very intellectual woman whom I greatly enjoyed learning to know when I crossed the Atlantic last summer. I found the Ermans well and as usual was with them a good deal. I used the Dictionary more than I ever have previously and worked through a difficult Middle Kingdom text on a grave stela which we have recently acquired. This will probably be published ere long. With the kindest greetings from mother and me,
 Sincerely yours | Caroline L. Ransom


**22 February 1913**                                    0026

Chicago | February 22, 1913
My dear Miss Ransom:
It was very pleasant to hear from you again. I ought to have written you before handing in your name to President Wilson, but they have been pestering me to death to get behind the Egyptian work of the Institute, and you see I endeavored to make you one of the first victims. I fear they will have difficulty in finding any one to look after the Egyptian department of their new Journal. If you have any one to suggest I should be very grateful, in their name, but as you say, everybody in our field is loaded to the gunnel.

Maspero sent me his new art book, but I have not heard from the Nation about it. You are quite right about the Davis comb, which I saw many years ago in his home at Newport, and recognized at once on opening the book a fortnight ago. But have you noticed how many of the legends under the cuts are wrong? I am inclined to be very charitable in such matters with busy men, for I know how often I have slipped myself, but it seems to me that the famous green head of Berlin, (Figure 476), <u>ought</u> not to have been attributed to the Louvre; the well-known granite statue of Ramses II at Turin ought not to masquerade as alabaster, (Figure 358); and <u>Sakhit</u> has

---

history.html (accessed 8 November 2016).

too long been understood to be <u>Sakhmet</u>, to appear as in Figure 564; etc., etc.

I am hoping to see you and your mother again around the week's end of March 8th, when I shall be returning from the completion of the Brown University course. I have very pleasant recollections of my visit a year ago. The news of the Ermans was welcome. What a charming little book his primer, 'Die Hieroglyphen',[61] is.

With pleasant regards to your mother and yourself, in which Mrs. Breasted joins, I am | Always very sincerely yours | JHB

**28 February 1913**                                          0027

February 28, 1913 | The Beresford | 
1 West Eighty-first Street

My dear Mr Breasted:-

It is very good news that you are coming to New York in the near future. Could you dine with us here Sunday evening March 9th at 6:30? Or if you are staying into the next week any evening after that would suit us if more convenient to you. I have an engagement for Saturday evening. Then about the Museum. Of course some of our 1912 accessions are on exhibition including the interesting Menthuweser stela in the Fifth Room but there is much down stairs that you ought to see including a most valuable set of coffins of the early XII. or possibly pre-XII. –polychrome with texts in hieratic and pictures with legends attached – inside – the usual sort only I think ours have some unique features. Now I have to be away from the Museum Friday all day and Saturday afternoon. I shall be there from 10-12 Saturday, all day Monday and thereafter. I take it you will not get here Friday so that doesn't matter but hope it will be possible for you to go to the Museum Saturday morning or Tuesday or later. Such few ideas as I have about the editorship for Egypt of the Institute's Bulletin, I'll impart when I see you. I wish Mrs Breasted were coming, too, but I fear she isn't since you didn't say so. Kindest regards from us both and anticipation of your coming.

---

[61] Adolf Erman, *Die Hieroglyphen* (Berlin un Leipzig: G.J. Göschn'sche Verlagshandlung, 1912).

Cordially yours | C. L. Ransom

I shall have things to tell you about the Ermans. I've had two letters from Professor Erman lately. Don't bother to answer until you know what will be convenient to you. I will hold the times free which I mentioned.

**5 March 1913**                                                    0028

March 5, 1913

My dear Miss Ransom:
Many thanks for your kind note and invitation. My New York programme is still a little uncertain, but I shall try to write you a card from the train, with further indication.

I have a lumbago back, so please excuse machine.

With kindest regards to yourself and to your mother, I am | Most sincerely yours | JHB

**18 March 1913**                                                    0029

March 18, 1913

My dear Miss Ransom:
Many thanks for the beautiful photograph of the new stela. It seems as good as the original. I am going to take it up with my youngsters next Quarter.

Wasn't it stupid of me not to look under 'hotels' for the telephone number of The Beresford, but I couldn't find it under the B's, so I ran away in a hurry, not knowing it was so late, and thinking surely to find you before you should have gone out. Too bad! But we had a delightful morning in the Museum at any rate.

Remember me kindly, please, to your mother.

Always very faithfully yours | JHB

**31 March 1913**                                                    **0030**

March 31, 1913

My dear Miss Ransom:

Have you noticed that the earliest specimens of glass in Northern and Central Italy are in several cases almost exact reproductions of the variegated blue glass bottle of Theodore M. Davis which you have on loan at the Metropolitan? 'Civilization Primitive on Italie', I Planches, Series B, Plate 103, No.7; also, ibid., Plate 298, No.1. The bottles shown on Plate 103, No.8; Plate 156, No.1; and Plate 361, No.14; are all interesting as practically identical with the Egyptian type of such bottles. I believe the Davis vase is published, is it not, in his Thutmose IV, or one of his volumes? Would it be too much trouble to secure a photograph of this bottle? The bill goes to my publisher, and if you would kindly attend to it I should very much like to have it, and publish it in the book beside my Italian example. But do please send me the bill. If my generous friends in the Metropolitan will insist on sending me photographs without a bill, my only recourse will be to cease asking, and I am sure you won't let me do that.

With kindest regards | Sincerely yours | JHB

**5 April 1913**                                                    **0031**

Metropolitan Museum of Art | New York |
Department of Egyptian Art | April 5, 1913

My dear Professor Breasted:-

It was a great disappointment to me to miss your call that Sunday morning, and I have been meaning to write to tell you so! Another time when you are in town I won't leave the house. There was still so much to talk over!

I am pleased that you find the Menthu-weser stela of sufficient interest to take up with your 'youngsters.' I worked through it, as best I could, in Berlin and handed the manuscript for its publication to the Director several weeks ago. He said then that it should be published at once. But when estimates were obtained, it was found that it would cost between seven and eight hundred dollars to bring it out with two collotype

them accessible through the ancient door from the Second Room. They descended upon me for a Bulletin article after I had committed myself to getting away on Friday. This is why I have not earlier acknowledged the arrival of the ms. with your interesting and helpful notes. I am more grateful to you than I can tell!

There are several things I should like to say about it, but my aunt has filled my program here so full that I must defer these until later. I shall have some photographs to mail you when I return to the Museum on the 26th. They were not quite ready when I left. I motored up from New York with friends on Friday, attended the Pageant here on Saturday (repeated from the 75th anniversary), an open-air rendering of 'As You Like It' in the evening and was with friends in Springfield yesterday. You see I am being very frivolous!

I enclose some stamps to cover the registering of my package. The desk of the college room where I am being entertained has paper, but no envelopes, hence this old one from my bag!

With warm regards, also to Mrs Breasted | Sincerely yours | Caroline L. Ransom

**28 May 1913**                                     **0041**

Metropolitan Museum of Art |
New York | May 28, 1913

My dear Professor Breasted:-

I have in mind to write to you at greater length soon. This is just to acknowledge your kind letter, which awaited me when I returned to the Museum and today that prints of Mr Davis's glass vase will reach you in due time. It takes a little time for the matter to go through the Photographic Department. It is a pleasure to attend to it for you.

With kindest greetings | Caroline L. Ransom

I picked out for you the photographs of the coffins that seemed the most likely to be useful, the choice being determined chiefly by the state of preservation of the originals.

**2 June 1913**                                        0042

Chicago | June 2, 1913

My dear Miss Ransom:

I have received your kind note from South Hadley, and the photographs have since arrived. They are superb and have whetted my appetite wonderfully, but really I hope you will send me a bill, for they must have been very expensive. I wish I could ever get time to develop a seminar on the coffin texts and thus to work this material through carefully. I have three advanced men now quite capable of doing such work.

Before I forget it, let me tell you that on the advice of the President, I am going to step out of the harness until January 1st, 1914,- that is, taking six months' vacation. If your assistant, Miss Cartland, comes on in the autumn, I think I can arrange for Luckenbill to give the beginning course, as there are other applicants, I understand. I would then take up the class on the 1st of January, and do not think Miss Cartland would suffer any delay.

With kindest regards | Very faithfully yours | JHB

**10 June 1913**                                       0043

Metropolitan Museum of Art | New York | Department of Egyptian Art | June 10, 1913

My dear Professor Breasted:-

The photos of Mr. Davis's vase are being mailed to you today. The gilt-edged card 'Presented by the Trustees' etc is a frill of the Secretary of the Museum! The vase is considerably patched and the photos show its most favorable aspect, even though you might not think so. I had one ordinary silver print and one print of the kind used as copy for the Bulletin illustrations made. You caught the vase just in time, for the day after it was photographed, Mr. Davis sent for his things and it is now in Newport.

The ms. of the Menthu-weser stela is now in the hands of the Secretary of the Museum for publication. I think it will be out in the course of the summer. I want to thank you again for your kindness in looking it through. Your suggestions have taught me a good deal and I have adopted the majority of them. Where I didn't, I was probably foolish not to do so!

FIGURE 1: NSW, OR KING        FIGURE 2: : QN OR ḴN, MEANING MIGHT OR POWERFUL

When I was in Berlin last they were saying about Sethe's reading of [see figure 1] 'Erman glaubt es noch nicht.'[70] In view of your advice, I read Sethe's article in the ÄZ, which I ought of course to have done long ago, and found it convincing. I am grateful to you for stirring me up to be up to date on this point. With respect to the god referred to in the offering formula, unless I totally misunderstood them in Berlin, the interpretation I have given is a new result there. Dr Nöller gave me some late passage to support it but unfortunately I have mislaid the reference. In Erman's Hieroglyphen, p. 70, he translates 'möge er geben-----alle guten reinen Dingen, wovon ein Gott lebt.'[71] Wouldn't he be likely to say 'der Gott'[72] if he thought the word referred to Osiris, invoked at the beginning of the formula? I may have confused things, or, if not, they may be wrong, but I think I'll risk my text as I had it at this point and see what happens! I only hope the text will be considered interesting enough to awaken some discussion. I'm not sure that I understand what you mean with 'Fellow of the Mighty'. Do you understand it as Menthu-weser's way of saying that he was associated with the influential men of the king's government? That 'Powerful Second' was Professor Erman's suggestion, made with some hesitation, to be sure, and I've been uneasy about it. I haven't struck it out yet, but I may do so in the proof. So far as I thought about the determinative of [see figure 2] I thought it belonged to the expression as a whole.[73] Your translation seems

---

[70] Translation: 'Erman does not believe it yet.'

[71] Translation: 'May he give ----- all good pure things, of which a God lives'

[72] Translation: 'The God'

[73] These signs are difficult to translate without the rest of the context of the line. But the transliteration presented above is as close as I can get. The determinatives have to do with powerful qualities. In the published work, she remarked that this determinative could mean

a less far-fetched one, only I did not know before that 'neighbor' or 'fellow' was established for the first of the two words. It would seem to me as if the second word ought to be in the plural. I cannot tell you what a comfort it was to have your approval of the general character of the essay. Without it, I should not have had the courage to publish the thing.[74]

It is very tantalizing to hear of your plan for a Seminar in 'Coffin Texts' when I should so much like to be a member of it. If only you were at Columbia! I presume it will be my next task to work through the texts in Berlin which our coffins contain. Since you were here I have spent all the time I could spare from routine work on them.

I am delighted to hear that you are to take some time off this year. Miss Cartland will not be able to go to Chicago before the Autumn of 1914, if she can manage it then. Shall you be in Chicago when not teaching? I hope you are going to let me help on the proof of your Ancient History, as well as of the Nile book.

So far as I know now, Mr. Lythgoe will not be back until the middle of August. I may not try to go to Berlin before the middle of October. In that case I shall be here all summer and shall stay abroad until into January.

With kindest greetings, also to Mrs. Breasted | Sincerely yours | Caroline L. Ransom

**16 June 1913**                                                                                   **0044**

Chicago | June 16, 1913

My dear Miss Ransom:

I am very glad to have your letter of June 10th, and wish to thank you very much for the photograph of the Davis vase, which has duly arrived; but I

---

might or power. See Caroline Ransom, *The Stela of Menthu-Weser* (New York: Metropolitan Museum of Art, 1913), 18-19. The MMA presents a newer translation, in the form of 'decisive character' and not powerful or mighty (see http://www.metmuseum.org/art/collection/search/544320 Accessed 22 December 2016).

[74] In the first edition, she is noted as being the Assistant Curator of the Department of Egyptian Art on the title page; on the back page, there is a note that 300 copies of the book were printed in December 1913.

notice again that I do not receive any bill, and I shall have to devise some method of retaliation.

By 'fellow of the mighty' I meant 'comrade,' 'companion,' attaining the meaning 'companion' from the use of 'second' as 'like---equal, etc.' in the phrase 'without his like,' –literally, 'without his second.' One eye may be called the 'second' of the other, establishing the meaning of 'fellow,' or 'companion.' It seems to me, therefore, that he means to say he is the companion of the strong men of his time. 'kn' usually indicates physical strength, but I have no doubt might equally well indicate political or official power. The fact that 'kn' is not indicated as plural is, I admit, against this rendering.

Yes, I shall be in Chicago between August and January 1st next. I appreciate very much your kind offer of help in the proof reading, but I should be loath to impose upon you when I know you are so over-loaded already.

Mrs. Breasted joins me in kindest greetings to yourself and your mother. I envy you very much your coming trip to Berlin, and when the pot-boilers are done I shall be doing likewise.

Sincerely yours | JHB

**24 October 1913**                                                    **0045**

Chicago | October 24, 1913

My dear Miss Ransom:

Just a line to thank you for your two copies of the Metropolitan Bulletin with your interesting reports on your Nubian accessions and the new stela.[75] It looks stunning. I am grinding away on my text-book and feel as if I had migrated to foreign parts every time I look at Egypt.

With kindest regards | Very sincerely yours | JHB

---

[75] C.L.R. 'Nubian Objects Acquired by the Egyptian Department,' *MMAB* 8:9 (September 1913): 200-208; C.L.R. 'The Stela of Menthu-Weser,' *MMAB* 8:10 (October 1913): 213, 216-218.

**9 February 1914**  0046

Chicago | February 9, 1914

My dear Miss Ransom:

Many thanks for your copy of the long-expected stela. I congratulate you on its appearance, a sentiment which is based on both content and exterior.

I expect to be in New York during the latter half of March. I have a lecture at Yale on the 14th and two in Philadelphia on the 21st and 28th. The intervals I hope to spend in New York at the home of my good friend, Professor T. C. Hall of Union Theological Seminary. Of course I am looking forward to seeing you and your mother, and hope that we may have a pleasant visit.

With kindest regards to your mother and yourself | I am | Very faithfully yours | JHB

**7 March 1914**  0047

Chicago | March 7, 1914

Dear Miss Ransom:

Will you kindly have mailed an unmounted photographic print of the 'Great Etruscan Bronze Chariot' of the Metropolitan Museum,[76] to Mr. E. K. Robinson, Care of Ginn & Company, 29 Beacon Street, Boston? I will settle for it when I see you in New York. I am just rushing off last things in the way of illustration, and shall appreciate your assistance in the matter.

I am looking forward with great pleasure to a visit in New York.

With kindest regards to yourself and your mother | I am | Sincerely yours | JHB

---

[76] See for more information http://www.metmuseum.org/art/collection/search/247020 accessed 11 November 2016

9 March 1914                                                    0048

Metropolitan Museum of Art |
New York | March 9, 1914

Dear Professor Breasted:-

It was a pleasure to hear on my return from Berlin, about a month ago now, that you are to spend some time in New York this Spring. Indeed we shall see you next week, shall we not?

Do give us all the time you can both in the Museum and at the Beresford. My mother is looking forward to your coming as much as I am! Here in the Museum two rooms have been installed and opened to the public since you saw the collections and we have some beautiful new objects.

Your letter about the photograph has just come and I will attend to the matter with pleasure.

With anticipation and regards | Sincerely yours | Caroline L. Ransom

Isn't Mrs. Breasted coming this time? Please do give her my warm greetings. I have many messages for you both from Berlin.

29 May 1914                                                    0049

Chicago | May 29, 1914

My dear Miss Ransom:

Owing to my forgetfulness I failed to select from the available photographs of the Etruscan Chariot one suitable for my text-book.[77] Would you kindly use your own judgement in the matter, selecting the one which is most obvious and clear, so that a young person would discern what it is at once?

I am still regretting that we did not have another final session at the Museum.

With kindest regards to yourself and your mother, I am | Very faithfully yours | JHB

---

[77] James H. Breasted, *Ancient Times: A History of the Early World* (Boston, Mass.: Ginn and Company, 1916). He was repeatedly asked to write a textbook for high school-level history, he finally relented and *Ancient Times* 'established Breasted's reputation as one of the nation's leading experts in the field and the figure most commonly associated with ancient Near Eastern archaeology for many Americans' (Abt, *American Egyptologist*, 205). President Theodore Roosevelt was one of the books most ardent admirers, and by 1920 the book was selling 100,000 copies per year. See Abt, *American Egyptologist*, 195-206.

P.S. Kindly have photograph mailed, with bill, to <u>Mr. E. K. Robinson, Care Ginn & Company, 29 Beacon Street, Boston.</u> If the Museum does not issue bills, will you please liquidate and let me know the amount, and I will respond at once. Please do not fail to let me know the amount of expense, as you know it falls on the publishers and not me.

**19 April 1915**                                                                   **0050**

The Beresford | 1 West Eighty-first Street |
April 19, 1915

My dear Professor Breasted:
It has given me pleasure to read Professor Erman's letter which I have translated to Mother and which I now return to you with many thanks.

I made inquiries at the Museum this morning about the cast of Xerxes enthroned from the Hall of Columns at Persepolis, and learn that it was bought from Brucciani, London.[78] The upper part of the scene with the figure of the king cost £40 and the lower part, which in our Museum is separately exhibited at the left, cost <words missing> by Sir Cecil Smith entitled <u>Catalogue of Casts of Sculptures from Persepolis and the Neighborhood</u> with list of prices, in which account is given of a private expedition send out from England in the winter of 1891 to secure the moulds. The high price of the casts is accounted for by the heavy expense of this expedition. It is not even certain that the casts are longer obtainable as it was the intention to break the moulds when a certain number of impressions had been obtained, but if, despite the price, you are still interested, an inquiry of Brucciani or of Sir Cecil Smith would no doubt settle that point. I neglected to record Brucciani's address at the Museum this morning and am now writing at home, but I can easily get it for you as I have their catalogue, if you desire it. Very likely, however, you have it recorded yourself.

I hope that you had a comfortable journey home and found your family well. We both send warm greetings to you all-
Cordially yours | Caroline L. Ransom

---

[78] I have not found this item in the MMA database.

**28 April 1915**                                                        **0051**

Chicago | April 28, 1915

My dear Miss Ransom:

Many thanks for your prompt information regarding the Persian casts. I am sorry not to have returned your Erman letters before, but on my arrival I found our little girl quite sick, and since then Master James has followed suit. Both are now getting on well, but this complication has quite delayed me and I have not yet read the letters to Mrs. Breasted, which I hope to do at once and return them to you promptly.

I have carried home very delightful memories of my visit with your mother and you, and of all that I saw in the Museum. It is very gratifying to me to see a student of mind so satisfactorily situated and doing such substantial and successful work.

Please remember me most kindly to your mother, and believe me Always very faithfully yours | JHB

Many thanks for the Chamberlain book, which I am returning by same mail.


**N.D.**[79]                                                              **0052**

The Beresford | 1 West Eighty-first Street

My dear Mr Breasted:-

We are about starting west, Miss Randolph, my mother and I and I am planning to have Monday in Chicago. I must run about to the different collections of Egyptian objects and pick up any notes in color that the material affords, but would then be any time in the day when I could see

---

[79] This letter is not dated, but must have been written before she got married in 1916. She signed the letter CL Ransom, and talked about a trip west. The most telling evidence for dating this letter is her discussion of the installation of Perneb's tomb at the MMA and a publication she was working on in the summer. From this, one can assume that the letter must be from summer 1915. http://www.metmuseum.org/art/collection/search/543937 (accessed 13 July 2016). See also Caroline L. Ransom, *The Tomb of Perneb: With Illustrations* (New York: The Metropolitan Museum of Art, 1916); Caroline Ransom Williams, *The Decoration of the Tomb of Per-Neb: The Technique and the Color Conventions* (New York: The Metropolitan Museum of Art, 1932).

you for a few moments either at Haskell[80] or your home? We all expect to spend a couple of days in Chicago on our return, so if you are too busy to see me just at the opening of the academic year, don't hesitate to put me off. I've so little time on Monday that a brief call is all I could manage then any way. If I don't catch a glimpse of Mrs Breasted and those dear children Sunday; I shall hope to see them on my return journey. Would it bother you too much to send me just a post card to Toledo Ohio, c/o Hotel Secor, where we shall be Saturday, telling me when and where to catch you, if at all! Perneb's cult chambers are being installed and I have just finished a long chapter (of a proposed publication) on the technic [sic] of the decoration, a piece of work I have been engaged in all summer.

With kindest greetings to you both | Sincerely yours | C. L. Ransom


**18 January 1916**                                          **0053**

Metropolitan Museum of Art | New York |
Department of Egyptian Art | January 18, 1916

Dear Mr Breasted,

Ever since we returned I have wished to write to you and Mrs Breasted to tell you once more how greatly we all enjoyed the homey, delightful evening we spent with you. It was a great deal for you to do, to give us so much time just when your MS was so pressing. If I had been aware of the conditions under which you were working earlier, I don't think I should have let you know that we were in Chicago! I do hope the pressure is over now and the printing of the book will under way.

I plunged into so much work on my return that now the long journey seems very much of a happy dream and it is hard to believe that I have really been away. The installation of Perneb's tomb is nearly completed and the tomb is to be formally opened on the evening of February 3d with a large reception. Mr Lythgoe and I have rushed through a booklet on the tomb, which is now on the press and is promised for the evening of February 3d.

---

[80] Haskell Oriental Museum at the University of Chicago. It was completed in 1896 after Caroline E. Haskell donated funds for the museum to be dedicated to the memory of her husband. This museum and the collection displayed there formed the basis of the Oriental Institute 1919. There is also a library associated with the museum that bears the same name. See more here: https://oi.uchicago.edu/research/beginning#Institute

It is only a popular thing, but in a way I think such pieces of writing are a more responsible undertaking than a scientific work. If you make mistakes in writing for your fellow Egyptologists, they soon set you straight, but the public is so trusting and rarely goes into the more technical books! This little guide to Perneb's tomb is coming out in an edition of 2500 copies, to begin with, and Mr Harkness, who gave the tomb, has offered to make up the deficit if the Museum will sell it for ten cents a copy.[81]

I enclose the postcard which I gave to you in Chicago and then absent-mindedly gathered up with my notes! My mother sends her best greetings with mine to you and Mrs Breasted.

Ever sincerely yours | C. L. Ransom

**26 January 1916**                                                    **0054**

Chicago | January 26, 1916

My dear Miss Ransom:

Will you excuse a type-written note in reply to your very kind letter, which we were all very glad to receive? Many thanks for the San Francisco painted relief, which is very welcome.

I am enclosing you a letter from Erman, which has been sadly mutilated by the censor.[82] You will be interested in the Reisner[83] item.

I am greatly interested in your inauguration of the Perneb tomb. We will remember with the greatest pleasure the evening we had with you all, and the household joins me in kindest greetings to your mother, yourself and Miss Randolph.

---

[81] Lythgoe wrote the chapter about the history of the tomb, its description and its removal from Egypt and rebuilding in New York; Ransom Williams wrote the second chapter about its decorative and inscriptional features (49-79). Hers was the linguistic analytical work; Lythgoe's was the excavation method, further showing the gendered divide in workloads. There is a note on the back page, stating that 5000 copies were printed in February, and 5000 additional copies were printed in May. It was obviously quite popular among visitors.

[82] Not in files.

[83] George A. Reisner (1867-1942) was an American Egyptologist who studied under Erman and Sethe around the same time as Breasted (1894). He became the Curator of the Egyptian department of the Museum of Fine Arts in Boston 1910-1942. He excavated all over Egypt for the MFA and Harvard.

Very faithfully yours | JHB
Enclosure.


**29 January 1916**                                                0055

Chicago | January 29, 1916

My dear Miss Ransom:
I do not recall having made the acquaintance of the curator in charge of the
Classical Greek material at the Metropolitan, or I would not bother you with
the following matter. I wonder if you could put into the proper channel for
me a request for a photograph* of the beautiful new Dipylon vase published
in the <u>American Journal of Archaeology</u>, Vol. XIX, Plate 17.[84] I should very
much like to publish it in my Ancient History, if there is no objection.

Thanking you very much for your kindness in transmitting this
request, believe me, with pleasantest recollections of your recent visit,

Always sincerely yours | JHB
*Please send bill for my publisher.


**7 February 1916**                                                0056

Metropolitan Museum of Art |
New York | Department of Egyptian Art |
February 7, 1916

My dear Professor Breasted,
It was most good of you to let me see the censored letter! Have you read
the Reisner article to which Professor Erman refers? I was telling Mr
Winlock about it and he suggested that Professor Erman might have had
a garbled report of an article in which Reisner defended his nationality as
an American.[85] Some Englishman had attacked him in the Egyptian papers
as a German, ostensibly working for an American institution, but one who
should not be allowed in Egypt at this time, and he replied rather hotly

---

[84] http://www.metmuseum.org/art/collection/search/248904 (accessed 13 July 2016).
[85] Despite a concerted effort, I could not find this article.

disclaiming German nationality, that he and his parents before him were born in the United States and were American citizens.

The opening of Perneb's tomb took place with great éclat and the interest of the public has not yet subsided. My cousin, Mr Gay of Harvard, whom you know, I believe, was with us yesterday and I took him over to see the tomb. People were formed in line two abreast all the way back to the Fifth avenue entrance to get into the chambers. Glass positions electrically lighted illustrate the former position and the taking down of the tomb. There are two cases of the objects found in the course of the excavations including the greater part of Perneb's skull. A model of the entire tomb makes clear the position of the burial chamber. I am sending you and Mr Allen[86] copies of our little handbook. The whole department is distressed over the cover design which quite belies the claim for excellence which I make for the preliminary sketch, being such a travesty of the original! There were circumstances beyond our control or it would never have been used.

How good to know that the dear Erman family has been spared any immediate loss. I have a lighter heart every time they are heard from and I know that the young men are all safe. But what a strain to live under all the time, for those at home. I understand that Professor Erman has passed the half-way mark in his work on the dictionary.

I hope that we shall see you here before many months. Mother joins me in greeting to you and Mrs Breasted.

Very sincerely yours | Caroline L. Ransom

---

[86] Thomas George Allen (1885-1969) was an American Egyptologist who studied under Breasted and earned his PhD from Chicago in 1915. He worked alongside Breasted and, from the evidence in later letters, fielded much of Breasted's correspondence while he was away in the field. He was also the Assistant Curator of the Field Museum. In 1916, however, he was the Secretary of the Haskell Oriental Museum.

**10 February 1916**                                          **0057**

Chicago | February 10, 1916

My dear Miss Ransom:

Very many thanks for your prompt attention to the photograph, which has already arrived.

I have never seen the Reisner article to which Prof. Erman refers but I knew of the incident which Mr. Winlock mentions, and the possibility of the same explanation which he suggests had also occurred to me. I shall write to Erman making this suggestion.

I am delighted with the Perneb pamphlet which you so kindly sent me. It is going to be useful in ways probably quite different from those which you and Mr. Lythgoe had in mind preparing it, for I am going to secure a number of copies and use them as propaganda here in Chicago among those interested in Egypt – especially with a view to securing effective installation of the Field Museum mastaba chambers.[87] I have handed on the other copy of the Perneb pamphlet which you so kindly sent, to Mr. Allen, and he is very much interested. I fancy the task of overseeing the installation of the Chicago mastabas is not unlikely to fall into his hands.

I have a very brief last official report of the dictionary by Erman, stating that the work is over half finished, and I presume this is what you refer to in your letter.

Again heartiest thanks for the 'Sendungen', which have been very much enjoyed, and with kindest regards to you both, I am

Very sincerely yours | JHB


**12 February 1916**                                          **0058**

Metropolitan Museum of Art |
New York | February 12, 1916

Dear Dr. Breasted,

---

[87] To my knowledge, there is no scholarly work done on these mastabas. There is evidence that after the Field Museum underwent some renovations to the Egyptian displays, the mastaba of Unis-Ankh was hidden behind some modern walls. See http://www.atlasobscura. com/places/hidden-egyptian-temple-in-field-museum-break-room (accessed 13 July 2016).

When I wrote to you some days ago I quite forgot to mention the photograph of the Dipylon vase. I hope it has reached you safely. I took up the matter at once with the photographic department and have been told that a glossy gray print from the same negative from which this illustration in the American Journal was derived was sent to you a week ago today. If by chance they have not served you satisfactorily, please let me know. The Classical Department is very glad to have you publish the vase in your history.

    Sincerely yours | Caroline L. Ransom

**25 April 1916**                                    **0059**

Chicago | April 25, 1916

My dear Miss Ransom:

I am in the midst of mountains of proof and beginning to see the end of this vexatious textbook campaign. I wonder if I may trouble you once more – and I think for the last time for this book – to ask you if you recall a wonderful encaustic portrait[88] of a woman in the Berlin Museum which has been very beautifully reproduced in colored lithograph. Unfortunately we do not possess this publication and I do not even recall its exact title. May I ask if you have this publication in the Museum library? If you have it and the three-color engraver could be allowed to take negatives of it at the Museum, it would be a matter of very great accommodation to me. Unfortunately our time is now very short, and if you find this publication available, will you kindly send me a night letter, at my expense?

    I might say that my illustration scheme calls rather for the portrait of a man than of a woman. You may not have noticed that a papyrus letter of a young Roman soldier of the Second Century, written from Italy to his father in Egypt, states that he is sending home also a 'little picture' of himself. He was then at the Roman war harbor of Misenum but the picture must have been one of the encaustic portraits such as we are accustomed to in Egypt. There is also a very fine head of a man at Berlin, which I believe was lithographed. As you of course know, we cannot make three-color halftone negatives from a plate which is itself done in three-color halftone; we can

---

[88] This is a painting technique using pigmented hot wax. This technique was used throughout the ancient world.

only photograph from the original itself or a good colored lithograph.

Kindly let me know also whether you have the portrait of the bearded man (in Berlin, I believe) with face resembling somewhat the later Christ type.

I am sorry to trouble you with all this, but shall be very grateful if you can let me know about it in a night letter.

I am reading Old Kingdom texts with a group of excellent students, and we turn very often to the mastabas with reference both to the reliefs and beischriften, and I often think of you as we do so and wish we might share some of the light which you have been throwing on some of these matters lately.

Please give my kindest regards to your mother, and with greetings from us all, believe me

Very sincerely yours | JHB


**27 April 1916**                                                    **0060**

New York | April 27, 1916
[Night Lettergram]
Professor J. H. Breasted | 5615 University Ave. | Chicago

Excellent colored lithograph famous Aline Berlin Tempera on Linen[89] antike denkmaeler volume two plate thirteen in Tarbell's library but glad to have our copy reproduced. Colored lithograph Man's Head Berlin unknown to me. Why not use one of Bearded portrait panels in Metropolitan Museum? Sorry reply late. Letter received today.

C. L. Ransom

---

[89] For more, see Martin Kemp, ed. *The Oxford History of Western Art* (Oxford: Oxford University Press, 2000), 62.

**27 April 1916**                                                                **0061**

Metropolitan Museum of Art | New York |
Department of Egyptian Art | April 27, 1916

My dear Mr. Breasted,

It is always a pleasure to me when you let me do something for you.

I regret that the night letter is being sent 24 hours later than you expected that it would be. Your special delivery letter did not reach the museum until last evening at seven-thirty and did not come into my hands until this morning.

Mr. Lythgoe would be very glad to have you make use of any of the portrait panels in our collection in case you do not find what you wish in colored lithographs. The only thing I know of is the <u>Aline</u> in the <u>Antike Denkmäler</u> II, 13.[90] There used to be a portfolio of good reproductions of the Fayum portraits in Mr Tarbell's department library, but I can't recall whether any of them were colored or not; he could tell you. We have our portrait of a boy – beardless, technic good who would do well for a <u>young</u> Roman soldier sending his portrait home, and several bearded heads.[91] None is so pleasing as some in the Graf collection, still they would be newer than Aline who is illustrated in Wheeler and Fowler's Archaeology[92] and is not a beautiful lady, though well painted. You will note that 'Aline' is in the exceptional tempera technic on canvas. I fear that your book is keeping you from the meetings of the Oriental Society and that we shall not see you here! I pine to be in your class reading Old Kingdom inscriptions. Mother joins me in kindest greetings to you and Mrs Breasted.

Sincerely yours | Caroline L. Ransom

---

[90] Deutsches Archäologisches Institut, ed. *Antike Denkmäler, Band II* (Berlin: Verlag Georg Reimer, 1908).

[91] Portrait of the Boy Eutyches, http://www.metmuseum.org/art/collection/search/547951 (accessed 11 November 2016) was not officially accessioned to the MMA until 1918, but may have been on loan or display in 1916. However, this is the only portrait of a boy that they have.

[92] Harold North Fowler and James Rignall Wheeler, *A Handbook of Greek Archaeology* (New York: American Book Company, 1909).

**1 May 1916**                                                    **0062**

Chicago | May 1, 1916

My dear Miss Ransom:

I want to thank you <u>very</u> much for your prompt reply regarding encaustic portraits. I had forgotten, if I ever knew it, that the famous Berlin portrait is not in encaustic. The best of the beautiful Graf subjects are unfortunately all in black and white, for no intelligence was shown in selecting those given colors. If you have a photograph of the beardless boy which you mention as in your own collection, will you kindly send me a print? Or if not, would you kindly have it photographed, of course at my expense, and send me a print as soon as convenient? Unfortunately the new Petrie portfolio contains only three color halftones.

You are quite right – I was unable to get away from proof long enough to attend the meeting of the Oriental Society. Mrs. Breasted joins me in kindest regards to your mother and you.

Again, very many thanks for your trouble in this matter.

Very sincerely yours | JHB


**11 May 1916**                                                   **0063**

Metropolitan Museum of Art | New York |
Department of Egyptian Art | May 11, 1916

My dear Mr. Breasted,

Sometime ago, possibly when I saw you in Chicago, you told me that Professor Erman had been devoting attention to the legends of Old Kingdom reliefs. I do not now recall whether you said that he had already published, perhaps in the Abhandlungen of the Berliner Akademie, or whether he was about to publish.

I am at work again on our Old Kingdom reliefs as Mr. Lythgoe has asked me to write for the other two sets of mastaba relief owned by the Museum a small, popular handbook, comparable to the one on Perneb's tomb.[93] The Raemkaë chamber is now being built up, within the Third Egyptian Room, <u>as a chamber</u>. You will recall that it was exhibited before

---

[93]  It is unclear if this project was ever finished.

in detached walls.

It would help me immensely if I could get hold of Professor Erman's discussion of the legends. Would you mind letting me know, just on a postcard, the title etc, if it is already published? It is discouraging business ordering books from Germany just now, but I am going to try through Nijhoff in the Hague for a few things I most need.

I wonder if you happen to know that the Frau Klebs[94] who wrote in 'AZ 52 (1914) on „Die Tiefendimension in der Zeichnung des alten Reiches"[95] has published a sort of catalogue of the themes treated in Old Kingdom reliefs. She studied with Dr. Ranke[96] and at his request I once lent her photographs that I happened to have with me in Berlin. Now I have a card from 'Leutnant Ranke,' written from 'Falkenberg i. Lothr.' In which he tells me that her work, entitled „Reliefs des alten Reiches,' came out some time ago in the „Abhandlungen der Heidelberger Akademie.'[97]

I have not heard from the Ermans since February and am beginning to be uneasy about them again, but I trust that all is still well with them. The last thing I received was a review by Professor E. of Wreszinki's „Atlas zur Kulturgeschichte' in which he showed up all its weak points quite relentlessly!

I hope that the photo of the Fayum portrait reached you safely. There chanced to be a print already made and I was able to get it off at once. It was sent to your residence.

With kindest greetings from us both

Sincerely yours | Caroline L. Ransom

---

[94] Luise Klebs (1865-1931) was a German Egyptologist. She published 3 volumes about reliefs: *Reliefs des Alten Reiches* (1915); *Reliefs und Malereien des Mittleren Reiches* (1922); and *Die Reliefs und Malereien des neuen Reiches* (1934).

[95] Luise Klebs „Die Tiefendimension in der Zeichnung des alten Reiches' *Zeitschrift für Ägyptische Sprache und Altertumskude* 52:1 (December 1915): 19-34.

[96] Hermann Ranke (1878-1953) was a German Egyptologist and Assyriologist who got his PhD in Munich in 1902. He later studied with Erman in Berlin and joined the Berlin Museum in 1905. He was half Jewish, so his position at the university in Heidelberg ended. He then moved to the US in 1937 and became a visiting Professor at the University of Wisconsin in 1938, then at Pennsylvania 1938-1942. He moved back to Heidelberg in 1942 and resumed his position at the university in 1946.

[97] Luise Klebs, *Die Reliefs des alten Reiches*, (Heidelberg: Carl Winters Universitätsbuchhandlung, 1915).

**13 May 1916**                                    **0064**

Chicago | May 13, 1916

My dear Miss Ransom:

I am sorry to have been so tardy in acknowledging your kindness in sending me the print of the Metropolitan Museum encaustic portrait. I did not find any memorandum of expense enclosed. Perhaps the bill is yet to come from the Museum.

This morning I have your letter inquiring about Erman's essay on the mastaba legends. He wrote me that he was bringing out this material in the proceedings of the Akademie, and he promised to send it to me soon, but I have not received it and therefore only know of it from his letter. I presume the delay is due to the courteous attentions of the English censors, but as soon as it comes I will not fail to send it to you. I am very glad you are going to work up the further mastaba materials in your collections. I am glad too that Frau Klebs' catalogue of the mastaba subjects is out. I had heard of it but did not know when to expect it. I too have not heard from the Ermans for a long time. I have been so pushed that I have been derelict myself and that may be the reason, but the mails are outrageously interfered with by the English navy.

Again thanking you very much for the Fayum portrait, and regretting that I cannot give you anything further on the Erman essay, I am, with kindest regards from us all,

Always sincerely yours | JHB

**2 September 1916** **0065**

The Chesbrough Dwellings[98] | Toledo, Ohio |
September 2, 1916

My dear Mr Breasted,
The enclosed card reached me a few days ago. I am almost sure that you
have the inexpressibly sad news, for the 'Anzeiger'[99] followed the card in a
day or two and no doubt yours will have come through too.

I have not yet thanked you, except by message through Mrs
Breasted, for your friendly letter which followed the announcement of my
engagement.[100] I valued it very much and I am also truly grateful for the
handsome gift which you and Mrs Breasted were so good as to send me.

I hope that you have not been working all too hard this summer and
that you were able to escape to some cooler place during the long stretch
of hot weather.

Life in Toledo has opened pleasantly for me. At this moment I am busy
getting my study in order. We have settled in this comfortable apartment
hotel for the winter and besides our regular suite Mr Williams has taken
an extra room with large closet for me to use for my working library and
papers. I have had the closet shelved from floor to ceiling, and for the first
time since I left Bryn Mawr have a really commodious and healthful study.
You see, I do not intend to give up my old pursuits entirely! Within ten days
or so I shall be going to New York to help mother break up our apartment

---

[98] The Chesbrough Dwellings were a high-end apartment-hotel in Toledo. Not unlike the
Beresford in New York where CRW and her mother lived, these were like condominiums.
One author defined apartment hotels as an 'apartment home with hotel services, rather
than a hotel with apartments to lease' (John Wellborn Root, 'Hotels and Apartment Hotels,'
in *Forms and Functions of Twentieth Century Architecture, in Four Volumes: Volume III Building
Types*, ed. Talbot Hamlin (New York: Columbia University Press, 1952), 96-130 (quote on p.
121). http://www.oldwestendtoledo.com/index.php/toledo/apartment-buildings/123-
apartment-bldgs/detail/518-1505-jefferson-chesbrough-dwellings?tmpl=component
(accessed 22 December 2016).
[99] A newspaper from somewhere in Germany, or in the German language. This one
announced the death of the Erman's son, Peter, in the First World War.
[100] Caroline Ransom married Ulysses Grant Williams (1865-1942) on June 28, 1916 in Mercer,
Pennsylvania. Grant Williams was a real estate dealer in Toledo, Ohio. He had his own firm,
Grant Williams & Co., which dealt with railroad and insurance companies ('Obituary—Grant
Williams Taken by Death,' *Toledo Blade* [25 December 1942]: 18.)

there to bring her back with me to live in Toledo. She, too, will have rooms in this hotel for the present. I dare say we shall take a house eventually but I am glad not to plunge into too much that is new all at once. Do please stop to see us when you can. I hope that Mrs Breasted will come some day too.

With warm regards to you both | Sincerely yours | Caroline Ransom Williams


**24 September 1916**                                                    **0066**

New York | The Beresford | 1 West Eighty-first Street |
September 24, 1916

My dear Mr Breasted,
You will be surprised to receive a letter from me dated in New York. I am here for a little time to help my mother break up the apartment we had leased together until the first of October.

The volume 'Ancient Times' reached me here forwarded from Toledo and I am delighted to have it. I shall enjoy it the more because of this inscription you so kindly wrote in it. Permit me to extend congratulations on the completion of this valuable work. I almost wonder if it is not the finest thing you have done yet, for it will reach so many individuals just in their most impressionable years. I quite envy the high school students of the book, for I know how much it would have meant to me at that age. Instead I was struggling through all manner of heavy reading, such as Horace Greeley's Civil War! I like especially the term 'The Fertile Crescent.'[101] The book will have many older readers, among them just at present is my mother, who is fascinated with it! Its appearance is dignified and pleasing; the illustrations are quite remarkable in selection and quality.

I have also received your card from Canada. As soon as I return to Toledo I will send you the Anzeiger from our dear Ermans. It is touching in its wording and I know you will wish to see it. I can believe how deeply you feel for them with your own son just at University age, too, and your desires centering in his future. I, also, am full of sadness as I think of Peter,

---

[101] While this phrase is commonly used now to describe the crescent-shaped area that covers the Nile Valley and the Tigris and Euphrates Valleys, Breasted coined the term in his 1916 *Ancient Times*.

for I watched him with interest through his years in the gymnasium. He was of fine and sensitive nature and of brilliant promise intellectually; I cannot bear to think of the suffering his loss means to his parents.

I had the pleasure of meeting Mr Bull[102] the other day. You must be glad to see men of his sort going into Egyptology.

With sincerest thanks for the copy of your book and warm greetings to Mrs Breasted;

Gracefully yours | Caroline Ransom Williams

**14 November 1916**                                                    **0067**

The Chesbrough Dwellings | Toledo, Ohio | November 14, 1916

My dear Mr Breasted,

Here is the <u>Anzeige</u> which I am sorry not to have sent sooner. We have been very much occupied since returning from New York in getting our goods fitted with their new quarters and there has been much going on in other ways, too.

I was very glad to receive your letter a few weeks ago. It was kind of you to think of us in connection with the Abbott collection[103] and it would be a great privilege to do a catalogue of it. I am afraid, however, they will wish the cataloguing done by someone who could stay with them long enough to supervise the installation and renovations of the objects. They are in a deplorable condition, --the bronzes attacked by bronze disease, the limestone much disintegrated by sale etc.* It is true that I have some work to finish for the Metropolitan and I shall want to help them as much as they care to have me until Mr Lythgoe is able to make an appointment. I had an inquiry ten days ago from the Cleveland Museum whether I could

---

[102] Ludlow S. Bull (1886-1954) was an American Egyptologist who began his career working as a lawyer from 1910-1915. He got his PhD at Chicago under Breasted in 1922. He was a professor at Yale from 1925-36 and was an Associate Curator at the MMA.

[103] The collection that came to the NYHS in 1860, from Henry W. C. Abbott (1807-1859). Abbott was a British physician and collector. His collection was popular in Cairo, and he tried to sell it in the US in 1853 for around $60,000. In the end, the NYHS bought it for $5,000. It was the first Egyptian antiquities collection owned by an institution in the US. In 1937, the Brooklyn Museum took it on loan; they purchased it from the NYHS in 1948.

help them complete their records and may have a little work to do there, although I have heard nothing further from them as yet.

When I have settled down to a regular program of study as I hope to within a few days, I may find it necessary to consult books not in my collection and I thought I should enjoy going occasionally to Chicago for a day. I do not mind night travel and could go by our night train and return by the next, thus gaining a full day in Chicago without being very long absent from home. When you have time to write again will you perhaps tell me on what day in the week I could best work in the Haskell library; you see I am taking it for granted – I hope not with all too much assurance – that you will be willing that I should use the library! I am delighted to know that Mr Allen now has an assured position in Haskell and that you are not to lose his help. How good that the outlook for the future of H[askell]. Museum is so encouraging!

May I inquire whether you received in the summer sample pages of the Berlin Egyptian dictionary as it is to be issued in two series of volumes, one printed, one autographed. If by any chance yours did not come through I could send on mine.

Within the last fortnight I have received the first letters written by German friends since they knew of my marriage. It seems that our announcements did not reach Berlin until September 11th! I heard from Dr Roeder, who is comfortably placed in Hildesheim[104] now, from Professor Winnefeld of the Berlin Museum, from Freiherr Hiller von Gaertringen, from some of the women whom I knew well in Steglitz, but not a word from the Erman family! Of course the Ermans have written and I grieve that just their messages should be the ones to be lost.

Mr Williams appreciates your kindness in expressing the wish to see him in Chicago but we both hope you will come first to us, if possible with Mrs Breasted. But please don't leave us out when you go East, for we are on the main line from Chicago to Buffalo, as you know. I shall certainly take my husband to call on you whenever I can get him to Chicago!

With kind regards to Mrs Breasted and all good wishes for your winter's work.

Sincerely yours | Caroline Ransom Williams

---

[104] He would be there until 1945, when he was dismissed for being a Nazi supporter.

*Are the authorities of the N. Y. Historical Society ready to have the Abbott Collection catalogued immediately, do you chance to know? Your suggestion is an alluring one!

**2 December 1916**                                                **0068**

The Chesbrough Dwellings | Toledo, Ohio | December 2, 1916

My dear Mr Breasted,

I am sending under separate cover, registered, the sample sheets of the Berlin Dictionary. Please keep them until all your students have had a good chance to see them. It is a surprise that the published work is to be kept in such comparatively small compass.

Thank you for letting me see the enclosed card. It is heartbreaking to think of the Erman family without Peter. Have you any news of Dr Müller and Herr Ibscher[105] who also went to the front?

I have now a positive engagement to help the Cleveland Museum complete the records of their Egyptian objects and shall go there for a week either this month or early in January. Mr Lythgoe, too, would like to see me take hold of the Abbott collection and I am inclined to do it if I am offered the job! Mr Lythgoe would be very helpful in consultation about the problems of saving the limestone and bronzes which so badly need attention. My husband is unselfishly interested in my plans and encourages me to take any opportunity for congenial work that comes my way.

I don't know when I shall avail myself of the privilege of using your library, but I look forward to seeing you and Mrs Breasted in that connection before very long.

With kindest greetings to you both from us all | Sincerely yours | Caroline Ransom Williams

---

[105] Hugo Ibscher (1874-1943) was a German manuscript restorer. He mounted and stored papyri at the Berlin Museum, and museums around the world.

**21 December 1916**                                           **0069**

Chicago | December 21, 1916

My dear Mrs Williams:

I have received a letter from Mr. James Benedict, Domestic Corresponding Secretary of the New York Historical Society, accompanying a copy of the antiquated old catalogue of Dr. Abbott's collection, made by himself. The old gentleman—I mean Mr. Benedict—evidently thinks this catalogue quite sufficient. As tactfully as I could, I have indicated the necessity for a modern publication of the collection; and I must say that as I looked through Abbott's loose and wandering list, the unpublished things there made my mouth water. There is a chance for a large and beautiful monograph on these things. In view of your last reference to the matter, I mentioned your name, as together with Prof. William Milligan Sloane, I am storming the citadel of conservatism in the sleepy old Society, in the hope that we may succeed in giving them a jolt. I will let you know if any results ensue. Sloane thinks we <u>may</u> get an appropriation!

We have all been very much interested in looking over the advance pages of the dictionary which you so kindly sent on. I shall be returning it to you soon, registered to avoid all risk. I cannot but wonder what satisfaction the British censor has in holding up such material as this, for he did not allow my copy to come through.

I sincerely hope that you may be able to come out to the meeting of the Oriental Society, though I fear you would find much of it painfully philological. The family all joins me in warmest regards and warmest good wishes of the season.

Very sincerely yours | JHB

**11 January 1917**                                           **0070**

Chicago | January 11, 1917

My dear Mrs. Williams:

You will be interested in the enclosed letter from the New York Historical Society. What a delightful piece of work you could give us if your time and home duties would permit its completion! I am debating in my own mind whether to venture further counsel to the conservative old Society regarding the conservation of their antiquities, which must be in a sad way by this time. I fancy it would not hurry them any if I did so.

I was interested to see in the Cleveland Museum programme, that you were lecturing there. Mrs.Breasted joins me in kindest regards and best wishes of the season.

Very sincerely yours | JHB
Enclosure.


**16 January 1917**                                          **0071**

Cleveland, Ohio | January 16, 1917

My dear Mr Breasted,
Your kind letter of January 11th inclosing letters from the Secretary of the New York Historical Society was forwarded to me here. I return it herewith, together with the letter he wrote to me and some newspaper clippings sent to me by Mr Lythgoe, which may interest you.

Thus far I have only acknowledged the receipt of Mr Benedict's letter, telling him that I would give his inquiry careful consideration and write again in a week or ten days. I should very much prefer, naturally, to talk the matter over in all its bearings with my husband and mother. I have plenty of leisure, so far as that is concerned, but it is a bit hard on my family to have me go away so often. Yet they take pride in having me do such work and do not wish me to give it up.

I should value greatly, too, your counsel as to what it would be equitable to charge the Society. The Society has the reputation of being wealthy, but Mr Benedict writes as if they were feeling the high cost of living, like everybody else! I have been accustomed to work on a time basis and should prefer it. Do you think it would do to insist on this, with payment at the rate I receive from the Cleveland Museum and the Minneapolis Institute of Arts (where I am going in February), or must I respond to Mr Benedict's ardent preference and value a lump sum for which I would do the work, and if so, <u>what</u> should that sum be![106]

---

[106] It was during this time that CRW took on a number of extra positions to continue working in the field and, probably, to help make ends meet in caring for her mother. She worked at Cleveland and Minneapolis for 1916-1917.

I hope to stop in Chicago on my way to Minneapolis, perhaps the weekend of the 10-12 of February. In view of the two absences from home— then and now, I cannot consider going to the meeting of the central branch of the Oriental Society of which you kindly sent me a notice.

I am wondering if Dr. Allen would have the time and be interested to compare notes on his Art Institute collection and the one here. This is probably the smaller of the two but it has some delightful objects in it.

Please accept my sincere thanks for your friendly interest in furthering the project for me to do a catalogue of the Abbott Collection. If I undertake it I shall endeavor to endure to the end![107]

With my very best greetings to Mrs Breasted and to you | Sincerely yours | C. R. Williams

I return to Toledo on Saturday. I have received the first installment of M. Dévaud's new publication of the <u>Proverbs of Ptahhotep</u>. Have you this? If not, I will take it with me to Chicago.


**25 January 1917**                                                    **0072**

The Chesbrough Dwellings | 
Toledo, Ohio | January 25, 1917

My dear Mr Breasted,

A letter has come from Mr Breck asking me to delay my going to Minneapolis a week, because of a journey east which he finds that he must make. My plan now is to leave Toledo Sunday evening, February 18th, spend Monday in Chicago and go on Monday night to Minneapolis. I am going back to Cleveland next week for Monday to Saturday inclusive and hope that I shall be able to get over the remainder of the collection. I examined and made careful notes on about 2/3 of their objects when last there. The work

---

[107] Her involvement was announced in *The New York Historical Society Quarterly Bulletin* 1:1 (April 1917): 12. They said it would take 'a year or so' for her to do the exhaustive scientific catalogue…to replace the catalogue made by Dr. Abbott at the time the Society secured his collection, which is still in use.' In the end, it seems, it took 7 years to complete the catalogue and get it published. The final product was Caroline Ransom Williams, *Catalogue of Egyptian Antiquities* (New York: NYHS, 1924).

there and in Minneapolis is good preparation for the Abbott Collection! Of course in New York my time has largely given to selected objects, or single large tasks, such as Perneb's chambers. In these small collections I have to handle every bead and do something with it!

I have sent a letter today to Mr Benedict in which I spoke of the difficulty of deciding from the old catalogue on even an approximate cost for handling the collection. I called his attention to entry no. 3 on p. 1: 'A piece of linen, inscribed, from a Theban mummy' and said that I might be able to dispose of it in fifteen minutes or the inscription might involve days of close application! I asked if the Society would be willing to have me begin on a time basis (stating the terms made with the two museums in Cleveland and Minneapolis) with the understanding that after I had become acquainted with the conditions of work and had had a chance to examine the collection itself I should endeavor to give them an idea of the eventual cost to complete the task.

Since I wrote you last I have had touching letters from the Ermans. They were written in November and have just come into my hands!

My mother joins me in greetings to you all.

Sincerely yours | Caroline Ransom Williams

**30 January 1917**                                      0073

Chicago | January 30, 1917

My dear Mrs. Williams:

I am very sorry that I have been so long in replying to your inquiries of January 16th, and am now in receipt of your letter of January 25th, from which I see that I am too late to be of any assistance. It seems to me that you have made a very fair and reasonable proposition to the New York Historical Society People.

I am very interested to hear of your work on the Cleveland collection. Mrs. Breasted and I are delighted that you are expecting to spend a day in Chicago on your way to Minneapolis. I hope Mr. Williams is planning to be with you. Mrs. Breasted is writing to you, and of course we shall want you to come at once to our house and make it your headquarters for the day. We can then have a long talk over work and experiences.

We had a very successful meeting of the Western orientalists last Saturday, and organized for the permanent continuance of a Western Branch of the A. O. S. I hope you can join later on. The next meeting I presume will be held in Cincinnati.

Very sincerely yours | JHB

I should be greatly interested to see the Erman letters.

**19 July 1917**                                                                                        **0074**

The Chesbrough Dwellings |
Toledo, Ohio | July 19, 1917

My dear Mr Breasted,

Under separate cover I am sending you a brief article on the Abbott Collection.[108] The editor asked for a 'chatty' article and a statement of plans hence I wrote in the first person. We are to have the services of Mr Hoffmann, the head repair man of the Boston Museum, who is said to be very skillful. It chances, fortunately for the Abbott Collection, that he can be spared from his regular post.

Long ago you told me that you had tried in vain to get hold of a copy of Dr Rathgen's book on the care of Museum objects and at the moment I thought that I had a second copy, but I find to my regret that I no longer have it. I must have given it away for I certainly had at one time two copies. I should, however, be very glad to send the book on to you to keep until Autumn. I cannot possibly need it again until the middle of October when I return to New York. I have also a monograph of Dr. Rathgen's in German which is later than the handbook and which I could send with the latter, if you care for it.

Beginning early in August I should like to go to Chicago occasionally between Sundays for work in the library. May I ask whether the Egyptian books will be available continuously until the middle of October, or is there

---

[108] There are a few articles from this period she could be referring to, and as there was nothing in the correspondence archives to accompany this letter, it is unclear which article she means. The most likely option is: CRW, 'The Abbott Collection,' *NYHS Quarterly Bulletin* 1:2 (July 1917): 34-37.

any time which I would better avoid? I have not only the work on the Abbott Collection, but various oddments from Minneapolis and Cleveland to attend to.

I should like to ask you also whether it would be feasible, and whether you would consider it a good plan, for me to go over all the difficult inscriptional material I have in hand with Dr Allen. Perhaps his University salary is not yet so large that he would be adverse to earning a little on the side and I can perfectly well afford to compensate him adequately. My idea is to get as far as I can with each inscription first and to see if he can do more than I with difficult passages. I don't think the amount of help I should need would justify collaboration in authorship, but I should wish to make all just acknowledgement of his help when it came to publication. You can imagine that I miss the Dictionary sadly. I should dread the responsibility of publishing the material without some check on my results. Besides, it is much more interesting to talk over the material with others. I can hardly wait to show you the 50 8x10 photographic prints which I have from the first period of work! In the six weeks spent in New York I examined exhaustively all the statues and larger statuettes and the better ushebtis. The poorer ushebtis are in my possession here in Toledo, sent on for me to study at my leisure this summer. Thus I hope to make before I return to New York a first draft of the sections of the catalogue dealing with sculpture in the round and ushebtis.

We are having many good times with our car despite the frequent rains. Last Sunday Mr Williams and I were in the country and I drove all the way from the yard of my husband's brother into our garage in Toledo, a distance of over thirty-nine miles. Mother and I go out every morning about nine o'clock and I am quite proud to be managing the big touring car alone! I hope that Mrs Breasted and the children are well. Please give them our best greetings.

Sincerely yours | Caroline Ransom Williams

24 July 1917                                                    0075

July 24, 1917

My dear Mrs. Williams:-

Many thanks for your chatty account of revelations to be expected from the N. Y. Historical Society's collection, which I found very appetizing indeed. I quite envy you delving into such an archaeological cornucopiae, and I shall greatly enjoy seeing the photographs, which sound very attractive.

It is very kind of you to remember the Rathgen book. He certainly should be very glad indeed to be able to use a copy for a time. Are you not reluctant however, to trust your only copy to the mails? Perhaps if registered there would be no danger, but it might be safer to wait until you come in August and bring it with you, if not too burdensome.

We are all delighted to hear that you are planning to come here in August to use the library. There will be nothing whatever to interfere with your complete control of our books. If a decorator or two should intrude, we can easily give you a table in a neighboring room on the same floor, so that it need not interfere with your work, at any hour of the day, or any day of the week. I have not yet had any vacation, and hence I may be away for a time in August; but if you are coming often, I shall surely not miss all your visits. It would be well to drop a card before you come the first time: one to Dr. Allen (Dr. T.G. Allen, 5547 Drexel Ave.), and one to me. You are sure to catch one or other of us that way.

I will talk to Allen about assisting in the translations. I think he might be of some aid, though for some time past he has not had such time for the language. The chief difficulty is likely to be lack of time, as he is still pegging away at the Art Institute catalogue or guide, and has also a number of other lesser enterprises to take care of. We can talk it over when you come; but I am sure he will be eager to participate.

Mrs. Breasted joins in kindest regards, and with pleasant anticipations of your visit, or better, visits, I am | Very sincerely yours | JHB

**17 August 1917**                                                    **0076**

The Chesbrough Dwellings | Toledo, Ohio |
August 17, 1917

My dear Mr Breasted,

My plans to go to Chicago <u>early</u> in August were shipwrecked, but I am now
getting off at last on Sunday night next and shall be able to stay this time
a week to ten days. I will send word to Dr. Allen as you suggested, for I
suppose that by now you are away on your holiday. I shall be going again in
September and October and so shall hope to see you later if I miss you this
time. I will deliver the Rathgen book to Dr Allen if you are away. If I had not
expected, when your kind letter came, to get off earlier, I should have sent
it by registered mail. After delaying, I was afraid to send it lest you be away
and the book follow you and prove a bother!

With kind regards, also to Mrs Breasted | Sincerely yours | Caroline
Ransom Williams

**5 February 1918**                                                   **0077**

Chicago | February 5, 1918

My dear Mrs. Williams:

What with lectures out of town and added responsibilities connected with
Charles' illnesses, besides the usual rush, I have not been able to write you
as I expected to do in explanation of Professor Shipley's[109] letter to you.

Those men in the Institute – especially Shipley – have been giving
me no rest regarding the Egyptian number of <u>Art and Archaeology</u>. If
you happen to recall the Egyptian number of the <u>American Geographic
Magazine,</u> you will at once understand how reluctant I have been to see such
a number of <u>Art and Archaeology</u> appear edited by incompetent hands, and
yet I know you have more than you can easily attend to, just as I have. Isn't
there some young person – perhaps connected with the Metropolitan –
who would be willing to relieve us of the work if we outlined the content
of the number and made suggestions regarding the illustrative matter? If

---

[109] F. W. Shipley, of Washington University, St. Louis, was the President of the American
Institute of Archaeology at this time.

there is not, I do not think you ought to be burdened with the matter, even if you were willing, and I fear I would be unable to carry it myself. I would appreciate it very much if you would think the matter over and see what you can suggest.

I am glad to say that Charles is steadily improving, though his latest trouble was pleurisy, and as a result of his long-continued illnesses, he is to be discharged from the army.

With kindest regards, in which Mrs. Breasted joins | I am | Very faithfully yours | JHB


**6 February 1918**                                                    **0078**

The Chesbrough Dwellings | Toledo, Ohio |
February 6, 1918

My dear Mr Breasted,
I have your letter of February 5th, and, like you, would be greatly relieved to be excused from case with respect to the number of Art and Archaeology. The only person connected with the Metropolitan who has sufficient knowledge to help us materially is Miss Bernice Cartland. Whether she would find that she had time for it, I do not know. She might regard it as an opportunity, as she has still her reputation to make. I could ask her if you wish, but I think the request would come with more authority from you and she would be gratified to be asked by you, so if you think well of the suggestion, will you not be the one to take it up?

I agree with you that it would be unfortunate to have this Egyptian number, like that of the Geographic Magazine, to which you refer, simply turned over to the Egypt Exploration Fund and I fear that would be the result, if you do not control the situation. It ought not to be an all too burdensome matter, as it involves only 28 pages of text, the other 28 pages to be devoted to illustrations, so Mr Shipley wrote to me. The only plan for the number which occurred to me was to make it a museum number, with as many collections as possibly represented by short articles. The articles might have a short introductory paragraph giving some idea of the scope and size of the collection and then treat in a popular way some one object, if possible one of aesthetic value. Would Dr Allen do such an article for the

Art Institute? However, please don't take this suggestion seriously, if you already have something in mind. I go on the 18th to New York and shall be engaged intensively on the Abbott Collection until the last of April, then I must stop in Cleveland on my way home. I should be unable to give any time to the matter until June, but could do so then if need be. I will certainly not fail to help you, if the case is thrown back on you. I have promised to send Dr Gardiner[110] two articles for the J.E.A., one on the Cleveland Collection, one on the Abbot Collection, before the expiration of 1918[111]; I must keep a certain number of articles going for the New York Historical Society's Quarterly and Mr Whiting is pressing me for something for his Bulletin! However I am sure I could squeeze in a little writing for this special number if the ms does not have to be ready before summer – say sometime in July.

I could go to Chicago in June, perhaps quite early in the month, to consult with you and at the same time work in the library – perhaps even before the expiration of May.

You must be relieved, now that Charles has done his world duty, that he is discharged from the Army, but I fear it is a bitter disappointment to him! Under separate cover I am sending to you and Mrs Breasted a copy of the Mt Holyoke Quarterly which contains an article by my Aunt and a picture of the gallery of casts lately renamed in honor of her.[112] I believe you knew something of her early struggles to get the building.

With all kind regards to you both | Sincerely yours | Caroline R. Williams

---

[110] Alan H. Gardiner (1879-1963) was a British Egyptologist who was taught at UCL by Petrie and Margaret Murray. He also studied under Erman in Berlin, and took a post at the University of Chicago from 1924-1934. His most famous work was *Egyptian Grammar* (1927) which he dedicated to his teacher, Murray.

[111] 'The Egyptian Collection in the Museum of Art at Cleveland Ohio,' *Journal of Egyptian Archaeology* 5:3 (1918): 166-78; 'The Egyptian Collection in the Museum of Art at Cleveland Ohio (Continued),' *Journal of Egyptian Archaeology* 5:4 (1918): 272-85. If she wrote on the Abbott Collection, it was never published in the *JEA*. They had taken a publication break in 1919 due to the war, and an article strictly on the Abbott Collection never materialized although she did mention the Abbott Collection in these articles.

[112] Louise Fitz-Randolph, 'History of the Department,' *Mount Holyoke Alumnae Quarterly* (January 1918): 197-202. For more information see, Victoria Schmidt-Scheuber, ' A History of the Mount Holyoke College Art Museum,' 16 November 2011 at https://www.mtholyoke. edu/org/artgoddesses/more%20articles/MHCAM%20135%20Retrospective.html (Accessed 18 November 2016) Also see http://www.plastercastcollection.org/en/database. php?d=lire&id=151 (Accessed 18 November 2016)

**13 February 1918**                                          **0079**

Chicago | February 13, 1918

My dear Mrs. Williams:

Many thanks for your kind letter of February 6th. I think the suggestion about Miss Cartland is a good one. If she would be willing to take the editorship, with what assistance you and I might give her, as proposed in your letter. I am writing Prof. Shipley about the matter and hope soon to hear from him.

I am very glad to hear that we are to see you later in Chicago. We could then discuss the project more fully.

Charles continues to improve, I am glad to be able to say, though he will not be allowed to leave the hospital for an indefinite period – yet I hope soon to be called East to bring him home.

Many thanks also for the Mt. Holyoke Quarterly which you kindly sent us. I enjoyed very much reading Miss Randolph's account of the history of her work at Mt. Holyoke. The magazine is really very creditably done – the article by Miss Hussey[113] is also useful.

Mrs. Breasted joins me in kindest regards | Very sincerely yours | JHB


**12 April 1918**                                             **0080**

Chicago | April 12, 1918

My dear Mrs. Williams:

Many thanks for the copy of your interesting essay in the bulletin of the New York Historical Society.[114] It demonstrates clearly what a treasure-house you are investigating. You will be interested to know that I met Prof. William Milligan Sloane at the University of California three weeks ago. Indeed, we stood up together as fellow alumni to receive the LL.D. at the hands of President Wheeler. Professor Sloane spoke with the utmost enthusiasm not only of the work that you were doing, but also of your

---

[113] Mary I. Hussey, 'Babylonian Tablets,' *Mount Holyoke Alumnae Quarterly* (January 1918): 211-216.
[114] Possibly, 'Some Bronze Statuettes in the Abbott Collection,' *New York Historical Society Quarterly Bulletin* 2:2 (July 1918): 43-53.

complete success in interesting and winning over the members of this very conservative old Society. He assured me that they would back up any plan you had in mind that was at all within reach of their means. From what he said I should think you might make your large scientific publication a very ambitions affair, and I congratulate you upon your success. I hope that we are to see you here in Chicago before long.

With kindest regards, in which Mrs. Breasted also joins, I am | Very sincerely yours | JHB

**21 May 1918**                                                    **0081**

The Chesbrough Dwellings |
Toledo, Ohio | May 21, 1918

My dear Mr Breasted,
Your kind letter of April 12th ought to have been acknowledged long ago! I was in New York when I received it and returned home shortly afterwards. Here I have been involved in house-cleaning and visits which have frustrated all my efforts to get away for a little time in Chicago.

Please accept my hearty congratulations on the Ll.D. The honor was surely never more worthily bestowed! It was kind of you to pass on to me Professor Sloane's verdict on my work thus far for the New York Historical Society and his opinion as to the prospects for the publication. My relations with individual members of the Society are bringing me much pleasure. Among those whom I saw frequently last winter is Mrs Schuyler Van Rensselaer,[115] who is delightful.

I am planning to go now, if I may, on May 31st to Chicago, to be there until the following Friday. This will enable me to do a few of the most immediately pressing things. But you will see me soon again, for I have quite an accumulation of work requiring library facilities. I would stay longer this time but we have guests coming on Saturday, June 8th.

Mother has been enjoying apple-blossom time in the Connecticut Valley and is still in South Hadley with Miss Randolph. This week they are

---

[115] Mariana Griswold (Mrs. Schuyler van Rensselaer) (1851-1934) was an American author and critic. She donated a bronze cast portrait of herself to the MMA in 1917 (see: http://www.metmuseum.org/toah/works-of-art/17.104/ [accessed 18 November 2016]).

going to Boston and will visit our Cambridge relatives, the Randolphs and the Gays. As soon as Mother returns I hope we may be able to persuade you and Mrs Breasted to motor here for a long weekend with us!

With greetings to you both | Sincerely yours | Caroline R. Williams

You will be interested, I am sure, in the enclosed card.[116]

---

**23 May 1918**                                                                    **0082**

Chicago | May 23, 1918

My dear Mrs. Williams:

We were very glad to have your letter of the 21st with information that we are soon to have the pleasure of seeing you here. We shall be very interested to hear all about the progress of the New York catalogue and to put at your disposal anything you want which our library supplies.

I was deeply interested in the card which you enclosed. I have not yet shown it to Mrs. Breasted, so am keeping it until your arrival.

With kindest regards, in which Mrs. Breasted joins, and pleasant anticipations, I am

Very sincerely yours | JHB

---

**20 November 1918**                                                               **0083**

Chicago | November 20, 1918

My dear Mrs. Williams:

I have been derelict in not acknowledging your kindness in sending me your last two publications – one from the New York Society and the other just now received, from the collection of the Cleveland Museum of Art.[117] I quite envy you delving to your heart's content in these things. I am tied up hand and foot with so many routine matters that I find it very discouraging.

I suppose you are greatly disturbed in mind, as I have been, regarding

---

[116] Not in archive.

[117] 'Wooden Statuettes of Gods in the Abbott Collection,' *New York Historical Society Quarterly Bulletin* 2:3 (October 1918): 75-88; 'Stela of a High-Priest of Memphis,' *Bulletin of the Cleveland Museum of Art* 5:8-9 (October-November 1918): 67-69.

our dear friends the Ermans. I fear that the publication of the dictionary will now be indefinitely postponed.[118] The overwhelming discouragement also will, I fear, be more than our friend can endure.

With kindest regards, I am | Very faithfully yours | JHB

**26 May 1919** **0084**

The Chesbrough Dwellings | Toledo, Ohio |
May 26, 1919

My dear Mr Breasted,

A fortnight or so ago I received through Monsieur Dévaud[119] a <u>Bericht</u> of the Prussian Academy, no longer 'königlich', issued the last of January 1919. It is a review by Professor Erman of the work in the Dictionary and is hopeful in the prospect it holds out of publication. Very likely you, too, have received a copy, but if by any chance yours did not get through, I should be glad to lend you the one that reached me.

It was with considerable grief that I learned that you spent a whole day at the MMA while we had no glimpse of you at the Historical Society! I have been home now a fortnight and it seems indeed good after the long absence in New York. A few days ago I sent you the first part of the long paper on the Cleveland Collection, on which I was working last summer.

With kind regards | Sincerely yours | Caroline R. Williams

---

[118] The concern these two share for their colleagues in Germany throughout the war is common, especially among scholars who, in the late 19th and early 20th centuries, had to go to Germany for graduate training and then return to the United States. The scholars themselves were not at war with their friends, but oftentimes were considered problematic in their institutions.

[119] Eugène Victor Dévaud (1878-1929) was a Swiss Egyptologist who trained under Pierre Loret in Lyons and then in Berlin. His main work was in the Coptic language.

**28 May 1919**                                                   **0085**

Chicago | May 28, 1919

My dear Mrs. Williams:

It was very kind of you to write me about the new Dictionary report, which fortunately, unlike the sample pages of the Dictionary, did reach me through the kindness of Dévaud.

I was very sorry to miss you at the Historical Society. Although I had definitely expected to go over there, I was so rushed with publication matters in New York and the Philadelphia session of the American Oriental Soc'y (presidential address, etc.), all followed by the Hale lectures which I had to give before the National Academy of Science in Washington – that my program was more than full. I hope next time we may have better luck.

I am studying your presentation of the Cleveland Collection with much interest. Congratulations and many thanks.

Very sincerely yours | JHB


**6 January 1920**                                                **0086**

The Chesbrough Dwellings |
Toledo, Ohio | January 6, 1920

My dear Mrs Breasted,

Would you be so good, on the inclosed card, to tell me the best way to address Mr Breasted just at present? There is a question with reference to the Abbott collection, one of the disposal of some of the material, which I need to ask him and which won't wait, as conditions have developed in New York, until his return. It is the greatest unworked storehouse of written documents from Egypt in this country and Mr Breasted was instrumental in giving me my present opportunity, hence I want him to have the first chance at anything that might interest him.

I hope that the year is slipping by for you without too great hardships in your husband's absence, especially I trust that Astrid is well again. You will be interested to know that I had a 21-page letter from Frau Erman shortly before Christmas, also a card from Professor Erman. Very likely you, too, have heard, but if not, when I get Frau Erman's letter back from my cousin Louis Gay to whom I lent it, I should be glad to send it to you.

With all kind greetings | Cordially yours | C. R. Williams

Mr Edwin F. Gay has recently taken over the administrative control of the <u>New York Evening Post.</u> It is a great joy to me to see my cousin and his family often in New York. Please don't be offended by my p[ost].c[ard].[120] It is to save you bother if you chance to be very occupied when my letter reaches you!

**27 October 1920**                                                                **0087**

Chicago | October 27, 1920

My dear Mrs. Williams:

Among the large accumulation on my desk during my absence, I find on my return your exceedingly interesting article in the April Bulletin of the New York Historical Society on early Egyptology in America.[121] I have often wanted to know more of Abbott, Gliddon and others of those old days. I wish your article might appear in one of our Oriental journals where it would gain wider circulation among Orientalists.

There is one episode of unusual interest that might be added—that is the collection of Egyptian antiquities purchased by Joseph Smith, the founder of Mormonism, somewhere in western New York as early, I think, as 1828. It included a mummy which was being exhibited by an itinerant showman at that time, some vignettes of a late corrupt Book of the Dead, translated by Smith as the Book of Abraham, and a hypocephalus similarly discussed by the father of Mormonism. The fraudulent translations were exposed by the Frenchman Deveria[122] many years ago and you probably know his essay on the subject republished by Maspero.[123]

---

[120] She sent this note on a post card.

[121] 'The Place of the New York Historical Society in the Growth of American Interest in Egyptology,' *New York Historical Society Quarterly Bulletin* 4:1 (April 1920): 3-20.

[122] Charles Théodule Devéria (1831-1871) was a French Egyptologist who studied Coptic and earned a place in the Egyptian Department at the Louvre in 1855 where he began to work with Mariette. He focused much of his work on cataloguing Egyptian papyri in the Louvre, but not much of his work was published.

[123] For more on this episode, see John Larson, 'Joseph Smith and Egyptology: An Early Episode in the History of American Speculation about Ancient Egypt, 1835-1844,' in *For His Ka: Essays*

I hope that we are to see you here soon and that you may be interested in looking through some of our new accessions, a number of which I think you will find of <u>unusual</u> interest.

Very sincerely yours | JHB

**22 November 1920**                                                      **0088**

The Chesbrough Dwellings | Toledo, Ohio |
November 22, 1920

My dear Mr Breasted,

It was most good of you to tell me that you found my paper on early Egyptology interesting and to call my attention to the Devéria exposé.

And now I have to thank you further for offprints of your recent lectures and convocation address. I am very particularly interested in your Washington lectures and the connection you make there between the work of the natural scientists and the archaeologists – as relates to Egypt. I am struggling with such problems as when the Egyptian first artificially alloyed metals, this in connection with the publication of the Abbott gold and silver objects. I know that my eagerly anticipated visit to Chicago will be of the greatest help and stimulus. I am also looking forward to seeing your new treasures. I am planning now to go next Monday, the 29th.

I hope you will not be too busy to talk with me about the medical papyrus of the Smith collection. In the winter, when the triennial election of officers took place, there was an attack on the management of the society in New York papers led by Mrs John K. Van Rensselaer. Dr von Oefele[124] took occasion to air his grievances in the press and I feel that it is imperative, if possible, to get work started soon on that medical papyrus by a competent authority, whose name on the title-page would carry conviction that the papyrus had been well handled. I am authorized by a sub-committee of the

_Offered in Memory of Klaus Baer_, ed. D. Silverman (Chicago: Oriental Institute, 1994), 159-78.

[124] Felix von Oefele was a physician in New York, associated with the New York Historical Society. He was so well known to them, and the readers of the Bulletin, that he was only referred to as 'von Oefele' in the 1922 article about the Edwin Smith Papyrus. James Breasted, 'The Edwin Smith Papyrus: An Egyptian Medical Treatise of the Seventeenth Century Before Christ,' _New York Historical Society Quarterly Bulletin_ 6:1 (April 1922): 5-31.

Executive Committee to ask you whether you would care to prepare the publication and would have time for it. The papyrus is probably the most valuable one owned by the Society and I am ready to waive my interest in it, in the hope that it may be published sooner and better than I could do it. If you are not interested I have in mind Dr Alan Gardiner or Professor Erman, but I should not wish us to turn over to any foreign scholar valuable scientific material that you would care to handle and could find time for. The Society ought, and would, I trust, pay an honorarium for the work. The purpose of mentioning the matter in this letter is to give you a few days to consider whether it appeals to you. The papyrus can be very satisfactorily reproduced in paper negatives and positives of which you could have duplicates to use in your seminar, if you considered it a suitable subject for seminar work.

How happy you and your family must be to be together for Thursday. Please give my regards to Mrs Breasted. With greetings from us all.
Sincerely yours | Caroline R. Williams


**3 January 1921**                                    **0089**

Chicago | January 3, 1921
My dear Mrs. Williams:
I am enclosing you herewith the Erman Dictionary notes which you kindly loaned me to copy and which I neglected to hand you before you left. If you have no objection I hope I may retain the Erman letters for a little while longer until Mrs. Breasted has had opportunity to read them all. I will return them by registered post or, if you are expecting to return here soon and do not need them, I can hand them to you on your arrival.

Mr. Hoffmann[125] has just given me to understand that you are not expecting to be in New York the 1st of February, and I cannot recall clearly what you told me of your plans for the new year. I hope I make it quite clear that I am only raising a question and not bringing up the matter with any pressure upon you or the Historical Society. I am therefore asking what is merely a question, namely, whether Mr. Hoffmann is correct in his further

---

[125] It is not clear who exactly Mr. Hoffmann is, but he is esteemed by both CRW and JHB for his work.

inference that you might not need him during February. If this is the case it would be of immense aid if we could have his services for another month, but I repeat, I am only raising the question, recognizing fully that we agreed he should return to New York to resume his work there February 1st.

Mrs. Breasted appreciated very much, as I did, your very kind letter and the delicious ginger that came with it. We both join in kindest regards and best wishes for the New Year to you and your husband and mother.

Very sincerely yours | JHB

Enclosures[126]

**3 January 1921**                                                         **0090**

The Chesbrough Dwellings |
Toledo, Ohio | January 3, 1921

Dear Mr Breasted,

It has become necessary for me to delay going to New York from the last of January to the last of February. If, under these circumstances, you would care to retain Mr Hoffmann through February, I should be glad to arrange to have the termination of his leave of absence shifted from February 1st to March 1st. May I hear soon what your wishes are?

I am sorry to mention again the New York Historical Society's papyri, but I find, now that I am home, that I have nothing tangible to say to the Committee appointed nearly a year ago. The impression I have from our conversation is that you think it hazardous to intrust the papyri to Hoffmann and that you discourage making any attempt to bring over Herr Ibscher, on account of the unlikelihood that the Berlin Museum would spare him, and the great expense involved if one could get him! But the papyri cannot lie indefinitely, if they are to be saved for science! Could you tell me very briefly by letter what you would like me to report as your opinion?

If you would prefer to reserve your opinion until you could see the papyri and would have time to visit the collection when you go East in the Spring, I will simply delay the matter until then on the ground that you

---

[126] Not in archive.

wish first to see the papyri and will also wait until March with respect to the medical papyrus to give you every chance to undertake it, if you care to do so and find yourself in a position to do so.

I am sure you will understand that it distresses me to trouble you when your time is so taken with important affairs of your won. If you wish to be rid of the matter a letter declining to undertake the medical papyrus would close it. If, at the same time, you included a warning against intrusting the mounting of the papyri to inexperienced hands, emphasizing the highly specialized character of such work, such a letter would no doubt give me support in dealing with the situation, for which I should be very grateful.

Sincerely yours | Caroline R. Williams

**5 January 1921**                                                 **0091**

Chicago | January 5, 1921

My dear Mrs. Williams:

How curious that our letters should have crossed in the matter of Mr. Hoffmann! I assure you I appreciate very much the opportunity of retaining him here for another month, as our new material is desperately in need of the kind of care he can give it.

Now regarding the papyri, I think it would be unsafe to express a final opinion about the feasibility of Hoffmann's undertaking the mounting of the medical papyrus until I have seen it. If it is in as good a state of preservation as our new Book of the Dead it would be perfectly feasible for Hoffmann to undertake to mount it. Indeed, if it is all in as good a state of preservation as the page of which you left the photostat reproduction here, I should think that Hoffmann could do the work. On the other hand, if the roll is tattered and fragmentary and much crushed together, successful mounting would be possible only to a man of long-continued intimate experience with such work. This I think Mr. Hoffman has not yet had.

It might seem a reflection on Mr. Hoffmann to report verbatim what I have said unless perhaps accompanied by an expression of my confidence in his unusual skill as a preparatory of long experience, which however has not included a specialty like the unrolling and mounting of papyri. It may be better therefore to do as you suggest, and merely report that it would be necessary for me to see the papyri before reaching a final opinion.

I may add that I am more and more inclined to undertake the editing of the papyrus myself, for the enterprise is very attractive to me and I appreciate very much your having given me the opportunity. Will it meet your purposes to state to the Museum, as far as the question of my editing the papyrus is concerned, that I am very much inclined to do it, but that I would like the opportunity of seeing it sometime within the next ninety days before making a final decision?

Please make use of what I have said in this letter in any way deemed wise, without of course creating the impression among the Historical Society people that I am in the least reflecting on Mr. Hoffmann because of the fact that he has had little or no experience in the difficult specialty of papyrus mounting.

With kindest regards, I am | Very sincerely yours | JHB

**7 January 1921**                                                     **0092**

1501 Jefferson Avenue | January 7, 1921

Dear Mr Breasted,

I have to thank you for two kind letters of January 3rd and 5th respectively. I have written today asking that Mr Hoffmann's leave of absence be extended through the month of February. The Trustees will pass on this request at their next meeting, January 18th. I anticipate, of course, a favorable reply and will let you know when I have it.

I have also reported that you wish to defer your decision whether or not you could edit the medical papyrus until you are able, sometime within the next ninety days, to see it. I have never raised the question with the Committee of Mr Hoffmann's ability to mount the papyri, although it has been very much on my mind, and I certainly shall be most careful not to use your words in a way to discredit him in their eyes, if it becomes necessary to do so. Again with thanks and with kind regards,

Sincerely yours | Caroline R. Williams

**19 January 1921**                                        **0093**

Chicago | January 19, 1921
My dear Mrs. Williams:
I am very glad to have your letter of January 7th, and shall hope to hear of
the favorable action of the Trustees of the Historical Society after January
18th.

Again thanking you for your most valuable coöperation in getting
this matter arranged, I am, with kind regards,
        Very sincerely yours | JHB


**21 January 1921**                                        **0094**

The Chesbrough Dwellings |
Toledo, Ohio | January 21, 1921
Dear Mr Breasted,
This morning I received word from the Acting Librarian of the New York
Historical Society saying: 'I read your letter to the Board yesterday and Mr
Hoffmann's leave of absence was extended to March 1st.' I hope this added
leave will enable to him to take care of your most urgent needs.

I inclose one letter which I think you may like to read because of
what is said of the Austrian president and conditions there. If you receive
news of the Berlin Dictionary and what the prospects are of bringing it to
completion, I should be grateful to be told about it.

Please tell Mrs Breasted that I appreciate her kind letter written
under such difficult circumstances. I hope Jamie is having a light case and
that the little girl will escape, but I feel concerned about them! It must be
an anxious time for you both.

With kind regards | Sincerely yours | Caroline R. Williams

**22 January 1921**                                                0095

Chicago | January 22, 1921

Dear Mrs. Williams:

I am exceedingly grateful to you for your good offices in securing for us an extension of Mr. Hoffmann's time here to the first of March. There were several important pieces which very much needed his attention and which he will now be able to finish, I hope, before he leaves us.

I shall read with much interest the letter from Austria which you have kindly enclosed. I fear the suffering there is beyond our comprehension, from all I hear.

I have had a long letter from Sethe which would interest you. I have not yet answered it, but after I have done so perhaps you may care to see it. He has accomplished a prodigious amount of work under war conditions, especially a third volume on the writing and paleography of the Pyramid Texts, which there is no money to publish.[127] Bull and I are sending him what we can, and a similar amount also to the Dictionary. It is more important than I realized that these men should be encouraged at this terribly depressing juncture.

Answering your kind inquiries, I am glad to say that Jamie is now dressed, and though still confined to his room, we have no further anxiety, but his mother is very much overworked and weary.

With kindest regards, believe me | Very sincerely yours | JHB

**16 March 1921**                                                0096

Chicago | March 16, 1921

My dear Mrs. Williams:

I find that it has been impossible for me to reach New York in March, as I had expected to do, but I am now expecting to lecture there on the 20th of April and shall probably spend some further part of that same week in New York. I think I ought to let you know therefore that there will be a slight

---

[127] This work appeared as Kurt Sethe, *Die altaegyptischen Pyramidentexte nach den Papierabdrücken und Photographien des Berliner Museums*, Bd. 3 (Leipzig: J.C. Heinrichs'sche Buchhandlung, 1922).

delay in my seeing the Historical Society's papyri,--that is, a delay beyond the ninety days which I mentioned to you. If this delay is of consequence to you, please do not hesitate to make other arrangements about the papyri.

It may interest you to know that Mr. Bull and I have been able to send a sufficient fund to Sethe to insure the publication of the third volume of his Pyramid Texts, which has been lying in manuscript awaiting publication for a long time. At the same time we have sent the same amount to the Dictionary, and I have received from Erman a statement of the financial condition of the Dictionary, which does not seem very hopeful. I mention these remittances of ours because I hope in the future we may be able to work together in the matter. You have evidently been doing nobly in supporting the Dictionary, and I can now see that it will be necessary for us to stand by Erman and this work to the uttermost in order to bring the enterprise through. In saying this to you I know I am bringing coals to Newcastle, for you had discerned it long ago, and I am very grateful for what you have already done. I am casting about for some practical plan for collecting more money here in Chicago, and I am confident it can be done.

With kindest regards to you and Mr Williams, in which Mrs. Breasted joins, I am | Always very sincerely yours | JHB


**21 March 1921**                                                    0097

The New York Historical Society |
170 Central Park West | (76th-77th Sts.) |
New York | March 21, 1921

Dear Mr Breasted

Your letter of March 15th with all its welcome news reached me this morning. The 20th of April or thereabouts, as you find convenient, is entirely satisfactory for the consultation about the Abbott papyri. It is very good of you to consent to give us your valuable counsel.

Certainly it would be better that we should not act separately about the Dictionary and I shall be glad to cooperate in any plan which you will lead. Only yesterday I was telling Mr Gay about the preliminary Handwörterbuch now ready for publication, the doubt whether there would be funds to publish it and how greatly it is needed, and he suggested that I send a letter about it to the Literary Review of the Evening Post. He would like something informative about the inception and progress of the Dictionary, as well as present needs, and all my data on the subject are filed in Toledo. Hence I am glad to wait until I know more of your plans. If you they include writing anything about the Dictionary for the press, would you, perhaps, send your article also to the Post? I am sure Mr Gay would be very pleased.

I wish I knew whether you were to read the paper announced for the Baltimore meeting! I should like so much to hear it, but perhaps it will be printed immediately. And may I hear your New York lecture or is it not to be open to the public?

Please accept my thanks for the reprint of your account of the Mesopotamian trip, forwarded to me from Toledo.[128] I hope to write to Mrs Breasted in a day or two. In the meantime, may I send my greetings through you?

My family would wish to reciprocate your kind messages to them.
Sincerely yours | Caroline R. Williams

**28 March 1921**                                                    **0098**

Chicago | March 28, 1921

My dear Mrs. Williams:
I am very glad to have your letter of March 21st from New York. I appreciate very much Mr. Gay's kind offer of coöperation.

If I remember your plans correctly, you were expecting to be in Chicago again for a short time before summer. I wish at that time we might talk over the matter of a campaign on behalf of the Berlin dictionary. A great deal depends upon the state of public opinion which is difficult for

---

[128] The recounting of this first trip of the new Oriental Institute at the University of Chicago is in the Oriental Institute Archives. JHB, 'Report of the First Expedition of the Oriental Institute of the University of Chicago,' N.D. (ca. 1920). It is also fully reprinted in Geoff Emberling, ed. *Pioneers to the Past: American Archaeologists in the Middle East, 1919-1920* Oriental Institute Museum Publications, 30 (Chicago: The Oriental Institute, 2010), 121-146. See http://oi.uchicago.edu/sites/oi.uchicago.edu/files/uploads/shared/docs/oimp30.pdf (accessed 23 August 2016).

a single person to gauge correctly. In view of this uncertainty it may be better to undertake a quiet and more personal campaign among those of one's one circle who might be interested to contribute.

The family has just been laid waste by a visitation of influenza, which however I hope has left no permanent damage behind. Mrs. Breasted joins me in kindest regards.

Very sincerely yours | JHB

---

**4 April 1921**                                                           **0099**

Chicago | April 4, 1921

My dear Mrs. Williams:

Many thanks for your kind letter. Please don't bother to acknowledge this, but in view of your very interesting survey of early American interest in Egyptian studies, I trust you may be interested in the enclosed correspondence, especially the excerpts from the Mormon records. I think Mr. Williams would also be interested in this.

With kindest regards to you both, I am | Very sincerely yours | JHB
Enclosures.[129]

---

**7 May 1921**                                                            **0100**

Chicago | May 7, 1921

My dear Mrs. Williams:

Schäfer's address is

Im Gertenheim 3,
Berlin-Steglitz.

I do not have at hand the stipulations of the Commonwealth Fund. Do you happen to know whether any of its income is available for science? I have been wondering whether any of it would be available for the Dictionary. Ever since leaving New York I have been vexed with myself for having forgotten to talk over with you the possibility of securing support for the Dictionary here in America. I fear we were altogether too much absorbed

---

[129] Not in archives.

in the interesting problems of the Historical Society's Collection. I have succeeded in getting Mr. John M. Wulfing of St. Louis, now in Germany, interested, and I am sure he will look the matter up in Berlin and enlist some of the money available in St. Louis for such purposes. While it is quite possible to enlist men of means like this by personal pressure, I am greatly puzzled as to whether public opinion makes it wise to attempt a general appeal. Mr. Gay would know far more about this, and his wide knowledge of the public situation would be very valuable.

You will be interested to know that my Institute plans are making good progress. It now looks as if we would be able to undertake the compilation of an Assyrian dictionary similar to the Egyptian Wb,[130] and also the collection and publication of the Middle Kingdom Book of the Dead, which I call 'The Coffin Texts'.[131] The prospects for excavation are also very good. For the present, however, we are keeping these matters quiet.

With kindest regards, I am | Very sincerely yours | JHB

---

[130] 'Wb,' meaning wörterbuch or dictionary. This 'Chicago Assyrian Dictionary' project began in earnest, with Luckenbill formally at the helm, on 3 October 1921. There was a team of collaborators working on the project of surveying all available cuneiform documents and recording their words. By the Spring of 1922, the team was producing around 2000 cards per week. Due to workloads and JHB's rigorous standards, the first volume was finally published in the early 1960s. There are currently 21 volumes and over 6 million cards. See Abt, *American Egyptologist*, 255-56; http://oi.uchicago.edu/research/publications/assyrian-dictionary-oriental-institute-university-chicago-cad (accessed 21 November 2016).

[131] JHB had wanted to begin this project much earlier, in 1912, when he argued that the mortuary texts present in pyramids, known as 'Pyramid Texts,' had moved in the Middle Kingdom to the insides of coffins, therefore he called them 'Coffin Texts.' As with the Assyrian Dictionary, all known coffin texts had to be collected, studied, and published together. Again, JHB produced standardized forms to help with collation and recording. Working with Alan Gardiner and T. George Allen, the texts were finally published in 7 volumes from 1935-1961. See Abt, *American Egyptologist*, 256-65.

**18 May 1921**                                     **0101**

The New York Historical Society |
170 Central Park West | (76th-77th Sts.) |
New York | May 18, 1921

Dear Mr Breasted

I am sorry to have left your inquiry so long unanswered. Mr Gay is away on a holiday but I am sure he would expect us to be the judges whether it were worth while to make a public appeal for an Egyptian Dictionary. I am growing very doubtful of it myself in view of the present multiplicity of demands.

I don't know the applicability of the Commonwealth Fund. I was rather hasty in mentioning the Fund in my letter, as I find now that there is no immediate hope from that source. For my own part I wish I knew how far our German friends were suffering for food <u>now</u>. I keep an occasional package going to the Ermans and I hope to be able to make some gift to the Dictionary, but I am somewhat held back by the Mount Holyoke drive. Last year the alumnae were called on and my husband and I pledged all that we could. This year in addition to our pledges we (the alumnae) have been assigned a quota which we must each 'get or give' and there is no escape!

If you have any plan in which I could help, I will do what I can, otherwise I will send directly to Professor Erman so far as I am able. I am very glad to hear that your own projects are working out favorably. I shall be going home at last early in June.

With kind regards | Sincerely yours | Caroline R. Williams


**5 August 1921**                                     **0102**

The Chesbrough Dwellings |
Toledo, Ohio | August 5, 1921

My dear Mr Breasted,

Mr Wall writes me that he has placed in your hands photostat copies of all the sheets of the medical papyrus which were mounted flat by their late owner. I think you may like to have copies, too, of the two sides of Us. 262, said to have been found with the medical papyrus and I inclose them herewith.

Shortly before I left New York, the New York Historical Society made Miss Leonora Smith, daughter of Edwin Smith and donor of the papyrus, a Life Member and informed her that they had named the document the 'Edwin Smith papyrus.' A cousin of hers, living in the Hotel Beresford, whom I had been beseeching for information about Edwin Smith's life, was stirred, on this occasion, to send me such meager information as she could and I copy this for you. A few other items about him which I dug out independently of the family are given in my Bulletin article on the progress of Egyptian studies in this country. I need not say how gratified I am that you are undertaking to edit the papyrus.

I am pegging away on the body of my catalogue of the jewelry. When I get it all in MS, I should like to go to Chicago to use books not in my library, but I don't know when that will be. I was able that last of June to send a contribution to the Dictionary. Professor Erman wrote that he should hold it in reserve to see whether or not they secured funds through the Academy; as yet the Prussian parliament had not yet voted the budget for 1921; if not needed to pay the assistants, he would use it for publication purposes. But I dare say he has written you in full of this situation.

Miss Randolph is spending the summer with us and recently she, my mother, a Toledo friend, and I went for a weeks' motoring trip in Canada. My husband unfortunately could not go, but insisted that Mother must have a change and I acted as chauffeur, driving 190 miles. Only 32 miles were a repetition; we crossed at Port Huron and returned to Windsor; the roads are about as in Michigan; much of the time we were in a grazing country, sparsely settled, with many pine trees and hills, just the sort of country roads with little traffic, which we enjoy better than the highways of travel. All went fortunately with us, and we were delighted with our 'trip abroad,' as mother called it!

I wish we might hope to see you and Mrs Breasted for a week-end, or, if you and Charles were motoring this way, that you would stop to see us! With kindest greetings from us all to you and Mrs Breasted,

Sincerely yours | Caroline Ransom Williams

Edwin Smith, the son of Sheldon Smith and his wife Polly Summers, was born in Bridgeport, Conn., April 27th 1822.

The family removed to Newark, N. J., when he was a child; thence to

New York City, where he was educated at the New York University.

He married Elma Doremus, of New York City, March 1st, 1849.

He became deeply interested in Egyptology and after studying the subject in both London and Paris, he went to Egypt about 1858.

He lived in Luxor and in Thebes from that time until 1876. Then, after a brief visit in this country he went to Naples, Italy, where he remained until his death, April 23rd, 1906.

Two daughters survive him, Mrs Eleanor Stölte, of Naples and Miss Leonora Sheldon Smith, who gave to the New York Historical Society (of which in his earlier years her father had been a member) the Edwin Smith Collection of Egyptian Curios and Papyri.

(written by Mrs Isabel Smith, a niece of Edwin Smith, June 1921, 1 W. 81 St., New York.)


**14 August 1921**                                                    0103


Chikaming Country Club |
Lakeside, Mich. | Aug. 14, 1921

My dear Mrs. Williams:-

I am very glad to have your kind letter of Aug. 5th, enclosing the two photographs of the papyrus fragment Us.262. I hope it may turn out to belong to the roll, though the writing looks larger and heavier at first glance.

Many thanks also for the additional data regarding Edwin Smith. These earlier people interest me very much. I wonder if anybody will ever be interested to look <u>us</u> up, after we have departed to    .[132] It is fascinating to sit down with the photostat prints of this big fine papyrus. But the minutes I have for it are so few, that I am dismayed when I contemplate my recklessness in having embarked on the task, or having ever allowed anybody to depend on me to do so. I have an abominably uncomfortable conscience.

You quite stirred our admiration at your prowess as a 'chauffeuse.'[133]

---

[132] JHB left the spot blank. But, to answer his question 95 years later: yes.

[133] For why this trip would have been so big for CRW, and so impressive for JHB, see, for example, Julie Wosk, *Women and the Machine: Representations from the Spinning Wheel to the*

I think we shall have to try it some time. Mrs. Breasted has now learned to drive our Cadillac and enjoys doing so very much. We live very quietly here, working in the morning and trying to get a little golf followed by a bath in the lake in the afternoon. Charles and the little folks enjoy it very much and James Jr. has developed surprisingly at golf, followed by his mother, who can do as well as 80 on the first nine, and hopes to graduate into the 70's next week.

We are glad to hear that you will be needing to use our library later on, and hope it may be soon. You will be interested to see the establishment of our Assyrian Dictionary staff, which begins work Oct. first. I hope that we shall also be attacking the Middle Kingdom B D [134] by that time. I think I wrote you of it. Gardiner is to join me in it.

Mrs. Breasted and the infants join in kindest greetings to you, and to your mother and Miss Randolph. Thanks for your kind invitation. If we are able to motor so far (being youthful and timid!), we certainly shall stop at Toledo to see you.

Very sincerely yours | JHB


**1 November 1921**                                                    **0104**

November 1, 1921
My dear Mrs. Williams:
I sent you last week a copy of a letter which I was sending to Mr. Wall, which perhaps needs no further comment except to express the hope that you approve of my desire that you should share in the memorial volume to be issued in celebration of the Champollion centennial. I very much hope that you can do this.

I find the photographs of the papyrus very satisfactory indeed. They are quite as good as the original except in the matter of rubrics. If you are going to New York soon I would like to give you the photographs and ask if you could draw a red line under each of the rubrics, marking, of course, in

---

*Electronic Age* (Baltimore: Johns Hopkins University Press, 2001). Also, Herbert Ladd Towle, 'The Woman At the Wheel,' *Scribner's Magazine* 57:2 (Feb. 1915): 214–33.

[134] B. D. being Book of the Dead. Although it is likely that he means the Coffin Texts, which contained the Middle Kingdom versions of the Book of the Dead.

each case, the exact extent of the rubricized words.

The papyrus is fascinatingly interesting and I only wish I had more time for it.

Are we not soon to see you in Chicago? Mrs. Breasted joins me in kindest regards.

Always sincerely yours | JHB

**6 November 1921**                                                    **0105**

The New York Historical Society |
170 Central Park West | (76th-77th Sts.) |
New York City | November 6, 1921

Dear Mr Breasted,

The copy of your letter to Mr Wall and your letter to me of November 1st have reached me here and I think [sic] you warmly for both. We are all delighted with your important and interesting results from the study of the Edwin Smith papyrus. Certainly I shall be most happy to underline the rubrics for you. If you can forward your photographs at once I shall be able to do it before going home, shortly before Thanksgiving. I shall not be in New York again until <words missing>

It would be a pleasure, [I'm] sure, to participate in the Champollion memorial volume. The only question would be one of time and strength and I should need to know when the MS of such a paper must be ready. It is imperative that I get the first part of my catalogue on the press at the earliest possible moment. I have in mind the Semkhkere relief of which we now have some beautiful photographs; it is the best example of the monumental art of Egypt in the Society's possession and monuments of that king's reign are little known. Please believe me appreciative of your friendly interest to have me included in the list of contributors. With your own plan to publish a preliminary account of the medical papyrus, I am heartily in sympathy.

May I trouble you with a question which is perplexing me at this moment? Signor de Ricci[135] called on me last evening just at the closing

---

[135] Seymour Montefiore Robert Rosso de Ricci (1881-1942) was a British antiquary. His interest was in rare books and manuscripts, and he went to Egypt a number of times to buy

hour with the request that he be permitted to examine papyrus No. 66 of the 1915 catalogue. I spoke of its especially fragile condition and he made very light of this, offering [to do] the unrolling and mounting [of] it, and reading glibly from it the names 'Romulus', 'Martinus' etc. He says it is one of the rare papyri inscribed in Latin. He also showed considerable excitement over the inedited [sic] late ostraca of the Anderson collection and the Abbott schoolboy's tablets. Can you tell me anything of Signor de Ricci's reputation as a scholar? He seems conversant with Egyptological literature but was overbearing and fairly discourteous in the insistence of his advice and demands. Should he be allowed carte blanch with the Society's late documents? I wish I was in a position to name some American scholar of competence who had asked the privilege of examining them! My fear is that Mr de Ricci may simply pick out a few treasures to use for his own purposes and spoil the material for systematic editing and publishing later. But if he is an authority on the text of the Roman period from Egypt, perhaps the Society ought to try to engage his services.

My kindest regards to you and Mrs Breasted.

Sincerely yours, | Caroline R. Williams

**8 November 1921**                                                                 **0106**

November 8, 1921

My dear Mrs. Williams:

I am very glad to have your letter of November 6 and especially to learn that you may be able to contribute to the Champollion memorial volumes. At this juncture I should not forget what I believe I mentioned in the letter to Mr. Wall – that Moret[136] stated that the French Government had granted the subvention for the volume to be contributed by French scholars but that they had not yet done so for the second volume, to be furnished by non-

---

mainly Greek papyri. He published a few of them.

[136] Alexandre Moret (1868-1938) was a French Egyptologist who studied under Maspero and focused on philology, law, and religion. He took his Doctorat és-Lettres in 1903. He held a number of important positions such as Director at the École des Hautes Études 1899-1938, Keeper of the Musée Guimet 1918-1938. One of his major works was *Histoire de l'Orient* (G. Glotz: 1929-1930), which has only been surpassed by *Cambridge Ancient History*.

French scholars. It is evidently very difficult to put through a government subvention in these financially stringent times and of course it may be that our French colleagues will fail in securing government support for the second volume.

Moret spoke of desiring the manuscripts early in 1922 but such enterprises are always notoriously belated, as you know. I think the Smenkhkere relief would be a beautiful thing to use for this purpose. I am glad you like the idea, also, of a preliminary notice of the Edwin Smith Papyrus in the proposed memorial volume.

With regard to De Ricci, I wish I might have a <u>talk</u> with you, for I don't like to put anything on paper that is unfavorable to anybody. It is, however, imperative and only fair that you and the Society should know at least something of the facts.

There is a strain of insanity in De Ricci's family, which, if I am correctly informed, has swept away all the members of this generation of his family but him, and some of the preceding generation. His mother has led a tragic life and lives at present under the possibility of seeing her son afflicted as all the other De Ricci's have been. I understand that she is devoting her life to him. He is a man of uncanny brilliancy but so erratic that his judgment is very unreliable. His mistakes of judgment made me a great deal of trouble when I was working for the dictionary on the Paris collections, though we are on perfectly good terms now. I have never heard that De Ricci has had the slightest experience in unrolling or mounting a papyrus though he certainly possesses great talent in paleography. Your reference to his being 'overbearing and fairly discourteous' quite confirms my own experience with him.

Your inquiry about this matter reminds me that recently my colleague, Professor E. J. Goodspeed,[137] in discussing the Society's collection, mentioned that he had published the Society's Greek papyri.

---

[137] Edgar J. Goodspeed (1871-1962) was a classical scholar who studied and worked at the University of Chicago from the late 1890s to 1937. He was a student of William Rainey Harper's at Yale for a year, 1890-91, and therefore a close friend and colleague of JHB. The Goodspeed Manuscript Collection at the University of Chicago bears his name (http://goodspeed.lib.uchicago.edu/collection.php, accessed 21 November 2016). He is not to be confused with George Stephen Goodspeed, who was also a student of Harper's and a friend of JHB (Abt, American Egyptologist, 36).

In this connection he expressed the desire to recollate some of the documents. Under these circumstances does not Professor Goodspeed's prior publication of the Greek documents and demonstrated interest in the collections give him a prior claim which may be very timely and convenient for the Society to use in dealing with De Ricci? I am bringing the matter to Professor Goodspeed's attention and if I can serve the Society in any way in this connection I shall be glad to do so.

Please impress upon Mr. Wall, and any members of the Executive Committee who may read what I have written you about De Ricci, with the necessity of keeping the entire matter strictly confidential. De Ricci is the last man in the world with whom I would want to be involved in a controversy.

Many thanks for your kind offer to underline the rubrics for me. I am mailing you the photographs today by registered post. Will you kindly, at the same time, mark 'reverse' on all the photographs taken from the back of the papyrus?

Thanking you very much for your help, I am | Very faithfully yours | JHB

**13 November 1921**                                                      **0107**

The New York Historical Society |
170 Central Park West | (76th-77th Sts.) |
New York City | November 13, 1921

Dear Mr Breasted,

Please accept my sincerest thanks for your understanding and helpful response to my inquiry.

I am just getting off to Boston where I am to consult with the Heliotype Company about the plates of my publication and see some things in the Boston Museum, but I want without delay to assure you that the contents of your letter probably will not be known to more than three other people, Mr Wall, the President of the Society and the Chairman of the Art Committee. I have Mr Wall's promise not to use it in the open Executive Committee unless some wholly unexpected opposition should develop and after that meeting your letter with the one I have written giving various data which I obtained at the M.M.A will be destroyed and not a word reflecting on Mr de Ricci will appear in the written records of the Society. I shall never mention to others what you have told me but I am grateful to know it for it clears up and explains so much. I have been astounded at the range of the man's writing; he has appeared as so many kinds of an expert! He wrote us that he had unrolled and catalogued the papyri belonging to M. Théodor Reinach but I have been unable to find the publication in New York. Perhaps it is very new.

Gratefully and Sincerely yours | Caroline R. Williams

Professor Goodspeed's letter to Mr Wall puts the matter in excellent shape to go before the committee at their regular meeting on Tuesday next. I shall write to thank him very soon. I return to N.Y. at the end of the week when I look <words missing> your photographs and will give them my most careful attention.

**4 December 1921**                                                        **0108**

December 4, 1921

Dear Mr Breasted,

The inclosed letter came to me this morning from Mr Newberry.[138] I copy for your information the part of my reply to him which concerns the papyrus:

'The Society has lately intrusted the publication of the medical papyrus to Professor James H. Breasted of the University of Chicago and if you are to see it and make notes on it, this privilege would necessarily, under the circumstances, have to come as a courtesy from Professor Breasted. Mr Breasted has made considerable progress in his study of the document and has promised the Society a preliminary account for its April or July <u>Bulletin</u> of next year;[139] he is planning to publish a somewhat fuller preliminary

---

[138] Percy E. Newberry (1868-1949) was a British Egyptologist from the earliest days of the discipline in Britain. He was an assistant to Petrie and excavated in Egypt for Lord Amherst, Margaret Benson, Theodore Davis, and more. He was the Brunner Professor of Egyptology in Liverpool 1906-1919, Professor of Ancient History and Archaeology at Cairo University, 1929-1933, and was associated with the EES for 65 years.

[139] James Breasted, 'The Edwin Smith Papyrus: An Egyptian Medical Treatise of the

paper elsewhere in the near future and his final full publication will be issued in due time by the Society in a handsome folio volume giving the text in facsimile and full size. Professor Breasted's address is 5615 University Avenue, Chicago, if you wish to write to him.' At the same time I am sending Mr Wall a copy of Mr Newberry's letter, my reply to it, and telling him that I have sent the letter and my reply to you. I have sent Mr Newberry an introduction to Mr Wall and offered him a chance to see the gold objects which are withdrawn from exhibition and which include the ring of which he published an adequate line cut in Scarabs, fig. 114.

By this time, presumably, you are in possession again of the photographs of the medical papyrus. If my underlining of the rubrics is at any passage unsatisfactory, perhaps we can talk over the matter in Chicago before I return to New York and I can take some of the photos back with me and go over the text once more. That part which was mounted by Edwin Smith on paper was here and there slightly smeared in the process making certain passages written in black ink take in the photos much as those in red ink, because the black was no longer so intense as it was originally. I was extremely hurried because of the rush of last things to attend to but I worked carefully and am confident that I did not make any important omissions. In one or two more instances of single signs or small groups in red underlying black I wanted to make drawings on the reverse of your photos and did not have time – drawings of the red signs and black signs separated, I mean. I can do this later, if it would be helpful to you.

In planning for Hoffmann's work, Mr Wall and I thought we should be glad to have him demount the sheets of this papyrus, which are now pasted to paper and remount between glass. He talks about using damp blotting paper to separate the papyrus from the old paper mount and is perfectly confident he can do it successfully. There is not the slightest prospect that the Society will ever be in a financial position to bring over a man already trained to do such work from Europe, even if such a person could be found, and every month we delay having Hoffmann work on the papyri, if eventually he is to mount them, only subjects the Society to further criticism from people like de Ricci. Mr Wall and I picked out the medical papyrus because it is already successfully recorded in photographs and

Seventeenth Century Before Christ,' *New York Historical Society Quarterly Bulletin* 6:1 (April 1922): 5-31.

most things which Mr Hoffmann must work on cannot be photographed until he has handled them and got them flat and the loose fragments collected. However, I have had misgivings since coming home, whether you would wish the mounting of the separate columns undertaken until after you had your publication completed. I hardly need say that only one sheet would be intrusted to Hoffmann first and Mr Wall would stop with that, if he appeared to be doing damage to the papyrus. It is not too late to make a change of plan for he was not to begin before Christmas, so please let me know in case you wish the work delayed.

With all kind greetings to you and your family | Sincerely yours | Caroline Ransom Williams

P.S. Do you go to the Archaeological Institute Meeting in Ann Arbor? If so couldn't you find time to come to us here, if only for a few hours? You have had, of course, the sad news of the death on October 2 of Georg Möller.[140]

**5 December 1921**                                               **0109**

December 5, 1921

My dear Mrs. Williams:

The photographs of the Edwin Smith Medical Papyrus have again reached me in safety and I want to thank you very much for your kindness in marking the rubrics, which must have consumed a good deal of time.

I hope that we are to see you in Chicago soon. I think you would be interested in the developments in our workshop, by which I mean the Institute as a whole.

With kindest regards, I am | Very sincerely yours, | JHB

---

[140] Georg Christian Julius Möller (1876-1921) was a German Egyptologist who took his PhD at Berlin under Erman in 1900. He was on staff at the Berlin Museum from 1901 and became the Assistant Director of the Egyptian collections there in 1907. His most important work was on hieratic texts and palaeography. His death was sudden.

**6 December 1921**                                                    **0110**

December 6, 1921.

My dear Mrs. Williams:

I am glad to learn from your letter of December 4 that we are soon to see you in Chicago.

With regard to the request of Professor Newberry, I appreciate your sending me his letter and a copy of your reply. I hope we shall have an opportunity to discuss Newberry's request more fully when you are here. I think a great deal of him and, as far as I am concerned, he is most welcome to study the papyrus to his heart's content I take it, however, that the Society will not want the essentially valuable things in the papyrus dissipated in any more preliminary publications than those which they have already consented to in my case. This is about the substance of what I should like to write to Newberry but would be glad to know if you agree.

Evidently my little note thanking you for your kind assistance in the matter of the rubrics had not reached you when you wrote. You have given me all that I wanted and I find it very helpful to be quite certain of the extent of the rubrics.

The question of Hoffman's demounting the sheets of this papyrus is a difficult one. I have nothing on which to base a conclusion regarding his ability in this direction. I should think, however, that his long experience as a preparatory should enable him to take care of a papyrus, which is in such a good state of preservation, but I would, by all means, follow the plan you have suggested of trying him out on one sheet. Perhaps I shall be able to visit New York after the holidays and in that case I could examine the results of his attempt on the single sheet. I think it would be safer to know exactly what these results are before going beyond the first sheet.

It would, indeed, be a great pleasure to accept your kind invitation to stop off for a visit at Toledo. Unfortunately I have been enlisted to organize and preside at a conference of the American Historical Association on 'The History of Civilization', meeting at St. Louis at the same time as the Institute meeting at Ann Arbor. I am, therefore, cut out of the Ann Arbor meeting.

I have been very much depressed at the news of Moeller's death, which is an irreparable loss. He was doing things which none of us can hope to undertake.

I am looking forward to your visit, as there is much which we shall need to discuss.

With kindest regards to you and your mother and Mr. Williams, I am | Very sincerely yours | JHB

Have just received wire from Newberry. He will arrive here next Friday.

**8 December 1921**                                                                          **0111**

The Chesbrough Dwellings | Toledo, Ohio | December 8, 1921

My dear Mr Breasted

Your letter of the 6th reached me in the morning mail. I am entirely in sympathy with your attitude about Professor Newberry's request. I have been in the same position myself repeatedly with respect to the archaeological material and rather than appear selfish, I let Mr Winlock have the bronze 'Soul of Pe', Mr Petrie have numerous subjects for his 'Ancient Egypt' etc. But it is not after all a personal question, but a question how far it is wise for the Society, in view of its own proposed publications, to permit the more interesting material to be made known in advance. I should think more of this might be possible with a papyrus with its many-sided interests than with the art objects. A bronze, once published, is published and that is the end of it, but until the text in facsimile of this papyrus is published there will always be scholars keen to get it, how ever [sic] much has been said about it in a general way before.

It seems to be perfectly simple for the Metropolitan Museum to take the stand that its excavation material is to be published by the members of the expedition and that other scholars are to keep hands off. I don't see why a Society which is putting so much money into the care and study of its Egyptian objects as the Historical Society is doing just now has not the same right, in view of its definite hopes to publish its material in full and the systematic plan on which it is proceeding. I have not even written preliminary papers about the jewelry in the Bulletin because I have come to feel that they might detract from the sale of the catalogue of the jewelry so soon to appear. There is, however, a kind of study of unpublished material and mention of it which is perfectly possible without detracting from its later publication. For instance, recently, in Boston, Professor Reisner permitted me to study some of his Nubian jewelry and I am allowed to mention in my publication the existence of certain dated pieces as an indication of the probable date of certain of mine. I have told Mr Wall to let Mr Newberry handle and make notes on anything in the collection he wants to see, with the understanding that we are planning to publish it; he may make any reference he cares to to the things short of publication. But perhaps the medical papyrus is all he is interested in at present! The matter is entirely in your hands. But you have already devoted so much time to it and made such interesting observations with respect to it, I don't feel that it is fair either to you or to the Society that your results should be in any way anticipated in any one else's publication. I am glad we are dealing this time with such courteous gentlemen; he will not misunderstand our position and we can safely do for him the most that is possible under the circumstances. I will write again tomorrow about the De Ricci matter. I do not go to Chicago, I am sorry to say, until February.

With appreciation of your kind letter | Sincerely yours | C. R. Williams


**9 December 1921**                                                    **0112**

The Chesbrough Dwellings |
Toledo, Ohio | December 9, 1921

My dear Mr Breasted,
I am sorry to trouble you with a second letter, but an engagement yesterday prevented me from finishing matters. Were it not that I have only just returned to my family after a prolonged absence, I would go to Chicago to talk with you, but I haven't the heart to ask them to spare me just now.

By all means send your letter to Mr Wall, since this is your opinion. I fear the suggestion means that Mr de Ricci has been impositioning Professor Goodspeed and if the Committee is unwilling to give Mr de Ricci access to the papyrus, let the onus fall on the Society. I don't know whether they will reverse their decision or not. There was a formal resolution passed refusing Mr de Ricci's written application to be permitted to unroll and study the papyrus which he says is written in Latin (=No. 65 of Professor Goodspeed's paper in Mélanges Nicole p. 191).[141] He has not pointed out to us any other papyrus in Latin and I do not know of any other. In view of what you say, it might be well if Professor Goodspeed (to whom all Latin text were meant-to-be consigned in the Society's resolution) or the Society, on his suggestion, were to ask Mr de Ricci to write on the Latin text or texts for the same part of the catalogue as that containing the Greek texts edited by Professor Goodspeed. It is my impression that Mr de Ricci's reputation of being in league with the dealers and his personal peculiarities have led in New York to a perhaps undeserved disparagement of his abilities. In the Metropolitan Museum I was told that 'nobody took him seriously' and Dr Stillwell, the Chairman of the Society's Art Committee, whose word has great weight with the Executive Committee, knows Mr de Ricci by reputation, and perhaps personally, and was opposed to extending any courtesy to him. It remains to be seen, therefore, whether such a plan could be put through. Further the papyrus would have to be extended and flattened, a fact which presents some difficulties of which I'll spare you an account! If the matter comes up I will, of course, support any recommendation in which you and Professor Goodspeed have united. I am only so sorry the question should be intruded on your time and attention.

With kindest greetings to Mrs Breasted and the children | Sincerely yours | Caroline R. Williams

**14 December 1921**                                                    0113

December 14, 1921

My dear Mrs. Williams:

I have both your letters regarding the Historical Society's papyri. I am very glad that we are in such complete agreement about the matter. I think that nothing should be published which will in the least detract from the

---

[141] Goodspeed argued that the papyrus in question was written in demotic on the recto, and in Greek on the verso. Edgar J. Goodspeed, 'Greek Documents in the Museum of the New York Historical Society,' in *Mélanges Nicole: recueil de mémoires de philology classique et d'archéologie offerts à Jules Nicole à l'occasion de 30e anniversaire de son professorat* (Geneva: Imprimerie W. Kündig & Fils, 1905), 177-91.

value of the final publication to be issued in the name of the Society, and in order to be sure that this is the case I shall see to it that if anything is to be published from or about the medical papyrus, that the subject matter, or, if possible, the manuscript itself, shall be submitted to you and Mr. Wall before publication takes place.

With regard to De Ricci, I feel regretful that I troubled you with the matter at all. I do not think that it is of any consequence to make any effort to smooth down his ruffled plumage and mentioned that aspect of the matter only incidentally. What I had in mind was the possibility of getting the Latin manuscripts published and, for the moment, was thinking of De Ricci very impersonally; and that is not in his case a wise thing to do. In view of what you write I think I will not send my letter to Mr. Wall but will let the matter of the Latin manuscripts entirely alone. We can discuss the matter more fully when we next meet.

In resuming work on the medical papyrus I am discovering what a laborious task I exacted of you in asking you to mark the rubrics and I want to thank you again. I find the marks exceedingly useful and sometimes grammatically helpful.

With kindest regards, in which Mrs. Breasted joins, I am | Very sincerely yours | JHB

**7 January 1922**                                                  **0114**

January 7, 1922.

My dear Mrs. Williams:

I have just received a letter from Moret in which he now states finally and definitely that their French committee for the Champollion centenary celebration has secured the money for the desired memorial volumes. He asks me to send him a list of collaborators, and before doing so I want to be sure that I am right in concluding that you will be able to contribute to this memorial enterprise. Moret states that they will need the manuscripts by the first of April at the latest but, as of course you know, such dates are always elastic. I hope this is not loading an unwelcome burden upon you, but I should be very much pleased if you are able to participate and it would be very appropriate for a Historical Society to contribute something from its collections for publication at such a celebration. Kindly let me know your conclusion as soon as convenient as I must write Moret very soon.

With best wishes for the New Year to you, your mother and Mr. Williams, I am | Very sincerely yours | JHB

**10 January 1922**                                               **0115**

The Chesbrough Dwellings |
Toledo, Ohio | January 10, 1922

Dear Mr Breasted,

It is very good news that the French government is to finance a second volume of essays by foreign scholars! Unluckily for me, the early date at which the essays must be ready cuts me out. When you first wrote about the matter, I thought the papers would be presented in person or by title at the Champollion celebration in September and printed afterwards. Were it possible for me to write my contribution in July or August, after the first part of the Abbott catalogue goes on the press, I should so gladly do it, but under all the circumstances of the New York work, I ought not to delay the appearance of the catalogue to write a paper which would certainly cost several weeks of time. My text is about one-third done and I have begun the preparation of the copy for the 24 (or more) collotype plates. The Society has voted $2500 for the publication and it is all up to me now to get it out!

I am feeling the more pressure in that I have just given up a month to reading, and commenting on, two books, one a history of ancient painting (still in ms) by a former pupil and the other M. Capart's[142] 543 pages of Leçons which is to be brought out in a second illustrated edition and which he asked me to criticize. I could not refuse to help my student and I felt as if in so doing I were paying some of my debts to you which I can never discharge to you personally! M. Capart, too, has done me a number of favors and I hope my comments will seem to him some return for them. These

---

[142] Jean Capart (1877-1947) was a Belgian Egyptologist. He studied in Germany and was appointed assistant Conservator in the Egyptian collections at the Musées Royaux du Cinquantenaire in Brussels in 1900 and Chief Conservator in 1925. He took the Queen of the Belgians to the tomb of Tutankhamun in 1923 as it was being excavated. His specialty was Egyptian art.

seemed to me obligations that I ought not to put aside. My withdrawal from the Champollion volume is a loss only to myself, for the Committee will no doubt have difficulty in keeping the choice of contributions within the limits of what can be printed.

   With appreciation of your kindness | Regretfully yours | Caroline R. Williams

**13 January 1922**                                                    **0116**

                                                              January 13, 1922
My dear Mrs. Williams:
I can quite understand that you cannot at this juncture turn aside from your work on the Abbott catalogue. I am delighted to learn that the first volume is so near completion. Of course I very much regret that the first volume is so near completion. Of course I very much regret that your name is not to appear in the Champollion volume.[143] I am hoping that the delay so usual in such publications may nevertheless eventually permit your participation.

   The Cambridge editors laid it very solemnly on my conscience that the manuscript of my contribution to the Cambridge Ancient History must be ready by January 1921. I sent them the manuscript in July 1921 and not a paragraph has yet appeared in proof, or is likely to do so for another six months. If this happens to be the case with the Champollion memorial volume I shall certainly hope to see your contribution also included. I hope you will not mind my mentioning the matter in this way to Moret.

   With kindest regards, I am | Very sincerely yours | JHB

---

[143] *Recueil d'études égyptologiques dédiées à la mémoire de Jean-François Champollion à l'occasion du centenaire de la lettre à M. Dacier relative à l'alphabet des hiéroglyphes phonétiques, lue à l'Académie des inscriptions et belles-lettres le 27 septembre 1822* (Paris: E. Champion, 1922).

1 February 1922                                                     0117

Mrs. Grant Williams | 1505 Jefferson Avenue |
Toledo, Ohio | February 1, 1922

Dear Mr Breasted,

From New York I hear that Dr Nath. Reich[144] has been studying demotic texts belonging to the Metropolitan Museum and would like to publish those belonging to the Historical Society. I think I could find a way to meet the financial question if I were sure of his competence.

I had never heard of him before. Surely, as yet, he has no such reputation as Spiegelberg,[145] Griffith,[146] and a few others of whom one thinks immediately, but it is such an advantage to have him in New York that if his work commands respect, the opportunity is perhaps one that we should not miss. From the Journ. Of Eg. Archaeology, vol. VI (1920), p. 280, I learn that in 1911 he presented a paper to the Vienna Academy on 16 demotic and 'abnormal hieratic legal documents in the British Museum which afterwards was printed as Denkschrift, No. 55, of the Vienna Academy. Mr Griffith speaks of 'elaborate commentaries' but says nothing of their quality, but their publication by the Vienna Academy no doubt bespeaks considerable competence on the author's part.

Would you consider Dr Reich qualified to direct Hoffman in mounting

---

[144] Nathaniel Julius Reich (1876-1943) was an American Egyptologist and he took his PhD in Vienna in 1904 and worked with Spiegelberg in 1907-1908 and Griffith in 1909. He held positions in institutions all over Austria-Hungary until he emigrated to the US in 1922. He became assistant curator at the University Museum of the University of Pennsylvania, and reader at Johns Hopkins University from 1926. The evidence shows no activity with the NYHS or in Cleveland (see below).

[145] Wilhelm Spiegelberg (1870-1930) was a German Egyptologist and Demotist. He studied under Erman and Maspero and got his PhD in 1892. He was a professor at universities in Strassburg, Heidelberg, and Munich. His specialty was on Coptic and Demotic studies and published hundreds of short articles in his time. He, along with Griffith, was the leading Demotist in Europe.

[146] Francis Llewellyn Griffith (1862-1934) was a British Egyptologist. He attended Oxford, graduating in 1884. He then went on to work with Petrie from 1884-88 in Egypt. He worked at University College, London, as Assistant to the Professor of Egyptology from 1892-1901, then went to Oxford to take up the post of Reader in Egyptology. He spent the rest of his career there. He was a noted linguist and published a great deal on the topic of texts and language. The Griffith Institute of Egyptology at Oxford is his legacy.

some of the papyri?[147] The question where to cut some of the papyri and other complications cannot be left to Hoffmann entirely and I do not see how I can be in New York to work with him. I do not know what Dr Reich would be willing to do yet. He has not written to me but has told both Mr Lythgoe and Mr Wall that he intends to do so, and he also said to Mr Wall that he knew you. Is he perhaps a pupil of Professor Junker?

I regret very much to trouble you with this question, but should be very grateful indeed to know your opinion, which if unfavorable will not be communicated to anyone else. If desirable, Dr Reich's request can be refused on the ground that the Society is undertaking at present all it can financially.

With all kind regards | Sincerely yours | Caroline R. Willlams

**6 February 1922**                                             **0118**

February 6, 1922

My dear Mrs. Williams:

Replying to your inquiry about Dr. Reich, it happens that I had been trying to do something for him and had therefore got together all the information I could regarding him. He was a pupil of Griffith and is without doubt a man of some attainments. I enclose you a 'Vita' which at my request he wrote out, which gives you his career, his bibliography, his photograph, etc. For my own part, I would not hesitate to recommend him for the publication of the Demotic papyri of the New York Historical Society.

I am rather reluctant to enclose a letter of his to me. It is filled with what is, I fear, a characteristically servile attitude sometimes found among people of his race.[148] You will see that his English is now exceedingly faulty. Griffith writes me it used to be much better.

I might add that he has sent me his publications, which I have not yet had time to look at sufficiently to possess an independent judgement on his ability. I am judging his qualifications chiefly from letters sent me by Griffith.

With regard to Reich's qualifications 'to direct Hoffmann in mounting

---

[147] Breasted underlined this statement on the original letter in blue pencil and wrote 'no' next to it.

[148] He was Hungarian and Jewish.

some of the papyri' I would not want to express any judgment. I should be exceedingly reluctant to entrust a practical mechanical matter to a man with German philological training. If, however, it is merely a question of where the papyri should be cut, Reich, I have no doubt, would be competent to settle such questions.

The only unfavorable comment on Reich which I have had I received from Gardiner. It was not at all serious, merely stating that Reich was rather sensitive, somewhat inclined to overestimate his own abilities, and easily tempted to regard himself as not sufficiently appreciated. These are doubtless frailties common to most of us. I should think his chief fault is his servility.

With regard to the finances, if I may express an opinion, I do not think the Society would be committing itself very seriously to take on Reich. He would undoubtedly regard it as a generous interposition of Divine Providence on his behalf if he were offered $100.00 a month or even $1000.00 a year.

Finally, while none of our American organizations, like the universities or the New York Historical Society, can be regarded as charitable institutions, it should be mentioned in connection with your attitude or mine toward Reich that some kind of work at this juncture would be a godsend to him. I have hitherto been deeply disappointed at not being able to secure him some kind of a post and if my budget here would have permitted, I would have given him some kind of work here in the Oriental Institute.

With kindest regards, I am | Very sincerely yours, | JHB

**9 February 1922**                                                      **0119**

The Chesbrough Dwellings |
Toledo, Ohio | February 9, 1922

Dear Mr Breasted,

The inclosed papers have interested me very much and I thank you for letting me see them, as well as for your letter which accompanied them.

My way of meeting the expense of having Dr Reich do the demotic texts, and perhaps some others, belonging to the New York Historical Society would be to propose to the Society that I drop their work wholly or partly in 1923 and that they use the customary appropriation for Dr Reich. I have had this in mind, too, as a way to offer proper compensation to Professor Smith, when he is ready to do the Greek texts. The Society is running on a very close budget, barely enough to cover salaries and maintenance of the building. It would not do, under their circumstances, to ask for even a slight increase in the expenditure on the Egyptian collections. They are able to cover your work on the medical papyrus and mine (or its equivalent) and no more. I should, however, be very glad to have a respite in 1923, and indeed I am ready to turn over New York Historical Society work or any other job, to any competent person who needs the work for his livelihood. But in Dr Reich's case it would evidently be well to go a bit cautiously and see how he fits into the situation, how much adaptability he would show with respect to museum routine and installation, whether his English improves etc. He has not written to me as yet. Very likely this is because Mr Wall gave him no hope of compensation. Mr Wall, as I have heard since, failed to show him the demotic texts in the Edwin Smith collection. If Dr Reich does not write to me, I will try to get into communication with him when I go to New York. It would be rather difficult to arrange work for him under the 1922 budget because I must continue until the catalogue of the gold objects is off the press. Yet I would try what could be done if he were likely otherwise to leave the country.

Home conditions are such that I cannot go to New York until the last of April; I hope before then to see you in Chicago to talk of this and other matters.

Sincerely and gratefully yours | Caroline Ransom Williams

P.S One other thought occurs to me. Mr Whiting of the Cleveland Museum has been waiting a long time for me to help him with fresh material which has recently come in and I see no prospect of being able to do so in the near future. I should be perfectly willing to write to him of Dr Reich's pressure in this country and need for work and refer him to you and to Mr Lythgoe, who has so recently had personal contact with Dr Reich if you think this advisable. Of course the material in Cleveland is largely archaeological and I don't know how far Dr Reich's courses in „Orientalische Kunstgeschichte und Archäologie,' „Museal-und Bibliothekskunde' have prepared him for American Museum conditions!

I should think it in many ways better for the New York Historical Society to have some one in residence to meet the various questions which arise unexpectedly, if they could get a thoroughly competent person for a salary within their means. But before I lay down their work entirely, if I do, some dovetailing would be necessary that I might finish pieces of work which I have already carried so far that I ought, in their interests, to finish them. I should feel no reluctance to drop their work if it were to be adequately continued by some one who needs the work.

**11 February 1922**                                                      **0120**

February 11, 1922

My dear Mrs. Williams:

While I very much regret to hear that you are about to relinquish your work on the Historical Society's collections I can quite understand your desiring to do so.

I write especially to say that I think you are quite right about proceeding rather cautiously in Reich's case. I have no doubt he can do the work and the uncertainty I have in mind is simply whether he may personally prove acceptable and fit into the situation. He has been writing me hoping that something might be found for him to do and would be possible for him at the Historical Society. Perhaps I should not have done this, but there is, of course, nothing binding about it.

About Reich's availability at Cleveland, let me say that I am very glad you brought up the matter. If I ever knew it, I had totally forgotten that Mr. Whiting was depending on your for help with his Egyptian things. Consequently I wrote him a day or two ago in the interests of my student Edgerton, who has been looking for a post, as he is about to make his Doctor's degree.[149] I have not yet heard from Mr. Whiting but I very much fear he may want Edgerton, -- I say 'fear' because I am offering him a post

---

[149] William Franklin Edgerton (1893-1970) was an American Egyptologist, trained at Cornell and then took his PhD at Chicago in 1922. He took part in the first expedition with Breasted, Luckenbill and others in 1919-1920. He was Assistant in the Oriental Institute from 1922-23, epigrapher with the Oriental Institute at Luxor from 1926-29, and held a number of posts at the University of Chicago until 1954.

in the Oriental Institute which I hope he may accept. I take it your thought is the possibility of Reich's taking the post until 1923 and then shifting back to New York. I will let you know when I hear from Mr. Whiting.

Always very sincerely yours, | JHB

**19 February 1922**                                                     0121

The Chesbrough Dwellings |
Toledo, Ohio | February 19, 1922

Dear Mr Breasted,

It had been In my thought when I should see you to ask about Mr Edgerton's plans. I did not know that he would be ready for a position quite so soon! From your recent letter I judge that you intend to keep him in Chicago. However, to cover any possible shift in your plans I should like to say that, knowing intimately both the Cleveland collection and the New York Historical Society's collection, I should think the work in New York the more desirable of the two.

I did not intend to imply that there was work in Cleveland to bring Dr Reich to the end of the year, but it might take care of him for some weeks. About a year ago Mr Whiting asked me if I would consider being 'Non-Resident Curator' of his Egyptian department at a nominal salary, this to regularize the intermittent requests for advice about purchases, Bulletin articles etc which he had been in the habit of making since 1917. I have handled (and furnished data for the inventory on) every object in the original collection and all material received prior to 1921. But of late it has been very trying for him that I was often not available when he needed me and I think he would be very grateful to make an arrangement with you that would take care of his periodic needs. I shall be surprised, however, if he has a regular post in Egyptology to offer. I stopped in Cleveland on my way home from New York in November and saw the new things from the Amherst sale – and from Egypt. The collection is not large and Mr Whiting wishes to emphasize only the aesthetic side, having little regard for the historical or archaeological aspects. Mr Wall, on the other hand, leaves everything to his Egyptologist and is ambitious to see the collection published.

Sincerely yours | C. R. Williams

**3 April 1922**                                          0122

The Chesbrough Dwellings |
Toledo, Ohio | April 3, 1922

Dear Mr Breasted,

Before returning to New York in the first week of May, I should like to go to Chicago for about a week's work in Haskell library, if I may, also to consult with you about various matters.

I have in mind to go two weeks from Thursday, April 20th, and be ready for work the next morning. I am purposely avoiding the Oriental Society meeting in my plans, though with regret, because I must be away from home so much with the New York Historical Society's work, that I ought not to prolong the time by the meeting.

The purpose of this note, then, is to inquire whether I should find you in Chicago immediately after the meeting. If more convenient to you, I could revise my plans to go a week earlier.

With kind regards | Sincerely yours | Caroline R. Williams

**6 April 1922**                                          0123

April 6, 1922.

My dear Mrs. Williams:

We are all very glad to hear that you are soon coming to Chicago. It happens that the National Research Council holds its annual meeting and committee sessions on Monday, Tuesday and Wednesday, April 24 to 26, and I shall therefore be obliged to leave for Washington, D. C. early on Sunday, the 23d. If you think that will give us time enough to discuss the matters which I am also quite anxious to confer with you about, the date of your stay here would be otherwise quite convenient.

Incidentally I may mention that Reich is now here and is expecting to stay through the meeting of the Oriental Society, so that you might also have a consultation with him if you desire before you leave if you come the week end of April 22d.

With kindest regards from us all, I am | Very sincerely yours | JHB

**21 April 1922**                                      **0124**

The Chesbrough Dwellings |
Toledo, Ohio | April 21 1922

Dear Mr Breasted,

I reached Toledo early this morning in the midst of a snow storm. My husband was at the train and we had breakfast together. Now I am making the first business of the morning finding the letters etc which concern the von Oefele matter. Among the inclosures is Dr von Oefele's letter signed 'MD' printed in the World and the Evening Post and my reply to it. I asked the Treasurer of the Society, Mr Weekes, who had been writing to the papers about the Society, to sign it and he was kind enough to do so. You will see from the inclosures what a stupid mess of misunderstanding we have had. I spent a trying hour to convince one of the Trustees of the Society, whom Mrs John K. van Rensselaer had influenced, that the Society had <u>not</u> let the Abbott Papyrus of the British Museum get away from it, that the Abbott Papyrus had never formed a part of the main Abbott collection! You will note in one of the inclosures that Mr Plimpton was on a rival ticket at the last election, when the Old Guard was reinstated with a sweeping majority. My impression is that the public's attitude has been that the New York Historical Society needed awakening, that Mrs John K.'s accusations may have been extreme in some instances, but that the agitation was good for the Society. You see the question of the medical papyrus has inevitably been involved in the general situation. If only some of the critics would give the Society funds with which to operate, it would be easier to satisfy public opinion! But certainly adverse criticism has been unduly stirred up by Mrs. John K van Rensselaer <words missing>. I doubt if it would do to deal with von Oefele through a lawyer unless you receive from Professor Erman very definite and damaging details of his 'Process.' It would be just like him to complain in the papers that he had been threatened. I certainly should not advise trying to conciliate him, that would be useless. Anything you write to him, if you wish at all, he is likely to quote—any attempt to rebuke him would not reach him, for he is not sensitive, and he might use your words putting false construction on them. From the Society he has had simply formed politely worded refusals, but we have been careful not to give him honest grounds for saying that his requests were unheeded.

Personally, I don't believe he will stir up much trouble now; his boldness was occasioned by the other attacks on the Society and the public's attitude is less unfriendly now. After the sweeping defeat at the last election it is inconceivable that the van Rensselaer forces <words missing> up a rival ticket next winter. Now that he has carried his persistence so far and has already attacked the Society in the paper, I think you might well not reply to his letter, if you prefer that course.

I trust that you found the memorandum I left on your desk, having happened on references to Edwin Smith which suggested to me that von Oefele's statements were put together from what he had gleaned from the older literature of the period of the acquisition and publication of the Ebers papyrus.[150]

I am sending Mrs Breasted's keys by registered first-class mail. With grateful memories of all your kindness during my recent stay in Chicago,
Sincerely yours | Caroline R. Williams

P.S. I found a letter from Frau Schäfer awaiting me and she relates that the Möller library has been sold to Königsberg.

I find that I have a copy of the cat & cat drawing – an extra one – and am sending it to you & hoping it will save your writing for one.

**24 April 1922**                                                                    **0125**

April 24, 1922
My dear Mrs. Williams:
It was exceedingly kind of you to leave your helpful notes on the Edwin Smith matter and especially to send me so promptly the very full information with your excellent letter of April 21, all of which arrived Saturday morning.

---

[150] The Ebers Papyrus is an Egyptian medical papyrus, reportedly acquired by Georg M. Ebers (1837-1898) from Edwin Smith in Luxor in 1873-74. Ebers first published a facsimile with an introduction and a glossary by Ludwig Stern in 1875. *Papyros Ebers: Das hermetische Buch über die Arzeneimittel der alten Ägypter in hieratischer Schrift, herausgegeben mit Inhaltsangabe und Einleitung versehen von Georg Ebers, mit Hieroglyphisch-Lateinischem Glossar von Ludwig Stern, mit Unterstützung des Königlich Sächsischen Cultusministerium.* (Leipzig: W. Englemann, 1875).

Curiously enough we have both reached the same conclusion since our last conversation on the matter. The confident tone of Oefele's letter and his failure to distinguish between fact and fancy quite misled me in the beginning, --especially so for two reasons; first, I had completely forgotten that Ebers accuses Edwin Smith of misrepresentation, and second, Oefele's assertion that the Edwin Smith Papyrus was found in the same tomb with the Ebers Papyrus. I concluded, therefore, that Oefele had personal sources of information that had not been accessible to us. It is perfectly evident to me now that he has done nothing but use the alleged facts published by Ebers in his introduction. I do not think, therefore, that we need apprehend any further consequences from his interference,

I can now reply to Oefele with the assurance that if he had known the literature or studied it carefully he would not have been able to characterize Mr. Edwin Smith as a 'bluffer.' But of course I shall not give him the satisfaction of drawing me into a controversy.

I had great difficulty in condensing an account of the content and scientific significance of the Edwin Smith Papyrus into the limits of a Bulletin article and I therefore intentionally cut down the account of the external history of the document. On looking over my notes I find a very interesting problem emerges which I shall be obliged to handle very carefully in the publication. In my notes I find that I have called attention to the fact that in the early publication of the Ebers calendar the Ebers Papyrus had begun to be called 'Papyrus Smith,' for example by Lepsius; or the 'Smith Papyrus,' for example by Goodwin, and this continued right down into the time after Ebers' purchase of the document.

Ebers was a very vain man, as is disclosed among other evidences, by the fact that he christened the papyrus after himself. It was important for him, therefore, to prove and make prominent that no European or non-Egyptian had ever owned or purchased the papyrus previous to his possession of it. I think this is a quite sufficient motive for his reflections on Edwin Smith for there is not anywhere in the correspondence a shred of evidence that Smith was trying to make money from the sale of the Ebers Papyrus. Anyone who has done any buying in Egypt will understand at once that Mr. Smith might very properly say nothing as to the ownership of the papyrus (in order to avoid competitive bidding at the hands of the Europeans who visited him), always hoping that he himself might be able to purchase it. There is no evidence that he authorized the statement on the part of anyone that he owned the papyrus, except the statement of Ebers, and the probable reason for that I have already indicated.

I have read the documents concerning the present situation in New York with the greatest interest and am inclosing them herewith. If Oefele attempts anything more I think we can easily meet whatever he may have to say.

We enjoyed your visit very much and hope that you may soon be coming again and bringing Mr. Williams with you.

Very sincerely yours | JHB


**6 May 1922**                                                                 **0126**

The New York Historical Society |
170 Central Park West | New York City |
May 6, 1922

My dear Mr. Breasted,

I have talked with Mr. Wall about the matter of giving the Berlin Dictionary the opportunity to make use of the Edwin Smith papyrus for dictionary purposes and he is in sympathy with our wish to do this and thinks there probably will be no opposition in the Committee. If you will write him a brief note speaking of the desirability from a scientific view point that this be done and the facts that the papyrus will be kept private and no extra expense caused the Society, Mr. Wall will be glad to present the letter at the May meeting of the Executive Committee on the third Tuesday of the month.

Mr. Lythgoe has recently received an appeal from Mr. Gardiner in behalf of Mr. Battiscombe Gunn.[151] Mr. Lythgoe has no post for him and it looks now as if it would be very difficult financially, if feasible at all, for the New York Historical Society to employ him, but nevertheless, I should like

---

[151] Battiscombe G. Gunn (1883-1950) was a British Egyptologist who started as a stockbroker and journalist but found he was good at language. He studied hieroglyphs under Margaret Murray at UCL and worked with Gardiner and Engelbach. He worked at Amarna for the EES in 1921-22, Saqqara for the Antiquities Service in 1924-27, and Assistant Curator at the Cairo Museum 1928-31. He ended up at Oxford, as Professor of Egyptology from 1934-50.

to ask you whether you know him personally (Mr. Lythgoe does not) and, if so, whether you think he would take up museum installation successfully and adapt himself pleasantly to the somewhat limited facilities here – as to space and funds. I suppose that there can be no doubt of his sound philological training. I don't care to ask these questions of Mr. Gardiner because it is still so uncertain whether the financial question could be solved.

I have not yet been able to communicate with Mr. Moeller who was at work on <u>Die Hieroglyphen</u> but if I learn that his Ms could be available for your friend, I will let you know. But in the meantime, may I say, that if you think it would be a pleasure to her to see the gold things on which I am working, I should be very glad to have you give her an invitation from me to call here. If she could make an appointment with me for some Sunday afternoon at two or three o'clock, I should be able to do more for her than on a week day. I suggest this because I know that people often enjoy looking behind the scenes on museum work and coming in direct contact with material not in cases.

Please accept my sincere thanks for your recent letter which I received in Toledo. All that you said was most interesting and convincing. I hope Dr. von Oefele has not annoyed you further.

With all kind regards to you and Mrs. Breasted | Sincerely yours | Caroline R. Williams

**11 May 1922**                                                    **0127**

The New York Historical Society |
170 Central Park West | New York City |
May 11, 1922

My dear Mr. Breasted:
Please accept my sincere thanks for your kind letter of May 9 which reached me this morning.[152] The letter is already destroyed and I assure you that I shall not need to use its contents. I simply shall not push efforts to get the necessary funds to bring Mr. Gunn here. I might not have succeeded in any

---

[152] No copy in the archives.

event, so you do not need to feel that he has necessarily lost an opportunity here.

When in Chicago I mentioned to you a Mr. Smith who gave a valuable collection to the city of Springfield, Massachusetts. As you seemed interested in his relationship to Edwin Smith I have made inquiries. I learn from Edwin Smith's niece, Mrs. Isabel Smith who lives in the Beresford, that the Springfield gentleman is a first cousin of Edwin Smith born ten years later and still living, past 90 years. I copy the following from a letter of Miss Randolph's: 'I have known Mr. Smith in his more active years when he was busy installing his treasures, mostly of Chinese and Japanese Art in the Art Museum, built by private subscription because he promised to give the collection to the city if a building were provided. I have heard connoisseurs say that the collection, tho' small, is throughout of rare worth and interest.' I inclose also a copy which my mother made of the entry in the New England Who's Who. I think you will be glad to know that your Bulletin paper has made the various members of the family very happy. Mr. Wall tells me that requests have come in from them for extra copies; Mr. George W. V. Smith was one of those who wrote and Mrs. Isabel Smith in the Beresford (who is past 80) talked to me with shining eyes of the joy it gave her. Miss Leonora Smith, the donor of the papyrus, is going this summer to Naples to visit her sister, the one at whose home Edwin Smith lived during the last years of his life. It does seem as if the family ought to have papers or letters which would be of interest to the Society, but I have asked the daughter more than once and she always said no.

I shall be in New York until June 30 and am looking forward to seeing you and Mrs. Breasted again before you sail.

With all kind regards to you both | Sincerely yours | Caroline R. Williams

**11 May 1922**                                      **0128**

Beresford | One West 81st Street |
May 11, 1922

Dear Mr Breasted

Since writing to you earlier in the day I have looked over a pamphlet on Egyptian medicine sent to the New York Historical Society during my absence in Toledo. I inclose just a few penciled notes to show you its character. Inasmuch as you intend touching on Edwin Smith's connection with the Ebers papyrus in your article for the Champollion volume, you may care to see this, if you have not already done so. Two copies were sent. One of them is filed in the library, the other Mr Wall handed to me, thinking that it was perhaps intended for me. I should send it to you at once, did I not think that you may be in possession of a copy, as the principal author, Dr Holmes, now lives in Chicago at 30 N. Michigan Avenue. You will let me know, will you not, if you wish the copy now in my hands?

Sincerely yours | Caroline R. Williams

Bayard Holmes, M.D. and P. Gad Kitterman, M.D. Medicine in Ancient Egypt. Cincinnati. The Lancet Clinic Press 1914. 250 copies printed. Copyrighted 1914.

**15 May 1922**                                      **0129**

May 15, 1922

Dear Mrs. Williams:

It is exceedingly kind of you to send me the reference to Dr. Barrett Holmes' essay on medicine in ancient Egypt. It was mentioned to me by someone some time ago but I have never seen a copy and the author did not send me one, as far as I recollect. If you could spare your copy and would post it to me I would be very glad and of course I would post it back to you as soon as possible.

I hope you may be able to reach some definite plan which you will find satisfactory about the continuance of the work in the Society's collections. I am very sorry that the question of Gunn should have proved so difficult to settle. I have just had a letter from Gardiner and he doesn't mention Gunn at all. If I should learn anything further about him this summer I will try to let you know.

Poor Reich is still hanging on here but I have secured a definite statement from the Philadelphia people that they will make him an offer as soon as the Demotic papyri which Fisher discovered have arrived in America.

We are all very much pleased that you will be in New York when we arrive and are looking forward to seeing you. Mrs. Breasted joins me in kindest greetings.

Very sincerely yours | JHB

P.S. In dictating the above letter I did not have your typewritten letter of May 11 at hand and hence I neglected to thank you for your thoughtfulness in sending me additional material about the family of Mr. Edwin Smith. The new facts are very much appreciated nevertheless. I am very glad also to know that the surviving relatives of Mr. Smith have taken pleasure in learning of his services to science. It occurs to me that on our way either to or from Egypt I shall certainly be in Naples (as I expect to go to Palermo) and if I had the Naples address of Miss Smith it might be that I could visit the two sisters and learn further of Mr. Smith's family history.

J. H. B.

**4 June 1922**                                                    0130

The New York Historical Society |
170 Central Park West | New York City |
June 4, 1922

My dear Mr Breasted,

Since I wrote to you last I have heard from Mr Werner Mueller that he has completed his translation of Professor Erman's <u>Hieroglyphen</u>. His wife is now typewriting it and is making a carbon for your friend Miss Roman, which Mr Mueller suggests that she keep and take with her on her journey, if she cares to do so. As it would be laborious to put in all the hieroglyphs by hand, especially the solid pages at the back, it would be well for her to have a copy of the last German edition. I possess only the 1912 edition. I have not seen the translation yet, but am hopeful, since Mr Mueller invites an idiomatic, almost faultless English letter, that it may be good, or at least furnish the foundation for a good translation. I shall wait to write for Professor Ermans' permission, until I have seen it.

I now have the name and address of Edwin Smith's daughter in Naples, which I will transmit to you now, lest I forget it when you are here –

Mrs Frederick A Stolte

7 Via Pontano

A little judicious questioning of this daughter, at whose home Edwin Smith died, might clear up any obscure points about his last years in Egypt that you wished to understand, with a view to the Ebers statements. Edwin Smith's niece, Mrs Isabel Smith, aged 82, has just returned with her daughter, from Springfield, Massachusetts, where she went to help Mr George Vincent Smith[153] celebrate his 90th birthday! I think I ought to tell you that Mrs Schuyler van Rensselaer has an unpleasant memory of Edwin Smith. She called here recently to see me and I took occasion to refresh my memory as to what she had told me previously. When a girl she was in Luxor with her father and was taken to Edwin Smith's house. She recalls unwrapped mummies standing about on the terrace which quite horrified her. She says Edwin Smith had antiquities for sale and she thinks she is not mistaken that he was suspected of selling forgeries. This last, however, I take, with some grains of salt. Mrs van Rensselaer's visit to Egypt was in 1872.

I am holding open in the plans for next year the opportunity for Dr Reich to do the demotic texts. Mr Hoffmann is to leave us at the close of the present calendar year. The Executive Committee of the Society has been

---

[153] Smith was an eclectic collector himself, and much of his collection is housed in the George Walter Vincent Smith Museum in Springfield, Massachusetts. According to the museum website, 'The vast holdings include excellent examples of Japanese lacquer, arms and armor, ceramics and bronzes; one of the largest collections of Chinese cloisonné outside of Asia; Chinese jade and ceramics; and a superb collection of 19th-century Middle Eastern carpets. In addition, the collection contains significant American 19th-century paintings (especially landscape and genre), Italian 19th-century watercolors, a fine assembly of Greek and Roman antiquities, a rare plaster cast collection, objects created for 19th-century International Expositions and examples of lace and early textiles' (https://springfieldmuseums.org/about/smith-art-museum/ accessed 21 November 2016).

informed that I cannot, after this year, come to New York for long stays and they have given the Librarian and me to act, within the limits of the usual appropriation, to keep the work moving. I have someone in mind to do the textiles, someone to do the Greek texts, and I can finish in Toledo, without making any long visit here, four further parts of the catalogue. There are a number of new cases needed and it is my purpose that each part of the catalogue, as it is ready, shall be published promptly, even if some part of the yearly appropriation goes to that. Thus, as long as the Society cannot afford to spend more at present on its Egyptian collections, I don't see that any better plan can be made. Later, when they have more money, perhaps someone will be available to take up the work that must be done here in the Society's rooms.

You must be very busy these days. If you are not to be with friends in New York, I wonder if you would care to consider coming to the Hotel Beresford, 1 West 81st St., which now has rooms for transients. The airy ninth floor dining-room and near-by park would be pleasant for Mrs Breasted and the children; but if Mrs Breasted has shopping to do, of course a downtown hotel would be more convenient.

With happy anticipations of seeing you all | Sincerely yours | Caroline R. Williams


**9 June 1922**                                           **0131**

June 9, 1922

My dear Mrs. Williams:
It is exceedingly kind of you to have taken so much trouble regarding a typewritten copy of the translation of Erman's little book for Miss Roman. I am sure she will very much appreciate it. I hope it is to be published.

I am noting the address of Edwin Smith's daughter at Naples, which you have kindly sent me, and I hope I may be able to learn further facts regarding his life in Egypt. Many thanks also for the additional information you give me, which I have found very interesting.

Now regarding the future work on the Egyptian collections of the Historical Society, I do not remember whether I mentioned to you a possible combination between the Historical Society and our Museum for sharing the services of Mr. Burtch. Burtch has been with us now for several months and has been doing very satisfactory work. We have been keeping him on from month to month and paying him $125.00 a month, which I know is what he was receiving in his permanent position at the Field Museum. The reason he left there was because he asked for more, but I presume his refusal at the Field Museum will probably discourage him in any future efforts to secure an increase. I wish we could afford to keep him the year round, for he is exceedingly useful. Do you think it would be possible for the Historical Society to take on Burtch for half the year at the above salary while our Museum uses him the other half? His home is in Chicago and I suppose some provision would have to be made for his traveling expenses to and from New York but this would not be a serious addition to his salary. I do not know how he would like the proposition, as, of course, I have not felt authorized as yet to take up the matter with him. Such a combination would enable the Historical Society to go on with its work of preparation and installation at a really very low rate of expense, lower, I think, than any other arrangement they would be likely to find available. If you think favorably of the suggestion, would you kindly take it up with Mr. Wall? The arrangement could be more successfully launched if I could hear from you and Mr. Wall regarding anything you might want done in putting it through before I leave Chicago. I expect to leave here not later than the 22d and if possible on the 20th.

Mrs. Breasted and I were very much pleased to hear that transient guests are now received at the Beresford. Miss Roman, who had just passed through here before the arrival of your letter, had already volunteered to find us quarters at the Hotel Lorraine but the Beresford would be much more feasible for us and we should both be very much pleased also if we might be near you while we are in New York. Hence I wired Miss Roman requesting her to telephone to you, which I presume she has already done. If you have not heard from her would you kindly ask the management to reserve two rooms (four beds) for us beginning Friday, the 23d. It is possible that we may be able to reach New York a day or two earlier but I shall not be able to settle that matter until a little later. If we push forward the date of our arrival I will take the liberty of wiring to you and I presume the hotel can take care of us even if we do arrive ahead of the date arranged.

With pleasant anticipations and kindest regards from us all, I am | Very sincerely yours | JHB

**11 June 1922**                                                    **0132**

Beresford | One West 81st Street |
June 11, 1922

Dear Mr Breasted,

You will like to know what you are coming to at this hotel! The room-clerk (who consulted the manager) says they will take good care of you and your family at ten dollars a day. Your rooms will be above the ground floor, will be connecting, with a bath opening from one of them. If there is no two-room suite vacant at the time, they will put you into a three-room suite at no additional cost to you. The rates are four dollars for each adult and a dollar for each of the children. I have been accustomed in the last years to pay four and five dollars for a single room and bath on a stretch of eight weeks and doubt if you could do better. It is not Miss Roman's fault, but I am a little confused as to whether it was the 23rd or 24th that you were to arrive. The clerk has made the reservation temporarily for the 24th-28th but if you can come a day earlier, will you let me know? If we hear at this end by next Monday they will arrange to take care of you beginning on the 23rd. The hotel is European plan and you can go as much or as little as you care to to the dining-room which has only à la carte service now a days. I hope it has not been so hot in Chicago as here for all your last labors! It will be such a pleasure to see you all!

Sincerely yours | Caroline R. Williams

**13 June 1922**                                                    **0133**

The New York Historical Society |
170 Central Park West | New York City |
June 13, 1922

My dear Mr. Breasted,

Your kind letter of June 9th awaited me at the Society's rooms this morning.

I will immediately change your reservation to the 23rd and if you let the hotel or me know two days or so in advance, I am sure they will take care of you, whenever you can come. I will tell them, too, to provide four beds.

It is a desirable opportunity for the Society to be able to cooperate with you in employing Mr. Burtch and I do wish I could see how this could be done. Of course his rates are very reasonable and we could readily include six months in the 1923 budget, except for the fact that there will be no one here to direct his work. I do not see how that difficulty could be overcome. I am not coming to New York in 1923; Mr. Hoffmann will be here until the end of the present year and I shall not have time to do more than get the records of the material he has worked on (and will handle before the end of the year) in order to leave. I should not be able to undertake to assign Mr. Burtch material to put in order and keep in touch with it. It has been a most difficult and unfortunate arrangement for me to have the preparatory working on a yearly engagement and to come myself to New York for only a few months of the year; I have many arrears to bring up as it is.

The only chance I see for the Society to employ Mr. Burtch in 1923 would be if Dr. Reich could give us six months or longer and could then direct him in mounting papyri, at least in a temporary way, if you thought Mr. Burtch capable of doing that under Dr. Reich's directions. But as yet, Dr. Reich gives me no answer, no doubt because he is hoping to get a permanent, full-time post in Philadelphia. By the time you come back from Europe the situation may be different, if, by chance, some other place could be worked out for Mr. Burtch for next year. There is a great deal of work to be done here eventually and I wish we could have Mr. Burtch do it. If you had an Egyptologist to spare for six months along with Mr. Burtch over a period of several years (to give continually to the work) that would work out admirably and we could enter on such a plan in 1923!

I greatly appreciate your kind suggestion and I am sorry to send so unsatisfactory an answer, but it is the best I can do.

Sincerely yours | Caroline R. Williams


**14 June 1922**                                                    **0134**

June 14, 1922

My dear Mrs. Williams:

It was exceedingly kind of you to go to all this trouble to engage rooms for us and write us a special letter about it. The arrangements you are making will be very satisfactory indeed. I am sorry there was uncertainty about the dates. We expect to arrive on the Century Friday, June 23, and this date is now definitely settled.

I am sorry you have been burdened with any details regarding the Papyrus but it is a relief to be assured that the matter is receiving the proper care.

We are looking forward with the greatest pleasure to the visit in New York and not least to being with you in the same hotel. With kindest regards from us all, I am

Very sincerely yours | JHB


**22 November 1922**                                                **0135**

November 22, 1922.

Dear Mrs. Williams:

The University of Chicago Press is now at work on my Art Institute book. They say it will probably be ready about the first of the year.

Have you made any further progress in finding a publisher for the translation of Erman's <u>Hieroglyphen</u>?

Very truly yours | JHB


**25 June 1923**                                                **0136**

The New York Historical Society |
170 Central Park West | New York City |
June 25, 1923[154]

Dear Professor Breasted,

I am venturing to inclose to you a copy of the preface to my jewelry catalogue which will go on the press in July. The plates are done and await binding. I should like to be sure that you are satisfied with my references to you, also that I have your consent to the use of some of your translations. In the latter, I have made a change or two such as substituting turquoise for

---

[154] She wrote in letter 0133 above that she would not be coming to New York in 1923, so her plans obviously changed, but it is unclear why.

malachite for Egyptian mfk3.t in passages referring to jewelry and inserting a question mark after 'fine' as a translation for nfr modifying gold, but I have indicated in the footnote that I did this. In the first draft of the preface, I quoted the title of Dr. Borchardt's book, in chronology, but the interest in that seems to have subsided and Mr Blackman[155], for one, who adopted B's early dates now has abandoned them for the minimum dates, likewise Professor Erman in his Literatur, so I'm inclined now to omit the reference. Please do not trouble to return this carbon unless you wish to mark on it some alteration that you wish made of course you will understand that the amount quoted from your Record is limited. I could not in such a book go into very many passages. From Dr Gardiner I used chiefly a passage from the Papyrus Koller and titles as given in his Catalogue of Theban Tombs.[156]

I should like to tell you that we have here a piece of stone inscribed in cursive hieroglyphs which I have long supposed to be a Middle Kingdom text. Now, following a clue given me by Mr Winlock, I find that it is from the Cairo tomb of Harhotep.[157] Line 1 begins 'Ho, Osiris Harhotep.' You will of course want to incorporate it in your Coffin Text material and if you will let me know when you are ready for it, I will see that you get a good photographic print. Mr Winlock has kindly offered to try to locate the block in the tomb for me, when he returns to Cairo, and if he succeeds, I shall do a brief article for the Society's Bulletin next April in order to let the members know what its interests are. But of course you may have it for your purposes as soon as you like. The block contains 24 vertical lines of writing.

It is a great pleasure to me to be seeing Mrs Breasted and the children daily. Astrid is a darling and I admire Jamie very much. My only regret is that I am not free to go about with them more. Could you perhaps send me

---

[155] Aylward Manley Blackman (1883-1956) was a British Egyptologist who studied under Griffith at Oxford and got his degree in 1906. He worked extensively in Egypt and before 1918 got his MA, and DLitt then taught with Griffith at Oxford. He was Brunner Professor of Egyptology at Liverpool 1934-48, and Emeritus until his death. He was a philologist with religion as his specialty.

[156] Alan Gardiner, Arthur Weigall, *A Topographical Catalogue of the Private Tombs of Thebes* (London: Bernard Quaritch, 1913).

[157] When she says 'here' she is talking about the NYHS. The block is now in the Brooklyn Museum, purchased in 1937 with the Charles Edwin Wilbour Fund. Now on display in the Egyptian Galleries on the third floor. See https://www.brooklynmuseum.org/opencollection/objects/118038 accessed 21 November 2016.

just a postcard in reply soon, as I shall be sending the book to press before long?

With kind regards | Sincerely yours | C. R. Williams

3 July 1923                                                        0137

Garland's Hotel | Suffolk St. |
Pall Mall | London | July 3, 1923

My dear Mrs. Williams:-

Very often I have wanted to write you during this past season in the East,- there has been so much of mutual interest which I know you would have found as absorbing as I have. Unfortunately I have been and still am quite unable to cope with my correspondence. It was a great pleasure however, this morning to receive your letter of June 25th with copy of the preface of your new book, which is going to be a real contribution to science. I have talked about it to a great many over here, and there will be many as eager as I am to see it.

Of course you are more than welcome to the translations you have used. In technical matters, as well as in a number of others they much need revision and I am glad you have made the necessary changes. As regards the chronology, I am still holding to the dates in my history and the possibility of change is, in my judgement still too uncertain to warrant any actual alteration. You may be interested to know that Sethe is much inclined toward a modification of Borchardt's views. He thinks that we should now push back Menes to synchronize with the introduction of the calendar,- an event which would have properly fallen at a time of stable unification. But since I found the ten pre-dynastic kings of Upper and Lower Egypt on the Cairo fragments of the Palermo Stone, I am inclined to think that their unification (a pre-dynastic unification) is more likely to have been the period at whose beginning the calendar was introduced. A footnote to the effect that an elaborately worked out system by Borchardt had produced earlier dates for the pre-Middle Kingdom period would be quite in place.

I am glad to hear that you have another fragment of the Harhotep texts, and as we have begun work on this tomb, I would indeed be very glad to have the photograph which you have so kindly promised. I hope very much that Winlock may be able to place it in the Cairo tomb chamber, where there is a good deal lacking.

The Edwin Smith Papyrus has turned out to be a very extraordinary document, as I have intimated in the two preliminary reports on it, but there is much I wish we could talk about. Men of science whom I have met over here are very much interested,-not least the members of the Royal Society, at whose official dinner I was asked to speak about it a fortnight ago. I only hope that I can devote my whole time to it when I return, so as to complete the edition at an early date. If we could only enlist a few 'shabbies' and duplicate ourselves![158]

I am so glad you are in New York, for I know Mrs. Breasted would be quite lonely without you. It is also a relief to hear that the 'enfants terribles' have not wholly disgraced the family! I shall be landing in N.Y. about the first of August, but I presume you will have left on your vacation before that time. I congratulate you warmly on having your volume ready for the printer and wish you rapid progress in the long task of proof-reading.

With kindest regards,-also to Mr. Williams, I am | Very sincerely yours | JHB

**6 November 1923**                                                    **0138**

Toledo, Ohio | November 6, 1923

Dear Mr Breasted,

When I wrote you Mrs Breasted a few days ago, I mentioned Miss Pratt's Ancient Egypt, A List of References to Material in the New York Public Library, but at the time I had not yet examined it.[159] Today I have written to Miss Pratt to acknowledge her courtesy in sending me the first installment, and I made bold to say that I disagreed absolutely with many things in Professor Gottheil's preface, and that I was particularly sorry to* have him

---

[158] He is talking about shabtis (ushabtis), which were funerary figurines in the likeness of the tomb owner, placed in Ancient Egyptian tombs to do the deceased's work in the afterlife.

[159] Ida A. Pratt, 'Ancient Egypt: A List of References to Material in the New York Public Library,' Foreword by Richard Gottheil, *Bulletin of the New York Public Library* 27:9 (September 1923): 723-766.

attribute your discovery of the Salihiyah paintings to French scholars.[160] This List is being published in successive numbers of the Bulletin of the New York Public Library and after it has all appeared in serial fashion, it will be reissued under one cover. Professor Gottheil ought to be made to correct his Foreword! Another thing that irritated me was his reference to the Egyptians as 'allied to the Negro Race'! I suppose that his error about the Salihiyah paintings is due to the mischievous political pamphlet of which you told me and which I have not seen. Do pardon me, if you have seen the Bulletin to which I refer. I thought there was a possibility that it had not come to your attention and that you would want to know about it.

We are much concerned here over the local issue whether Mayor Brough will be retained in office or the Catholic, yellow-paper candidate will go in. My husband and I are going tonight at the invitation of some friends to the theater where we shall stay and watch the returns flashing on the screen. 'The Hunch-back of Notre Dame' has been there this past week, but recalling Frances' adverse comment on it, we did not go. The week before we saw 'The Covered Wagon' and I should like to warn the Breasteds against it! It is full of vulgarities that spoil it; except for the fine riding I found nothing to enjoy in it. Even its supposed pièce de resistance, the crossing of the Platte River, I thought distressing, for I hated to see the animals struggling so. A movie like 'The Green Goddess' I can enjoy in the same way I would a detective story, but the Covered Wagon is not at all to my liking!

My love to Frances and Astrid | With greetings from us all | Ever sincerely yours | Caroline R. Williams

*I was of course not merely 'sorry,' but indignant; however, it would do no good to say so! If there is anything I can do in the matter I should be glad to do it. If he does not change his statement in the final publication, I shall review the 'List' and make the correction as prominent as I am!

---

[160] Richard James Horatio Gottheil (1862-1936) was an English Semiticist. He earned his PhD at Leipzig in 1886 and returned to the US to take up a position at Columbia University in 1887. He spent much of the rest of his career there, also taking on a position as the director of the Oriental Department at the New York Public Library in 1897. His papers are at the American Jewish Archives in Cincinnati, Ohio. http://collections.americanjewisharchives.org/ms/ms0127/ms0127.html , accessed 21 November 2016.

Bulletin of the New York Public Library, September, 1923

pp. 724-5: The two great powers that fought for the supremacy in the Near East during those far-off days were those of the Two Rivers, Mesopotamia, and of the One River, Egypt. Their fighting-ground was Syria and Palestine, and, in consequence, the peoples of these latter regions were either ground under foot or were driven out of their homes — Hittites, Phoenicians, Hebrews, Syrians. We are not well informed from Egyptian sources as regards the depths into which the Egyptians penetrated from the south. Their traces have been found in Judea and in Phoenicia — especially at Byblos. But the recent discoveries by French scholars of beautiful Roman frescos at Salihiyah on the Euphrates, show how far the west reached in this age-long struggle.

(From Professor Gottheil's Forword to Ancient Egypt, A list of References to Material in the New York Public Library.)


**9 November 1923**                                          **0139**

November 9, 1923.

My dear Mrs. Williams:

It was extraordinarily kind of you to write me about Gottheil's remarks in the Bulletin of the New York Public Library. Just between ourselves, Gottheil is a notoriously inaccurate man. All the work he has done swarms with serious mistakes, until it has become proverbial with us.

I had not yet seen the Bulletin and I am all the more grateful therefore that you have taken all the trouble to write me the full quotation which was certainly kind. I presume, in view of the French brochure, we can hardly hold him responsible for attributing the discovery to French scholars. Of course the remark about the race of the Egyptians is perfectly absurd.

I am writing Gottheil the circumstances and asking him to make the corrections.

It was also very kind of you to suggest a review making the correction. If you can do this in the midst of all that you are now involved in, I can assure you it will be very much appreciated, because even if Gottheil makes the correction, the error always goes much further than the subsequent correction.

Frances and I remember your visit with great pleasure only regretting that it was much too brief. The fates seem to be pursuing me, for I am laid up with a knee infection at the time when I ought to be most busily at work.

The text of the Salihiyah book, however, is in the hands of the Press and should appear early in the year.

With warmest greetings from us both, I am | Very gratefully yours | JHB

**23 November 1923**                                                    **0140**

Toledo, Ohio | November 23, 1923

Dear Mr. Breasted,

Through Mr Wall's courtesy, I am able to send you, with the N. Y. Historical Society's compliments, a photograph of the text from the tomb of [see figure 3] in the Society's possession. You will recall that I promised it long ago. I am not very much tied up with indexing my book. Many thanks for your recent letter. I hope the knee is better.

My kindest greetings to you all | C. R. Williams

FIGURE 3: HARHOTEP

**3 December 1923** 0141

The Chesbrough Dwellings |
Toledo, Ohio | December 3, 1923

Dear Mr Breasted,

Will you perhaps be so good as to look at the inclosed letters, one of which I propose to send to the New York Evening Post if it meets with your approval? If you care to suggest any changes in it, of course I should be glad to make such alterations. The Foreword contains many other mistakes, but it is an ungracious task to correct them, and I do not feel any call to do so; besides, it would weaken the effect of what I wish most to say to add any thing further.

I had a pleasant note from Frances the other day which I hope soon to answer. My labors on the Index of my book are being somewhat interrupted by Christmas doings and preparation for some talks on Egypt which I must give this month and next, but I hope to send the corrected page proofs and Index to the printer before the end of December. Will you be leaving as you hoped to do soon for Egypt?

With kindest regards from us all to you and your family | Sincerely yours | Caroline R. Williams.


**5 December 1923** 0142

The University of Chicago | Haskell Oriental Museum |
Office of the Director | December 5, 1923.

My dear Mrs. Williams:

It was very kind of you to remember that we are interested in the text of Harhotep. The photograph has duly arrived and we thank you very much for your trouble. Please give Mr. Wall our thanks also when you are writing or see him.

All join in kindest regards.

Very cordially yours | JHB

**6 December 1923** 0143

December 6, 1923.

My dear Mrs. Williams:

It was exceedingly kind of you to go to the trouble to write the correction which I received last night. Two inscriptions available since our visit to the Fortress have dated the paintings definitely in the First Century, a date which also makes it evident that the Fortress is pre-Roman, I ventured to make these two alterations. We shall avoid the difficulty about Cumont's being a Belgian by saying the <u>French Expedition</u>.

Since we last discussed the matter, I have had an amiable letter from Gottheil agreeing to make the correction in his publication, but I am very grateful to you for your statement in the <u>Post</u> because such errors always circulate far beyond the reach of the subsequent correction. Personally, I do not care, but it is important at this juncture that the Institute, for the sake of its future, should get all the credit which honestly belongs to it. I fear this matter must have been a burden to you in the midst of all your work on the Index of your new book.

I have been very much interested in the photograph of the Harhotep texts which you have so kindly sent to us. I think it fills a very awkward gap which we were regretting at Cairo, and Gardiner will also be very much pleased.

With heartiest thanks for all your many kindnesses, and many good wishes for you and yours for the happy Holiday Season, in which Frances joins me, I am

Very sincerely yours | JHB

1 Enc.

P.S. I am reluctant to trouble you at a time when I know you are so busy, but I remember with much interest your statement that you had observed unquestionable evidences of the painting of light and shadows in the VXIII. D. palace wall paintings in the Metropolitan Museum. May I quote you to that effect in this first volume of the Oriental Institute on the Salihiyah paintings? Please do not go to the trouble of writing a letter; a line on a post-card is all that is necessary. – J.H.B.

**18 December 1923**                                                     **0144**

December 18, 1923.

Dear Mrs. Williams:

I feel very guilty in having sent you an inquiry which obliged you to write me such a long and full account of the present situation in the matter of the Amenhotep III paintings, etc.[161] It was exceedingly kind of you to take all this trouble, and I assure you that this full statement of the published discussions of the question is very useful to me.

Perhaps my letter of inquiry was not clear in one point. I did not intend to indicate that Mrs. Davis' opinion is at variance with that of her husband. I think they are in complete agreement on this point.

I am filing your letter with our records as it is a convenient summary of the state of knowledge, especially because of your own information regarding the Amenhotep III paintings in the Metropolitan Museum. I hope sometime that these examples may be subjected to a thorough examination such as you suggest.

I believe Frances has sent you the last letters we have received from the Ermans. I am very much distressed about them. It is quite clear that there has been a moral breakdown as a result of the hardships to which they have been so long subjected. I wish M. Poincare might look into such a home.

With regard to Erman's little note on the Dictionary finances, I want to keep you informed of what we who are interested are trying to do. Perhaps I told you when you were here that last summer in England the following agreed to contribute to the Dictionary's support:

Alan H. Gardiner – £10
A. M. Blackman – £10
Percy E. Newberry – £10
The American contributors are Ludlow S. Bull – £10
T. George Allen – £5
James H. Breasted – £10

We think that a few more similar subscriptions will probably keep the Dictionary going and the assurance that these are coming will have much to

---

[161] Not in archive. It was common for JHB to file correspondence in his research files when they contained useful information, as he stated a few lines below this remark.

do with their ability to go on. I mean that the continuance of the Dictionary is partly an archaeological matter, and such support is a powerful influence in rousing and maintaining their courage.

As you know, I am sailing on the 29th of December and I fear we shall not meet until after my return. Please give my warmest holiday greetings to your mother and Mr. Williams, and, with many good wishes of the season to yourself, I am

Very sincerely yours | JHB


**12 January 1924**                                                    0145

The Chesbrough Dwellings |
Toledo, Ohio | January 12, 1924

Dear Professor Breasted,

About the time you so kindly sent me through Mrs Breasted letters you had had from Professor Erman, I, too, had letters from the Ermans. The one from Professor Erman contained a warning about forgeries and I sent it to Frances <u>before</u> Christmas, thinking it would reach Chicago before you left. But apparently it did not, for when Frances returned it, about the 7th of January, she expressed the wish that a copy of the section on forgeries might be sent to you. I inclose the copy, herewith, and I also send a copy to Mr Lythgoe. I fancy that this matter of the forged Egyptian art objects is already well known to you, but the data Professor Erman gives about the scribe's statue seen in two stages are especially valuable. I have sent a copy to Dr Allen for the Institute files and I am communicating the information to a number of the smaller museums with which I have had dealings, which might conceivably need the warning.

I also received your kind letter telling me of the plans for helping the Dictionary. Perhaps you did not get my message that I too will give $50 to the Dictionary. I have already sent $10 of the sum in unfolded one dollar notes by registered letter to Professor Erman and I will send $10 each succeeding month through June. I wrote Frances in detail what we had done otherwise, since she thought it would be well for us to keep in touch in the matter. In all our family expended $150 for the German friends after October first last, chiefly on food packages sent through the Central

Relief Committee.[162] I missed Mr Griffith's name from your list. Surely he must be both able and friendly enough to the cause to join us! You will let me know, will you not when another £10 is due from each of us?

My Index is just about done, and I hope it will not now be many weeks before my jewelry book is out.[163] I watch the papers with intense interest for the Egyptian news especially the crucial matter with respect to excavations. I wish I could get a chance to work in Egypt next winter. My husband and mother would let me go, if there were any useful thing I could do. Of course I should not be willing to go out and merely be a nuisance and in the way!

With all good wishes to you | Sincerely yours | Caroline R. Williams

We have just had the pleasure of entertaining Director Wace[164] of the British School at Athens He lectured here for the Archaeological Institute

---

**8 February 1924**                                        **0146**

Winter Palace Hotel | Luxor |
Egypt | Friday, February the Eighth 1924

My dear Mrs. Williams:-

I have been very glad to have your letter of January 12th, in which you have so kindly enclosed a copy of Erman's report on the forged statues on sale by Géjou of Paris.[165] I am very glad to have this copy for our files. Luckily I had

---

[162] It is possible she is referring to the Central Relief Committee (CRC) which was founded in October 1914 to help Jews in Europe and Palestine who were endangered by the First World War. Yeshiva University has many of their records: http://libfindaids.yu.edu:8082/xtf/view?docId=ead/crc19/crc19.xml;query=;brand=default (accessed 23 November 2016).

[163] CRW, The New York Historical Society Catalogue of Egyptian Antiquities, Numbers 1-160: Gold and Silver Jewelry and Related Objects (New York: NYHS, 1924).

[164] Alan John Bayard Wace (1879-1957) was a British Archaeologist who studied classical archaeology at Cambridge and was attached to the British School at Athens throughout his career. He was director of the British School at Athens from 1914-23, a curator at the V&A from 1924-34, and Laurence Professor of Classical Archaeology at Cambridge from 1934-44. He evacuated from Greece to Cairo in 1941 where he took up teaching and administrative posts in Egypt.

[165] Isaac Élias Géjou is difficult to track down in the literature. According to the British Museum, he was an antiquities dealer who was active in Paris especially from 1895-1939. He is present in the archives at the British Museum where his name is on packing lists he

read very hastily the letter of Erman referring to the matter, which you had kindly enclosed to Mrs. Breasted; for on the very day when I left Paris, early in January, on my way to Egypt, Géjou called on me at my hotel, stating that he had some remarkable things to show me. I was much pressed for time, but I went with him and recognized at once the altered statue which Erman describes. He had also a second, smaller statue of the same material, in the style of the Tanitic Period. While they were remarkably well done, I do not believe I should have been inclined to accept them, even without the warning I had, for there was something about them decidedly un-Egyptian. Géjou protested that he had them on commission only. I told him that the people from whom he took them on commission were likely to get into trouble if they went on making that kind of thing in France.

You will see that the certainty with which I was able to make Géjou was due entirely to the information which you sent me, and as my admonitions to Géjou may do some good, the benefit we owe to you.

I hope you will forgive me for seeming to probe into your financial efforts on behalf of our friends in Germany. The Ermans are so generous, I know that if we send them more money than they need, they will share with others. I sent for some new blanks for food packages, addressing the New York Office before I sailed, but they have not yet responded with the desired order forms.

I am very glad that you have finished the bulk of the work on your index, and I am looking forward with the greatest interest to the appearance of your volume. I had not forgotten your former reference to your desire to come out to Egypt next winter, but was in hopes that I could write you something more definite after looking over the situation this season, here on the ground. I should be delighted if you could join us in the work on the Coffin Texts, which I am sure you would enjoy, after you once got started. I have laid out also another project for the rescue of the temple inscriptions of Thebes, - an inclusive work, including all the temples on both sides of the river. I am reluctant, however, to propose either of these projects to you because with my present commitments, the Institute is not able to do any more in the way of remunerations than to pay your travelling

---

offered or sold. He sold to the Louvre as well as trying to sell in New York and elsewhere. There is no mention of forgeries. http://www.britishmuseum.org/research/search_the_collection_database/term_details.aspx?bioId=93482 (accessed 23 November 2016).

expenses. This is also the basis on which Gardiner comes. We should be so pleased to have you come out that I have mentioned the matter in this way, notwithstanding the fact that this very unsatisfactory financial aspect of the project makes me very loathe to refer to it at all. I am trying to do so much with the Institute that its funds are unhappily spread out very thin. You can reach me probably till the middle of April care Thos. Cook & Son, Cairo.

With cordial greetings to you all, I am | Very sincerely yours | JHB

**17 March 1924**                                                    0147

The Chesbrough Dwellings |
Toledo, Ohio | March 17, 1924

Dear Mr Breasted,

Your very kind letter written from Luxor reached me some days ago. It would be a very great pleasure to me to join your staff at the Coffin Texts and I consider your offer to have the Institute pay my traveling expenses a generous one. Indeed, I don't know that, were I go to out, I ought to accept so much.

I must tell you, however, that my prospects for going to Egypt next winter are quite altered, since I wrote to you, by my mother's sudden, acute illness in February. She had previously always been so active that I had scarcely thought of her as older and ever especially needing me. But now, although to our great joy she is fast getting better, she cannot use her eyes freely nor go on the street alone, and I feel as if I could not again leave her for any length of time. So you see my plan for Egypt is really off! I shall never forget your kind response to my question, although I'm sorry now to have bothered you with it!

With kind regards from us all | Gratefully and sincerely yours | Caroline R. Williams

6 October 1924                                              0148

October 6, 1924

My dear Mrs. Williams:

I am so delighted with the external appearance of your beautiful volume that it has even raised my anticipation of the character of the content, which I assure you is saying a great deal. The accumulation of all sorts of correspondence and other papers on my desk has thus far prevented my doing anything more than a hasty glance through the book, but those preliminary tastes make one's mouth water. It is splendidly done and I congratulate you very heartily on your achievement. The volume will always be fundamental to future researches along this line. I have about three-quarters promised our American Journal of Semitic Languages to write the review for them, which is a piece of effrontery on my part, but I shall make the endeavor at any rate, and shall hope to say there a good many things which are far too numerous to say here.[166] I assure you the volume is a source of pride to us all here, and a source of great gratification. I have a keen feeling of regret that our dear friend Tarbell could not have lived to see it.

Lest I should forget it, let me introduce a totally different subject and remark that somehow or other last summer I succeeded in losing the New York Blue Book[167] which your husband so kindly loaned to us. We have ordered another from the bookshop, but they sent us the wrong one, or you

---

[166] JHB, 'Book Review: *The Art of the Ancient Craftsman in Gold, Silver, and Semi-Precious Stones: Gold and Silver Jewelry and Related Objects (The New York Historical Society Catalogue of Egyptian Antiquities, Numbers 1-160).* Caroline Ransom Williams." *The American Journal of Semitic Languages and Literatures* 41:3 (April 1925): 200-202. The American Journal of Semitic Languages and Literatures became *The Journal of Near Eastern Studies* in 1942 and continues to run.

[167] JHB refers to the 'Social Register,' a publication put out annually since the late 19th century listing prominent families in certain areas such as New York, Boston, Washington, D. C., St. Louis, and more. These registers of family names and sometimes addresses stem from early visiting lists so that people of the social elite could easily find and associate with one another. Published by the Social Register Association, they have fallen a bit out of fashion, but were extremely useful upper class directories in their time. CRW was clearly part of this group, or else at this time she would not have had a copy of the register for JHB to borrow. See Allison Ijams Sargent, 'The Social Register: Just a Circle of Friends,' *The New York Times*, Sunday Styles (21 December 1997): 1-2. Also, http://www.socialregisteronline.com/ (accessed 23 November 2016).

would have had it before. As soon as the proper book arrives, we shall send it on at once, accompanied by the New England Maps which Mr. Williams also loaned us and which we have found very useful indeed.

I hope we shall see you here before we leave for Egypt. There are so many things about which we ought to talk. Callender sends me photographs of the Luxor house which show the building far along toward completion, with parts of the roof on.[168] Nelson is already on the ground and Allen with him by this time. I wish we might see you in the new house next winter, but I can easily understand that you are, under the present circumstances, reluctant to cross the ocean.

Again thanking you for the copy of your beautiful volume in which I can assure you Frances is also taking great pleasure,

I am, as always | Very sincerely yours | JHB
JHB: ES

**8 October 1924**                                                          **0149**

October 8, 1924

Dear Mr Breasted

I am writing hastily in my husband's office, having just shown him your kind and delightful letter. He bids me write you at once that the Blue Book was an old one, we had already had much use of it, and should greatly prefer that you should not replace it. If it is possible for you to cancel the order please don't replace the book. I'm sorry you should have that to

---

[168] Arthur Robert Callender (1875-1936) was an architect and engineer who first started in Egypt as manager of the Egyptian branch railways. He assisted Carter in excavating Tutankhamun's tomb and likely met JHB there. He was the supervisor of the building of what is now referred to as old Chicago House on the West Bank at Luxor, near Medinet Habu. He also sold objects to the MMA and the Oriental Institute. Chicago House itself was meant to house staff for the Epigraphic Survey as well as occasional visitors. It also houses an Egyptological Library for research. The first building was on the West Bank; the second and present Chicago House was built on the East Bank, midway between Luxor and Karnak Temples. See Abt, American Egyptologist, 283-89 and 361-62. 'Chicago House' also refers to the style of epigraphy that JHB and his team devised specifically for copying tomb and temple inscriptions. See also, https://oi.uchicago.edu/research/projects/epigraphic-survey (accessed 23 November 2016).

bother about. Thank you a thousand times for your kind words about the jewelry book.

Every Sincerely yours | CR Williams

**23 October 1924**                                                                 **0150**

The Chesbrough Dwellings |
Toledo, Ohio | October 23, 1924

Dear Mr. Breasted,

I am acknowledging first for my husband the up-to-date and useful Blue Book which you have sent him in return for the last old one. I fear the old book was just a nuisance to you, and now you have gone to this expense to give us a new one! Thank you many, many times for this gift. I think we shall have to begin at once planning a trip east! Grant would write to you himself except that he is incapacited [sic] just now, taking his turn in the hospital. The old saying 'It never rains but it pours' applies to our family this year, but we all hope to be well presently. I am nearly so, only I have a little more to do just now than is good for me. Otherwise, I should not have failed to thank you earlier for your great kindness in contemplating reviewing my jewelry book in the <u>American Journal of Semitic Languages</u>. If only it does not tax you too much with all you have to do, nothing could give me greater pleasure. I am wondering how late I could see you and Frances in Chicago – whether you will still be there at the time of the Institute meetings in the last days of December. Just now I cannot leave home, and I am due to give some talks in the M. M. A. November 29th and December 6th. Probably I could not go to Chicago before I go east, but I hope very much to do so before you depart for Egypt, and may be able to manage it shortly before Christmas, if you would be there then, and would let me chat with you at table, not to interfere with working hours. I was immensely interested to know that Dr Allen is in Egypt and am wondering if he stays all winter, or must be back to hold the fort while you are away. This first journey must be of the highest consequence and interest to him and he is richly prepared to profit by it.

One thing I wished to tell you is that I am to do no work for the Historical Society in the calendar year 1925. This is to allow Mrs Richardson undisturbed use of my notes and the file of photographs and complete command of the budget so far as any demand on my part on the funds is concerned. For this reason I should be free to give occasional lectures on Egypt. I mention this in case there should be inquiries at your Institute and no one else at liberty to take advantage of them. Of course I can be quite content merely to catch up in reading and studying, but if I have a chance for some remuneration work I shall then be better able to help the Dictionary and the Ermans, not to mention other causes dear to me!

Your kind words about my recently published book touched me deeply, also your reference to Mr Tarbell. Everyone has been very friendly to the book thus far, and I hope it will gradually become known and the edition be sold out. I have reason to think that Mr Strunsky will make it the subject soon of his page 'About Books' in the New York Times, perhaps November 2nd. That should help bring it to the attention of librarians. The moneys coming in from its sale will be kept apart by the New York Historical Society as the nucleus of the fund for the publication of the next part of the scientific catalogue, which we are expecting will be your important work on the Edwin Smith papyrus. Mr Winlock, just before he sailed, sent me a carbon of a review he had written at the request of the <u>Saturday Review of Literature</u>. It is chiefly in Chicago at the University and among very old associated in the M. M. A. that the book has had a welcome and I am most grateful to the loyal friends in these two centers.

With our warm thanks again for the Blue Book and best wishes to you for all your important Institute work,

Ever Sincerely yours | Caroline R. Williams


**27 October 1924**                                              0151

Chicago | October 27, 1924.

My dear Mrs. Williams:

I have your kind letter of thanks regarding the Blue Book. I hope you have not felt any obligations to write merely on that account at a time when you are so very busy. I regret to hear that Mr. Williams is in the hospital, and I earnestly hope that this may find him rapidly improving.

I am glad to say that we shall be in Chicago at the date you indicate for your probable visit here. I shall be in Amherst, Mass., for the Henry Ward Beecher Lectures during the middle ten or twelve days of November, but otherwise we shall be in Chicago without interruption from now until we leave for the ship, shortly after New Year's Day. We should be delighted to see you, and I hope that you may be able to arrange to come.

I am interested in your remark that the Historical Society is already laying away funds for the publication of the Medical Papyrus. That is a wise precaution, for I fear that it will be a costly enterprise. There is so much commentary involving many hieroglyphic citations scattered through English texts.

I am very glad to hear that you are open for lectures on Egypt. I receive, and turn down, reams of such invitations. If you have no objections, I will ask such people to open correspondence with you, though I fancy that the number I shall receive in the future will decrease, in view of the fact that I have been turning them all down.

Now, about publicity in the matter of your book: I receive letters every now and again from Dr. Edwin E. Slosson, Director of Science Service, the publicity office of the National Academy of Sciences in Washington, inquiring whether he can get material on this or that subject for distribution to newspapers.[169] This service goes all over the country. I am writing him today and telling him something of your book and I am sure he would be interested to see that a bulletin about it goes out from his office. It will, of course, be very popular, and necessarily totally non-technical. Do not be horrified by the 'newspaper punch' that is likely to go into his notice. He is a thoroughly scientific man, but he understands publicity. If he writes a notice of it, he may ask you to look over a carbon of it in advance, and send him corrections, which I hope you may be able to do. His address is

    Dr. Edwin E. Slosson,

    Director, Science Service, Inc.,

---

[169] A scientist, but also a popularizer of science. He was an important author who wrote one of the first popular works on Einstein's theory of relativity. Edwin E. Slosson, *Easy Lessons in Einstein: A Discussion of the More Intelligible Features of the Theory of Relativity* (New York: Harcourt, Brace and Howe, 1920). His son, Preston W. Slosson, wrote a short biography of Edwin and included it at the end of his final book, published posthumously. *A Number of Things, arr. with a biographical memoir, by Preston W. Slosson* (New York: Harcourt, Brace, and Co., 1930).

B and Twenty-first Sts.,
Washington, D.C.
Frances is writing you, and has not yet seen your letter of October 23d.
      With warmest regards to you all | believe me, always | Very sincerely
yours | JHB
      JHB:ES


**16 November 1924**                                                    **0152**

The Chesbrough Dwellings |
Toledo, Ohio | November 16th, 1924

Dear Mr Breasted

This note is just to thank you for your very kind and practical suggestion
about publicity for my book. I acted upon it at once by sending a copy of the
book to Dr Slosson whose secretary acknowledged the book, saying that Dr
Slosson was away on a lecture tour, that he would bring it to his attention
on his return. I have not as yet heard from Dr Slosson himself. I shall, of
course, be glad to look over a type-written statement or do anything else in
my power to help, if Dr Slosson chooses to take up the book. I have already
offered to send photographs or extra plates if needed.

      Mr Winlock's review was printed in the <u>Saturday Review of Literature</u>
on November 1st and Mr Strunsky gave his page 'About Books' in the New
York times of November 2nd to the book[170] and I have word that today's
New York <u>World</u> may have something on it.

      I have in the meantime received a delightful letter from Frances and
shall write to her soon probably from New York.

      Again thanking you, and with kind regards to you both from us all,
Sincerely yours | C. Ransom Williams


      I haven't heard from Mr Wall whether the book is selling well or not,
but shall find out while in New York. And I shall also give him a hint that
the proper publication of the Edwin Smith papyrus will be costly and urge
him to make provision in good time.

---

[170] Simeon Strunsky, 'About Books, *More or Less: What They Wore in Egypt*,' *The New York Times
Book Review* (2 November 1924): 4.

**2 January 1925**                                                    **0153**

Chicago | January 2, 1924 [1925][171]

Dear Mrs. Williams:

I have just written a very summary notice of your admirable book for our American Journal of Semitic Languages, which will probably appear during my coming absence. Besides a heavy burden of Institute responsibilities, I have during the past three months been obliged to serve also as a kind of publicity organ for the financial campaign of the University of Chicago, which is out for seventeen and a half million dollars. I regret very much, therefore, that I have not been able to write on the basis of more careful of the volume, but I am sure that you will understand.

I promised to furnish a contribution to the memorial volume of the Zeitschrift, in honor of Erman's 70th birthday, using materials from the Edwin Smith Papyrus, but I have failed entirely in getting it ready. I may be able to do something on the ship.

Frances joins me in the warmest good wishes to you all for the New Year. I only wish you were all going with us.

Believe me, ever | Very sincerely yours | JHB
JHB:ES

P.S. I understand that Dr. Slosson has been absent from Washington, and presume that is the reason why I have not heard from him regarding a notice on your volume. – J.H.B.

---

[171] This letter is dated 1924, but references a number of topics that CRW and JHB spoke about throughout the autumn and winter of 1924. These references, specifically JHB's 'summary article' of the jewelry book, his 'coming absence', and Dr. Slosson, place the letter in January 1925. It is not uncommon to continue dating documents with the previous year well into January of the new year.

**23 February 1925**                                                    **0154**

The Chesbrough Dwellings |
Toledo, Ohio | February 23rd, 1925

Dear Professor Breasted:
I wish to acknowledge your last kind letter written to me from Chicago in which you explain that the review of my book was necessarily somewhat curtailed because of all the extra demands on your time.

Of course I understand how difficult it would be for you to find time for a longer review and I count myself most fortunate that you could give the book any attention whatsoever. I only hope it did not tax you too much to do what you did. I am quite unable to tell you adequately how much I appreciate your kindness. When I was in Chicago in January, Professor Smith told me that your review would appear in the July issue of the 'Journal of Semitic Languages.' M. Portier has kindly consented to present a copy to the French Academy which means that the book will be given a notice in the Compte rendus of the Academy.[172]

We enjoyed seeing M. Capart. I hope he showed you in Chicago the pictures of his family, he and his wife and the ten children ranging from twenty-six year old Pierre, a Jesuit priest, down to the six-year old twins, Marie Alix and Marie Magdaline!

With best wishes for your work in Egypt | Always sincerely yours | Caroline R. Williams


**30 March 1925**                                                       **0155**

March 30th, 1925

Dear Mrs. Williams,
Frances and I were very glad to have your recent interesting letters, and to this is now added a memorandum from my stenographer about Typewriters. I really do not know just what to recommend. I have perhaps abandoned my Hammond, in spite of the convenience of its advantage of any form of type desired, because, in plain English, the workmanship on

---

[172] The *Compte Rendus de l'Academie des sciences* is the journal for l'Academie des Sciences in France.

the recent machines I have had from the Hammond people has been simply rotten. I wrote to the President of the Hammond Company about it and received a very courteous but diplomatic reply.

I have taken out a Corona International, and find that on the whole it does very good work though subject to one fault. They delivered me a new machine but not in very good condition and it has caused me much annoyance. I do not think, however, that these difficulties in my particular Corona are at all necessary, and I would advise you to try a Corona International before buying one.

We are sailing on April 6th, arriving in New York April 23rd. We are both hoping very much that we may see you this summer.

With kindest regards to all your circle in which Frances joins | I am | Very sincerely yours JHB

P.S. Frances wishes me to add that she would have written except for the fact that she has been ill, - an attack of the prevalent Influenza with infected throat, etc. She has been two days in the Anglo-American Hospital on the Ghezira,[173] but is now back at the Hotel[174] and nearly as good as new.

**1 June 1925**                                                          **0156**

The Chesbrough Dwellings |
Toledo, Ohio | June 1, 1925

Dear Professor Breasted:-

The morning mail brought me a copy of the April number of the American Journal of Semitic Languages and Literatures containing your most kind review of my book on jewelry, and I wish to thank you again for writing it.[175] It was much for you to do for the book, considering all the manifold demands on your time, and I am more grateful to you than I can possibly say.

You must have passed through sad and trying days recently in the

---

[173] Gezira Island, Cairo. It is a small island in the Nile, just west of downtown Cairo. Today it contains Gezira and Zamalek districts of Cairo. The Anglo American Hospital is still there.
[174] Probably the Hotel Continental.
[175] See note above, 41:3 (April 1925): 200-202.

illness and death or your friend President Burton.[176] I should like to tell you that when Dr. Burton was in Toledo a few months ago in the interests of the Chicago campaign, in the course of his address he referred appreciatively, almost affectionately to you and your great accomplishment. I wish I could recall his exact words, but I can only say now that he was using you as an illustration of the kind of scholarship and personality the University wishes to keep before its students and to honor. You would have been touched and pleased, could you have been invisibly present to hear what he said.

I have been glad to have news – once from herself and several times from Mrs Marin – of the excellent progress Mrs Breasted has made since her operations.[177] I am so glad for her that the ordeal is over, and now she has the long summer months of possible out-of-door life to reestablish her strength.

I noted with interest your suggestion about a Handbook of Egyptian jewelry, but until the New York Historical Society has sold out the book which has cost so much to publish, I shouldn't feel that I ought to edit any of the material in it. The thing I covet more than anything else – I venture to think I may speak freely to you – is an opportunity to participate in some capacity in the publication of the gold work from Tutenkhamon's tomb. I have by no means had my say out on the subject of Egyptian jewelry, and this past winter I have been carrying on a stimulating correspondence with Professor Robert Zahn of the Berlin Antiquarium[178] and Mr. C. Densmore Curtis of our Academy at Rome. Of course it would be difficult for me to get away to go to Egypt, but I might be able to do so as if I did not plan to stay too long, and I could work much from photographs after once examining the jewels, and then go back again to verify and correct. My mother is better than she was a year ago, and my husband's imagination would be appealed to by anything in connection with 'King Tut.' Is it possible that Mr Carter[179]

---

[176] Ernest DeWitt Burton, President of the University of Chicago from 1923-1925. For more information, see https://president.uchicago.edu/directory/ernest-dewitt-burton, accessed 29 November 2016.

[177] Frances Hart Breasted was known for having anxiety, depression, and other health problems throughout her life. See Abt, *American Egyptologist*, 389; Charles Breasted, *Pioneer to the Past*, 100.

[178] Robert Zahn was a German expert on gold jewelry from Egypt. C. Densmore Curtis was an American expert on ancient gold.

[179] Howard Carter (1874-1939) was a British Egyptologist and artist. This is the first mention

sincerely yours | Caroline Ransom Williams


**20 February 1926**                                                   **0159**

The Chesbrough Dwellings |
Toledo, Ohio | February 20, 1926

Dear Professor Breasted:-

Two days ago Mrs. Breasted was good enough to send me these Erman letters to read. She had held them until she could answer them, and then asked me after reading them to forward them to you.

How good is it that Frau Erman is so much better! And what a satisfactory letter she writes. I am grateful indeed to Frances for giving me the pleasure of reading this letter written to her.

Of course we have all followed your great news in the papers with the keenest interest and are holding our breath for the final decision. It is wonderful, whatever the outcome, to have done so great a thing as you have accomplished.[184]

Our family is well and everything looks favorable for my going to Egypt next winter, starting if desirable before Christmas and remaining in the country for about three months. If the work you and I talked about for me is not possible next winter, I am wondering if you could let me do anything at Thebes under your Chicago Institute plans. I should like immensely, if you thought it well, to do a monograph on the temple treasuries, their reliefs and inscriptions—what remain of them. That would be in a line with my studies of jewelry and gold work.

In the meantime I am studying Egyptian daily for a couple of hours or longer, reviewing grammar, trying to enlarge my vocabulary and ability to read at sight, and at the same time making systematic notes of data veering on jewelry and the like in the texts I go over.

One other circumstance I should like to tell you of. Hearing of the way Mr. Bull is teaching at Yale, in addition to his Metropolitan Museum duties, it occurred to me that perhaps I could do something of the kind at our nearest institution, the University of Michigan, and I wrote to the new

---

[184] CRW refers to the museum proposal.

again and what an entertaining and informing letter she always writes.

It is most kind of both you and Mrs. Breasted to say that you would be glad to see me in Chicago some time in May. I should like very much to go to the Hotel del Prado[187] for a few days when I could see you both and also work a little in the library, and I could do so any time between the 10th and 22nd of the month, or if you liked better now, I could defer going until some time in June. I am to visit my classmate and old friend, President Small of Lake Erie College, on May 24th and immediately thereafter my plans are a little uncertain. I may go east with Mother for a short time.

Will all warm regards to you and Frances from our family | Most sincerely yours | Caroline R. Williams

**1 July 1926**                                                                                         **0162**

Chicago | July First 1926

Dear Mrs. Williams:

In order that I may notify the Auditor's office, will you let me know by return mail to what address you wish send your salary checks when they are due for your services to the University?

With kindest regards | I am | Very sincerely yours, | JHB

**4 July 1926**                                                                                         **0163**

Mount Holyoke College | South Hadley Massachusetts | Department of Art and Archaeology | July 4, 1926

Dear Professor Breasted:-

Your letter of July 1st came into my hands only late last evening when we reached South Hadley again after a brief absence in New Hampshire.

I am so very sorry that you have not had the reply by return mail for which you asked. I would have telegraphed last night, but concluded it

---

[187] They refer to the original Hotel del Prado on 59th and Dorchester in 1926. http://chicago. curbed.com/2013/1/31/10278626/cornerspotted-the-first-hotel-del-prado-at-59th-dorchester accessed 29 November 2016.

would not do any good with the university offices presumably closed over the holiday and you perhaps already away from the Del Prado.

The salary checks, if issued in this country, would better go to my bank in Toledo addressed as follows:

Account of C. L. R. Williams
Ohio Savings Bank and Trust Company
Ohio Building
Toledo, Ohio

'C. L. R. Williams' is the way I sign checks, and of course with a name so frequent as Williams it is important that the University use that form to prevent confusion at the Ohio Bank.

I have also received from the Secretary, Mr. Dickerson, a form to be filled out which I am mailing with the letter to you.

I start home Tuesday and shall not be away from Toledo again except to lecture at the summer session of Michigan University on July 16th and to make a flying trip to Philadelphia for Ohio Day, July 20th. But it will take me until July 10th to drive home.

We are trying to get passage on the 'Roma' of the Fabre Line, October 19th, for the sake of the continuous passage. The sailings of the City Line were still less convenient. If, by any chance, we do not get on the 'Roma,' I shall secure transportation via Naples that will assure my arrival on time in Luxor.

With kindest greetings to you and Mrs. Breasted | Most sincerely yours | C. L. R. Williams

**29 August 1926**                                                      **0164**

The Chesbrough Dwellings |
Toledo, Ohio | August 29, 1926

Dear Mr. Breasted:-

Ever since it came, I have been meaning to send on the inclosed letter from Frau Erman for you and Mrs. Breasted to read. You may by now have all its news and perhaps have later news of how Annemarie is, but I'll send it even now, for one never knows. With such family crises as our dear Ermans always seem to be going through, Frau Erman cannot always find the time to write.

I trust that you are all having a fortunate and enjoyable summer. Mine until recently has been a very active one. First a motoring trip east and then a shorter rail journey to Philadelphia and New York. I could wish that the motor trip had not taken place this year, for I should so much have liked to devote the month it took to study. But it had already been planned and two friends invited to go with us before I went to Chicago, and as other peoples' pleasure than my own was involved, there was no retreating. My husband said when I returned that I looked 100 per cent better, so perhaps it paid, even from the point of view of next winter's work.

Since the beginning of the last week of July, I have been at work on an uninterrupted program of every morning and most afternoons spent on Harris papyrus[188]—with the help of Sethe's Verbum—and lately, since they came, Medinet Habu Dictionary slips, which Professor Erman was good enough to send me[189]. The latter are only Reste von Resten, as Professor Erman put it, but they are very useful to me, and as numerous as I shall have time to utilize.

I have thought better to rely for such archaeological work as you may require of me on my general training and accumulated experience and to put in my preliminary study where I most need it on the language. I am intrigued by the idea that the Medinet Habu texts are so individual, representing Ramses III's language, or that of his court, and have started systematic notes on graphic and orthographic peculiarities (referring here of course to photographs and photographic reproductions) as well as grammatical forms, also my own glossary. I hope this way of studying will make me more alert as to what may be contained in injured passages.

---

[188] Bought in 1855 by Anthony Harris, then-British Commissioner to Alexandria, the Great Harris Papyrus is in the British Museum and has accounts of Ramesses IIIs works during his life. It was 42 meters long and one of the longest surviving papyrus rolls to come out of Egypt. See the British Museum website for more information http://www.britishmuseum. org/research/collection_online/collection_object_details.aspx?objectId=114412&partId=1 (accessed 29 November 2016) See also JHB Ancient Records of Egypt: Historical Documents from the Earliest Times to the Persian Conquest, Volume IV The Twentieth to the Twenty-Sixth Dynasties (Chicago: University of Chicago Press, 1906), 87-206.
[189] Kurt Sethe, Das Aegyptische Verbum im Altaegyptischen, Neuaegyptischen und Koptischen, 3 bd. (Leipzig: J.C. Hinrichs'sche Buchhandlung, 1899).

I only lament daily how little I can do in a single morning, and wish I had seven months before me instead of only the seven weeks that remain before Mother and I start for New York to take our steamer. We have engaged passage on the 'Roma' of the Fabre Line, sailing October 19th and I shall be at Luxor promptly on December 1st.

I should like to have the weekly edition of the London Times sent to me during those three months directly to the Chicago House, inasmuch as newspapers are not so promptly forwarded as letters. Would my name and Chicago House, Luxor, Egypt, be right to give the Times as my address?

I am not sending Professor Erman's last letter because it contains nothing that would interest you, unless it be this sentence: „Es ist doch sehr nett von Breasted, dass er mit dem Med. Habuunternehmen so viele Glückliche zu machen weiss.'[190]

I wonder if you chanced to see in The Saturday Review of Literature of July 31, 1926 a review of 'The Cambridge Ancient History' Vol. III by M. Rostovtzeff. I could not but wish as I read the last paragraph that it would come to Mr. Rockefeller's attention, and that if the Egyptian enterprise should never go through, he would nevertheless establish with large funds an Institute for Oriental Research and Excavations under your leadership. There are so many workers, in this country and Europe, who need financial backing to be fully useful. Just lately I have had an appeal from M. Dévaud of Fribourgh, Switzerland, who apparently thinks I command large means! But I cannot help him.

Here is the paragraph from the review in case you did not see it:

To sum up. After having read the three volumes of 'Cambridge Ancient History' one is struck by two facts: first, how different are our ideas of the ancient world, if compared, say with those e.g. of our contemporary Maspero, and how much more we know about it, and second how little it is that we do know in comparison with what we ought to know to have an adequate idea of the evolution of the ancient world. New problems arise one after another and in the facts which we know there is no solution for them. We need, bitterly need, more facts and more material. And there is only one source for increasing our knowledge; Spade work. The ancient history of

---

[190] Loosely translated, Erman wrote: 'It is very nice of Breasted that he can make so many people happy at Medinet Habu.'

Mommsen stood under the sign of epigraphy, our ancient history stands under the sign of Archaeology.

I wonder if we shall see you and your family when you drive home. I wish it might be so.

With my love to Frances and many kind greetings from us all to you both, | Most sincerely yours | Caroline R. Williams.


**22 September 1926**                                              **0165**

September 22, 1926

Dear Mrs. Williams:

I regret that the congestion on my desk since my return has delayed this reply to your kind letter of August 29 enclosing also a letter from Frau Erman. We have been very glad of the opportunity to read the letter.

I think we owe to your husband a debt of gratitude for pledging you to a summer vacation which made you look 'one hundred per cent better'.

Regarding our Medinet Habu work, I am keener than ever to put out volumes which will be equal to the best. Our English friends, especially Gardiner, are looking a little askance at us in view of the large equipment we are securing and the extensiveness of our external development. I am inclined to think Gardiner doubts our capacity to produce acceptable epigraphic work and I should enjoy proving him wrong. I am confident that you are going to aid us substantially in this direction.

With regard to your address in Egypt, Chicago House is now so well known to the Luxor Post Office that it will be quite enough to have on your mail, addressed Chicago House, Luxor, Egypt, as you have suggested.

It is very kind of you to have taken the trouble to send me the paragraph by Rostovtzeff. He is, of course, quite right. I am sorry for Devaud. He appealed to me also a year or so ago but I was unable to do anything for him. I shall make use of Rostovtzeff's paragraph in New York. Many thanks!

Our stay in the Virginia Mountains was not as successful as we had hoped owing to noise and disturbance arising from new buildings directly before our front door. The middle of August, therefore, we took our leave and returned home via the old Virginia Settlements on the James River and vicinity, Washington, D. C., Gettysburg, the Delaware Watergap, the Catskills, the Adirondacks, Montreal, Quebec, the Thousand Isles, Niagara Falls and Buffalo to Detroit by boat. We regretted very much that the boat trip prevented our seeing you as we passed Toledo. We are looking forward nevertheless with great anticipation to seeing you at Medinet Habu.

Frances joins me in kindest greetings to you and all your household. Very sincerely yours | JHB

JHB: MDS

P.S. Thanks for your article on the New Cylinder Seal of Userkere. It is a pity we cannot find some fuller documents of the Kings of this series.


**11 April 1927**                                                         **0166**

Naples | S.S. Belgenland | April 11, 1927[191]

Dear Professor Breasted:-

I am hoping that this letter will reach you before you leave Cairo permanently.

I wish to tell you, if I may, how the matter stands with the two fragments, supposedly from early ceremonial slate palettes, which I saw at Blanchard's.[192] You know how unexpectedly Mr. Blanchard can act, and when he saw I hesitated a little as to their genuineness, a fact I ought probably never to have revealed, he said he would not sell them to me.

Then suddenly, in quite a different mood, because of his friendly feeling for the Toledo Museum of Art, he said, he promised to hold the pieces for me until next season, and to try to gather in more of the fragments from the natives. I am wondering how the piece which came in to Professor Spiegelberg's hands relates itself, if at all, to these pieces.

---

[191] There is a large gap in letters here because CRW and JHB were working together in Luxor on the Epigraphic Survey. For more on that important season, see Abt, *American Egyptologist*, 281-301 (esp. 292-301); *Medinet Habu, Volume I, Earlier Historical Records of Ramses III* (Chicago: University of Chicago Press, 1930). CRW took over 40 photographs while there, which can be found at the OI's internet database photo archives: https://oi-idb.uchicago.edu/index.php.

[192] Ralph Huntington Blanchard (1875-1936) was an American antiquities dealer in Cairo. Buying from dealers in the early days of Egyptology was a common practice among Egyptologists. His shop was next to the old Shepheard's Hotel on the Ezbekiya.

I do not know that this will interest you, but I thought there was the possibility you might, if not too hurried in your last days in Cairo, and if in Blanchard's neighborhood, like to take a look at them.

I did not, of course, mention your name to Mr. Blanchard, nor Professor Spiegelberg's; nor the name of any Egyptologist to any Cairo dealer, let me hasten to say. But I did tell him that I had heard of another fragment in Cairo, the genuineness of which some competent authorities had questioned. I had not seen it and could tell him nothing about it. I am not sure that I did not shake his complete confidence in his own judgment by this tale and that he wanted to hold his own pieces to get further light on them. So if you should be interested and have time to look at them don't refer to me or to Toledo, but just lead up to seeing his early things. It is odd that the cleanness of the pieces had bothered me and the staining of the one you saw did not look right to you. There was nothing between Mr. Blanchard and me to prevent his showing the pieces to you. What he promised was to give us the refusal of them until next season and to guard for me the privilege of publication. No one is to have sketches or photos of them. I do not think he will go back on this. He really knows about Toledo, for the late Mr Libbey bought much from him.

I am writing thus at length because the matter seems to me really important. If they are genuine, some important site of the dawn of history is being robbed that such things should come on the market. If they are not genuine the forgers have gone on a new tack.

Tiny as the fragments are, I am interested in them as an exemplification of a style which antedates the Old Kingdom. Our fragment is more advanced than the other, but the upraised hand of that piece is so unlike Egyptian drawing of the historical period that I need to refresh my visual memory as to whether it is possible at this time. The strong vigorous head is more convincing to me. With the less advanced piece I was better satisfied, in fact inclined, but for what you told me, to take them.

With greetings to you both from Mother and me | Most sincerely yours | C. Ransom Williams

Written just as we leave Naples with many pleasant memories of the winter. I have your two consignments of mail safe and together to be posted at once in New York.

P.S. I am uncertain whether Prof. Spiegelberg is still in Cairo but if this letter reaches you there and you know him to be there, perhaps having looked at his piece, you would care to tell him of the ones at Blanchard's, if he has not already seen them. I haven't time before our vessel sails to write to him.

**11 May 1927**                                                                **0167**

On board S. S. 'Roma' | May 11, 1927

My dear Mrs. Williams:

I was very glad to receive your last letter before sailing from Alexandria, with regard to the prehistoric relief fragments in Blanchard's hands. I kept the item in my list of agenda for several days at the end of our Cairo stay, but unfortunately the rush was too much for me and I was unable to get over to see the pieces.

Incidentally I learned of one matter of concern to you which may not reach you directly. The funny old packer, Gratzinger, told me that on endeavoring to obtain the museum seal for the export of your purchases he found that one piece had been refused an export permit. It was a fragment of tomb wall relief which you had bought off Abemayor.[193] The ground for Lacau's[194] refusal was his statement that the relief was cut out of the wall of a tomb and that in order to stop such practices he was refusing an export permit for all such pieces.

---

[193] Probably Elie Albert Abemayor (1883-1941) or Joseph Abemayor (1894-1941). They were a family of Egyptian dealers in Cairo who had been dealing for generations. Their shop was in rue Kamel opposite Shepheard's Hotel. The last Abemayor to practice was Michel Abemayor (1912-1975) who became a naturalized US citizen in 1946. He established himself in New York and sold to museums and private collectors.

[194] Pierre Lucien Lacau (1873-1963) was a French Egyptologist who first studied geology, then philosophy at the Sorbonne (1897) then Coptic and Egyptian with Maspero. He became the Director of the Antiquities Service in October 1914 but took up his post only after his war service ended in 1917. He retained this position until 1936, and presided over the excavation and clearing of the Tomb of Tutankhamun. He secured the totality of the finds for the Egyptian Museum. In 1936 he returned to Paris to take over Moret's chair at the Collège de France until 1947. The issues that JHB and Carter had with Lacau during the battle over Tutankhamun's tomb soured the relationship that JHB had with Lacau (see Abt, 311-316).

I was very sorry to learn this and hope that it has not involved you seriously.

Our last weeks in the Near East were very strenuous and wearying in the extreme. Fisher broke down at Megiddo and I had to shift him into an advisory position, a measure which he resisted vigorously, and put into his place as field director, P. L. C. Guy, who has been acting director of the Department of Antiquities in Palestine since Garstang's departure. Bollacher also broke loose and made himself so important that his conduct was very demoralizing for the entire staff at Chicago House. I shall have to take some kind of disciplinary measure in his case but it is very difficult to decide just what course to pursue.

We are arriving in New York May 13th and hope to reach Chicago a few days later. It would be very agreeable for us if our summer outings might bring us at least in passing for a brief visit in Toledo or you and your husband to us at Chicago.

Frances joins me in warmest greetings to you all. With all good wishes, I am | Very sincerely yours | JHB


**27 July 1927**                                              **0168**

July 27, 1927

My dear Mrs. Williams:

I notice the announcement in the Chicago Tribune this morning that you are to fill a special lectureship at the University of Michigan this coming year. I hope they realize how much they are to be congratulated!

I am developing plans at the moment, some aspects of which I very much wish I could discuss with you. Remembering that you had indicated to me that there was probably very slight prospect that you would be able to return to Egypt again next season I did not venture to hope that we might see you again at Chicago House next winter. The plans which I am now hoping to see developed concern subsequent developments in a more permanent form. I do not know whether you have noticed that Johns Hopkins University is not appointing any successors either to Professor

Paul Haupt or Professor Aaron Ember.[195] Harvard University is paying $1000 a year to a young instructor in Boston University for giving a course in cuneiform at Harvard, but is not appointing a successor to Professor Lyon. There is a desperate need that a large and statesmanlike program of the development of Oriental science, both in education and in research, should be drafted by some one and brought to the notice of those who have the means to alter this situation and who might lay down a permanent foundation on which Oriental science of the future could build. The specific point that I have in mind is this: if such a program could be carried out and such a dream made practically possible, what share in it do you think your interests, your capabilities, and your family responsibilities might lead you or permit you to undertake? There is an appalling lack of trained people for assuming these new responsibilities, and I earnestly hope that you may be able to share in this future development of which I am now dreaming.

In view of responsibilities here I have not yet been able to think about getting away for any continuous vacation. I am endeavoring to play golf twice a week in the vicinity and run out for an occasional week end into the country. If you and your husband are taking a drive, and it should lead you in this direction, it would be very gratifying if we could see you both here.

Frances joins me in warmest greetings. Always | Very sincerely yours | JHB

---

[195] Paul Haupt (1858-1926) was a Sumerologist and Assyriologist who studied in Leipzig (PhD 1878) and was a professor at Göttingen. He held the W. W. Spence Chair in Semitic Languages at Johns Hopkins from 1886-1923. He was a mentor to Ember and a friend of William Rainey Harper (former President of University of Chicago and JHB's mentor) (see Cyrus Adler, 'Paul Haupt,' *Journal of the American Oriental Society* 47 (1927): 1-2; and http://neareast.jhu.edu/about/history-of-the-department/ accessed 1 December 2016). Aaron Ember (1878-1926) was an American Egyptologist who studied Hebrew with Haupt, and then studied Egyptian under Sethe at Göttingen in 1910. He died trying to save a manuscript he had been working on for years from his burning house.

**29 July 1927**                                                    **0169**

The Chesbrough Dwellings |
Toledo, Ohio | July 29, 1927

Dear Professor Breasted:-

I am truly sorry that word of my appointment should have reached you through the newspapers rather than directly from me. They were certainly prompt in making their announcements at Ann Arbor, for I sent my formal acceptance of the post only the day your kind letter reached me. But at least you knew of the possibility of my teaching there, for I recall telling you about it before I went out to Egypt.

It is good of you to give me an inkling of the plans you are developing and of course I am keenly interested in them. I hardly know what to say about myself in connection with them. My teaching at Ann Arbor is of course an experiment on both sides; neither the University nor I wished to make an engagement of more than one year at once. I am to give a three-hours' beginners' course in Egyptian and a two-hour course not in the language, of which the subject is still undetermined. On the University's side it will be a question partly of budget, partly of what demand for my subject develops, on my side a question of how profitable intellectually and how easy I find teaching there, whether I ever do so again.[196]

I have under consideration a part-time arrangement with the Toledo Museum of Art for the calendar year of 1928. This would fit in with my part-time work at Ann Arbor and presumably would be renewed indefinitely if I wished it. But as yet I have not committed myself to this even for one year.

The two positions together will give me a substantial income with which to develop my working apparatus and take care of other expenses in which work in Egyptology involves me and for which I do not like to call on my husband.

What I like best to do and perhaps am most fitted to do is research work and what I like least to do is the Museum work, that is, under the conditions which prevail here. But the latter is the best paid and for

---

[196] The second course she taught was on Egyptian art and archaeology and 'met with an enthusiastic response.' However, she did not continue to teach there after the 1927-28 academic year. (Wilfred B. Shaw, ed. *The University of Michigan: An Encyclopedic Survey*, Volume II [Ann Arbor: University of Michigan Press, 1951], 666.)

practical reasons I must consider it.

I am convinced that I ought not to plan to go to Egypt every winter, though I have come reluctantly to this decision. I probably shall be able to go occasionally, say every two or three years. If only air-plane service to Egypt were already inaugurated it would be easier for me to go, for I should not then have to be away from home so long each time.

I am afraid we are not likely to motor to Chicago. If later you were to chance to take a holiday any where in the state of Michigan, I might inveigle my husband to drive us over to call on you. Very much, however, I should like to go by train to Chicago for a few days in the Del Prado to see you both and make use of Haskell Library. I should like to go at a time when both you and Dr. Allen were there. If I should not be able to do this before the University of Michigan opens (September 19th), I might be able to do so some week-end later in the autumn. And of course you know how gladly we would welcome you and Frances here if your plans should alter bring you this way.

From all the foregoing, I think you will see that I am rather feeling my way toward some satisfying and practical activity within the field of Egyptology, and I haven't as yet any fully determined program. I have still the monograph on the color of Perneb's tomb to finish and hope I may compass that before many months have gone by. And Mr. Winlock, at least, (for he proposed it to me) would like to have me do another piece of work left unfinished when I left the Metropolitan Museum.

We are still very much upset because I am having my Bookroom reshelved. After making working drawings and consulting with factories and private carpenters, I learned that I could actually get Art Metal shelves cheaper than I could rebuild and increase my wooden ones, and they will have the great advantage that I shall not have to scrap them when we leave the Chesbrough Dwellings. Included in my outfit is a set of roller shelves big enough for Lepsius' Denkmäler, if I am ever fortunate enough to possess the work. I shall be able to proceed much more efficiently when once everything is in order. The steel shelves are due August 5th.

I hope I make you understand how sorry I am not to go out to Chicago House next winter. I should have liked to stand by at least until the first volume on Medinet Habu were issued, and I shall always be grateful to you for the pleasure and inspiration the sojourn there gave me. Mother joins me in warm greetings to you and Frances.

Most sincerely yours | Caroline Ransom Williams

I have not as yet written to M. Dévaud, although to do an archaeological commentary on the Harris papyrus appeals to me as strongly as ever.

**3 August 1927**                                                           **0170**

August 3, 1927

Dear Mrs. Williams:

I have been very glad to have your kind letter of July 29th, and to learn that there is a possibility of our seeing you here in Chicago before I leave for the next season in the Orient.

The situation here is requiring my presence pretty continuously during the summer. I am hoping, however, to get away during the last fortnight of August for an outing somewhere in the woods. It would be a great pleasure to us to see you either before or after that absence. My family are urging me to extend this proposed vacation somewhat at either end, and it is possible that I might leave here on Friday the twelfth and stay on a little into September. There is much to talk about, and I will not endeavor to summarize it in a letter, but will hope to see you either before or after my vacation.

Frances joins me in warm greetings to you and your household, and with pleasant anticipations, I am | Very sincerely yours | JHB

**18 August 1927**                                                          **0171**

August 18, 1927

Dear Mrs. Williams:

We are just making out a list of the personnel of the Oriental Institute for the official publications of the University and I thought I ought to tell you that I have taken the liberty of retaining your name in the list, in view of the fact that we are looking forward with hope to your return to our work in Egypt at such intervals as you find feasible. If, however, you think that we should not include your name in the published list kindly let me know and it can still be expunged from the proof. I hope very much, however, that you will consent to have it remain.

James, Jr., and I are just leaving for a short vacation in the Big Horn mountains in Wyoming, but I shall be returning by the middle of September, or possibly even earlier, and we shall look forward to your visit at that time. I hope that your new duties at Ann Arbor may not be beginning so soon that you will be prevented from coming.

Frances joins me in kindest greetings to you and the household.

Very sincerely yours | JHB

**21 August 1927**                                                    **0172**

The Chesbrough Dwellings |
Toledo, Ohio | August 21, 1927

Dear Professor Breasted:-

Of course I am delighted that you care to retain my name on the roster of the Oriental Institute.

The University of Michigan opens September 19th and my class appointments are scheduled for Tuesday, Wednesday and Thursday, five hours in all. I shall be able to go to Ann Arbor Tuesday morning and return Thursday evening.

If you should be back in Chicago in the week preceding the opening of the Michigan University, I could go to Chicago then to see you and Mrs. Breasted, but if not—and I hope for your sake that you are to have a longer time in the west—I could go for some week-end soon after you returned. Perhaps you will be good enough to let me know when you are back or Francis will send me a card to suggest when it would be convenient for you to have me come.

With appreciation of your kind letter and greetings from us all,

Sincerely yours | Caroline R. Williams

**18 October 1928**                                                    **0175**

The Chesbrough Dwellings |
Toledo, Ohio | October 18, 1928

Dear Professor Breasted:-

In writing late last evening I failed to thank you for thinking of Toledo in connection with the Liverpool collection. I have advised the Director of our Museum to look into the matter and he has, I believe, invited Mr. Lind to stop here on his way to New York.

I think it not impossible if the amount, quality, and condition of the material warrants the large outlay that a sale might be arranged. But I am puzzled that any institution should be willing to sell a perfectly good collection for the sake of pure science, as the pursuit of the Hittites would seem to be. Do you consider this a great opportunity?

Sincerely yours | C. R. Williams

**31 October 1928**                                                    **0176**

October 31, 1928

My dear Mrs. Williams:

Owing to my absence in New York this reply to your inquiry of October 17th has unfortunately been delayed. I hasten to enclose you the copy of the proposed statement in Dr. Swindler's new book, which seems to me quite in order. It would be wise, I think, to insert the word 'probably' as I have indicated on the same sheet.

It is very pleasant to hear from you again. I only wish that we might have had a visit from you all during the past summer. There is a great deal since my visit to England during August and September about which I wish we might have a talk, and I have a ream of things that I would like to write to you. I hope that you may be visiting us in Chicago before I leave immediately after New Years.

Meantime, with kindest regards to your mother and Mr. Williams from all our household, in which I heartily join, I am | Very sincerely yours | JHB

'The date 3400 for the First Dynasty is a minimum date. Professor Breasted has found the names of ten kings of the North who ruled over a united Egypt before the time of Menes. According to Professor Breasted, the calendar of Egypt was formed in a period of stability under these kings and the dating of Menes is probably not therefore to be pushed back beyond 3400, despite Borchardt's theories about the calendar. I owe the information to Mrs. C. Ransom Williams.'

Copied from Not 6, Galley six of Dr. Mary H. Swindler's book on the History of Ancient Painting now on the Yale University Press.

(My only suggestion would be to insert the word 'probably' before 'a minimum date.' J. H. B.)

**15 November 1928**                                                       **0177**

The Chesbrough Dwellings |
Toledo, Ohio | November 15, 1928[202]

My dear Mr. Breasted:-

Thank you so much for your recent kind letter in which you returned the note from Dr. Swindler's book with the one suggestion of a 'probably' to be inserted. This suggestion I have passed on to the author and I have no doubt she will be glad to act on it.

It would be a tremendous pleasure for me to go on to Chicago at some time before you leave for Egypt. I have one point that I ought to look up in the library and if you and Mrs. Breasted are at the Del Prado as usual, I should be pleased to go if it were only for one day there, if I could do so at a time when I would not find you too busy to chat at table or of an evening. I should like so much to know something of your new plans.

We are expecting Miss Randolph on Saturday to stay over Thanksgiving and the holidays with us. Just yesterday I had the pleasure of a considerable visit with my old fellow student and fellow traveller in Greece, Professor David Moore Robinson[203] of Johns Hopkins University. He

---

[202] The date on the letter is 1929, but based on the evidence and events CRW discussed in the letter, it appears to be a typo.

[203] David Moore Robinson (1880-1958) was a classical art historian and is credited with finding the city of Olynthus and published the report in 14 volumes over 22 years. He got

was here to lecture for the local Branch of the Archaeological Institute and gave us a very interesting account of his last season's work at Olynthus.

I have heard with great delight that you are now the President of the American Historical Association and are to give the presidential address in Indianapolis.[204] I hope I may be able to go.

Just at the present moment I am working again on the technique of the Old Kingdom decorators and hope I may be able to get that monograph done and publish also some Old Kingdom reliefs on which I began work many years ago when still in the Metropolitan Museum.

With the kindest greetings from us all to you and Mrs. Breasted | Most sincerely yours | Caroline R. Williams

**17 November 1928**                                                    **0178**

November 17, 1928

My dear Mrs. Williams:

I am very glad to have your kind letter of November 15th indicating that you are hoping to make a brief visit in Chicago before the holidays. I am called to New York for trustee meetings, etc., next week and shall be absent from Chicago from Wednesday the 21st until probably Monday the 26th of November. Otherwise I expect to remain in Chicago until I leave for the ship New Year's night.

Frances and I would be delighted to see you at any time. There is a great deal that I would like to talk over with you. I am very glad to hear that you are continuing your work on the Old Kingdom decorators, and should like to hear more about it.

With kindest greetings to you all, in which Frances joins me, I am | Very sincerely yours | JHB

---

his PhD at Chicago in 1904, one year before CRW did, and spent the majority of his career at Johns Hopkins (1905-1947). He finished his career at the University of Mississippi. (https://dictionaryofarthistorians.org/robinsond.htm accessed 1 December 2016).

[204] For his address, see https://www.historians.org/about-aha-and-membership/aha-history-and-archives/presidential-addresses/james-henry-breasted accessed 1 December 2016. The same text is in *American Historical Review* 34: 2 (January 1929): 215-36.

23 December 1928                                    0179

The Chesbrough Dwellings |
Toledo, Ohio | December 23, 1928

My dear Professor Breasted:-

Possibly the inclosed catalogue because of its illustrations will interest you. I found the exhibition really a most delightful and informing one.

I wonder if you and your family have noted in the weekly London Times of December 6th (p. 629) the account of Prime Minister Baldwin's speech at the American Thanksgiving party. He, like you, finds diversion in detective stories, and mentions an American favorite of his. I think that our family will read aloud the Irving description of an old English Christmas on Christmas day.

We all appreciated the Christmas greetings with which you and Frances remembered us individually. And my husband and I are grateful to Charles for his beautiful Medici-print card.

One never can tell what the future will bring forth, but at present I see no possibility of accepting the professorship which you were good enough to offer me. The reason I made some inquiries about courses was that I was turning over in my mind the question of the summer quarter, whether I could offer to fill in once, or more than once, when you had need, commuting from here. Even that would not be possible next summer, and perhaps on the following summer, but yet at some future time, should you have a necessary supply, I might be in a position to help out. I have a good collection of slides formed for the teaching of Egyptian art which would supplement what the Institute has.

This is only a tentative suggestion. In another year I shall know better whether or not I am to have any free time. If I do have, when I get the publications now projected out of the way, I might be able to undertake something for the Institute, working here as Professor Worrell, judging by your Circular No. 2, does in Ann Arbor. These are the only chances I see for cooperation in your new plans, and I mention them only to show my desire to be of use in projects which mean so much for the future of Egyptology in this country. But for your Institute, I fear the subject would be dropped entirely from American universities.

Grant and I are still expecting to go to Indianapolis. The more my husband hears about work in the Orient, the more chance he will encourage his wife to keep on, so I have an ulterior motive in asking him to go with me!

With kindest regards to you all | Sincerely yours | Caroline R. Williams

**3 April 1929**                                                              **0180**

From Dr. James H. Breasted | Oriental Institute U. of C. |
Midway 0800 Local 112 | Western Union Night Letter | April 3, 1929

Could you accept summer appointment for entire quarter June seventeenth to August thirtieth or for first term only June seventeenth to July twenty-fourth to teach two courses Egyptian language one beginning the other advanced Remuneration fifteen hundred dollars for entire quarter or eight hundred dollars for first term only STOP could assure you good classes and heartiest of welcomes from us all

James H. Breasted

**5 April 1929**                                                              **0181**

Western Union Telegram | Toledo Ohio 5 828A |
1929 Apr 5 AM 8 19

Professor James H Breasted, Director Oriental Institute=University of Chicago=

Regret not free to accept appointment this summer thanks for your most kind message=

Caroline R Williams.

8 April 1929                                              0182

The Chesbrough Dwellings |
Toledo, Ohio | April 8, 1929

My dear Professor Breasted:-

Today I wish to try to thank you more adequately than I did by telegram for the delightful opportunity you gave me for teaching at the University of Chicago this summer.

My situation had not changed since I wrote you last, but I took a day before replying to think whether it would do to ask for leave of absence from my New York work for the first term of your summer quarter. Your message reached me after my husband had gone to business, and I wanted to ask his judgment in the evening. It seemed to us both, however, in view of my definite commitment, that it would not be a courteous thing to do. Then there was the further consideration that the monograph 'The Technique of the Decoration and Conventions of the Colors in the Tomb of Perneb,'[205] which I am so eager to finish and get published, would have been delayed by two months, for I should have needed the first part of June to plan the courses and the rest of July for a holiday after teaching.

Had I been able to teach, I should have begged leave to take Old Egyptian for the advanced course—not Pyramid Texts, but the legends and longer inscriptions in the tombs, using as far as possible facsimile reproductions of the inscriptions and taking up not only their grammar, but their content, to gain, in connection with the reliefs, some idea of the conditions of life, the station and activities of some of the great men of the time.

Please believe that I am most deeply grateful for your fine offer, and that I am very sorry not to be able to take advantage of it.

Perhaps I may have the pleasure of seeing you in Bryn Mawr, for Miss Swindler has invited me there for the 19th and 20th of April. I am going Thursday of this week to New York where I am to consult with Mr. Jaffé of Vienna about some colored plates for my publications.

With the kindest regards to you and Mrs. Breasted from us all | Most sincerely yours | Caroline R. Williams

---

[205] CRW, *The Decoration of the Tomb of Per-nēb, the Technique and Color Conventions* (New York: Metropolitan Museum of Art, 1932). 750 copies were originally printed.

**29 April 1929**                                                    **0183**

The Panhellenic[206] | 3 Mitchell Place |
First Avenue and 49th Street |
New York City | April 29, 1929

Dear Professor Breasted:-

I have been so very sorry to hear of the phlebitis and want to express my concern and sympathy and send earnest wishes for „gute Besserung'

I am glad that you are where you will have the most skillful care and I hope they won't let you forth until you have had a thorough rest. Sometimes an illness is the best way to secure a rest!

I am off tomorrow night for Boston, then shall return here and go home either at the end of this week or beginning of next.

My love to Frances and again best wishes for a quick recovery.

Ever sincerely yours | 'Caroline'


**24 December 1929**                                                **0184**

The Chesbrough Dwellings |
Toledo, Ohio | December 24, 1929

My dear Professor Breasted:-

As proud dedicatee, and in behalf of Miss Swindler, who otherwise would send it herself, I have just ordered for you from the Yale University Press the recently issued <u>Ancient Painting</u>, Miss Swindler's long awaited book.

I think it remarkable that in the midst of the exacting conditions of teaching at Bryn Mawr, she has been able to bring to completion a book covering so many phases of ancient art and such a wide range of technical literature.

I have noticed with interest that you have taken on Dr. Frankfort[207]

---

[206] The Panhellenic was originally built from 1927-29 as a building with affordable and safe housing for single women, who had belonged to a sorority, in New York City. It is now called Beekman Tower and is no longer a hotel. See http://www.franbecque.com/panhellenic-house-to-beekman-tower-panhellenic-to-beekman-tower-hotel/ accessed 1 December 2016.

[207] Henri Frankfort (1897-1954) was a Dutch Egyptologist and orientalist who took his MA under Petrie at UCL in 1924 (which also means he would have been taught by Margaret

in your Oriental Institute work, and my only regret is that you seem to be withdrawing him from Egypt! I would so like to see him complete the job at Amarna. Of late, I have given attention to the Amarna material which the Metropolitan Museum acquired at the Amherst sale, including about one hundred and eighty-five fragments of the temple statues.[208] They are lovely in quality but sadly broken. There was just such a chance back in 1892 to recover the complete scheme of the temple statuary as that so brilliantly utilized by Mr. Winlock at Deir el-Bahri in respect of Hatshepsut's statues. But then, alas, no such methods as he has used prevailed. Only two fragments of all those found by Petrie have ever been published. I do not believe Mr. Davies[209] right in his suggestion that the 'Shade of Re of Tiy' may have been a part of the main temple. Not one of the numerous inscribed fragments from that site in New York contains Tiy's name, not one Amenhotep III's name, and all the Aten cartouches and fragments of titular are in the earlier form. If the 'Shade of Re of Tiy' is to be located, I should much sooner believe it to be the 'smaller temple,' as you suggested long ago. At least there Tiy's name has been found. I wonder if there is a 'favissa' of that temple not yet located and containing the remains of its statuary.

Please give my affectionate greetings to Frances to whom I hope to write ere long. I am sure she too will like to see Miss Swindler's book, but

---

Murray). He took his PhD at Leiden in 1927. In 1922 he was with Petrie in Qau el-Kebir; in 1924-25 he was at the British School in Athens; from 1925-29 he was the director of the EES excavations at Amarna, Abydos, and Armant. Here CRW is referring to JHB inviting Frankfort to be the director of the Oriental Institute Iraq expedition, a position he held until 1937. In 1932 he was a Research Professor of Oriental Archaeology at the OI, and then he became the chair of the Department of Oriental Languages and Literature at Chicago.

[208] Two publications came out of this work: CRW, 'Wall Decorations of the Main Temple of the Sun at El-Amarneh,' *Metropolitan Museum Studies* 2:2 (May 1930): 135-51; 'Two Egyptian Torsos from the Main Temple of the Sun at El 'Amarneh,' *Metropolitan Museum Studies* 3:1 (December 1930): 81-99.

[209] Norman de Garis Davies (1865-1941) was a British Egyptologist. He has been mentioned above, but only in the notes, so here he will get a fuller treatment. He started his career as Congregational Minister where he met Kate Bradbury who was the secretary to Amelia Edwards, one of the founders of the EES. She interested him in Egyptology and he joined Petrie at Dendera in 1898. He became an artist and copyist, and married an accomplished artist, Anna (Nina) Cummings (Nina Davies). The two worked together at Thebes for over 30 years.

not knowing whether or not you are at the Del Prado at this time, I thought it safer to address you at the University.

I trust that you are again quite well and that the New Year will bring the fulfillment of every wish you entertain both personally and for the Institute.

With all warm greetings from our house to yours | Most sincerely yours | Caroline Ransom Williams

**30 December 1929**                                                    **0185**

30 December 1929

My dear Mrs. Williams:

It is very pleasant to have your kind letter of December 24th announcing the appearance of Miss Swindler's new volume on Ancient Painting. I agree with you that she deserves a great deal of credit for the completion of so exacting a work while carrying the burden of full time teaching at Bryn Mawr. It is exceedingly kind of you to remember me with a copy of the book, in which I am greatly interested.

I sympathize with your regrets about the interruption of Dr. Frankfort's work in Egypt. This interruption is due to several causes. In the first place, the autocratic methods of Lacau have very seriously discouraged Frankfort; in the second place, the depleted treasury of the Egypt Exploration Society; in the third place, the embarrassing situation of the Institute in the matter of scientific-executive personnel. It is exceedingly difficult to find men of good scientific competence combined with average business ability to manage a field expedition. The finances of the Egypt Exploration Society were in such a sad condition that I hardly think they could have continued the work at Amarna, and I therefore finally called Frankfort to head our Iraq Expedition. Incidentally, I might mention that Gardiner was very much depressed about the epigraphic work of the E. E. S., and I do not remember whether I have written you that, after preliminary discussion with Mr. Rockefeller at Abydos itself (which continued at intervals until the voyage home) he finally consented, two or three days before we landed in New York, to finance a complete edition of the wall sculptures and inscriptions of Abydos <u>in color</u>.[210] And the work on that coming edition of Abydos, which I hope will be final and definitive, is now going forward in the field.

Returning to Amarna,--I am intensely interested in what you say about the Amarna material at the Metropolitan. How regrettable that methods adequate to such situations are so rarely applied, as Winlock has so successfully applied them. I wonder what has become of Petrie's fragments. Your conclusions about 'Shade of Re of Tiy' interest me greatly. What a pity that we cannot go on with the complete investigation of Amarna! Meantime, I do hope that you will continue your studies of the available materials and publish your results. Just as a possibility, your letter suggests to my mind the hope that, after we have completed our architectural investigations at Medinet-Habu, we might possibly be able to settle Hoelscher at Amarna, but of course this could only be done in some form of combination with our British colleagues and I fear that even a mention of it by me at this stage is rather an indiscretion.

You will be glad to know that the plates of Medinet-Habu Volume I are already printed, and the proofs of the descriptive matter and titles, legends, and the like have just passed over my desk. I must say that I think the group that produced this volume have done extraordinarily fine work. Seen in bulk, as they lay here on my table, these plates made a very gratifying impression. Nelson hopes to finish the plates for Volume II by next spring.

I have handed your interesting letter to Frances to read and she sends you affectionate greetings of the season for you and yours, in which of course I join very heartily.

There is much of Institute development that I wish we might discuss together. I take it you know that we have secured Duell's[211] services for a

---

[210] JHB is referring to the three-month tour through the Middle East that he planned for the Rockefeller family and staff. They stopped in Gibraltar, Algiers, Naples, and Syracuse before arriving in Alexandria. They spent two weeks in Cairo, then took a steam-powered dahabiyya up the Nile visiting major sites including Abydos, Luxor, Thebes, and the Chicago House operation there, finishing the Egyptian part of the trip at Abu Simbel. They went also to Jerusalem, Nazareth, Megiddo, Damascus, Beirut and Haifa. See Abt, *American Egyptologist*, 341-43 for more information.

[211] Prentice Duell (1894-1960) was an American archaeologist who got degrees from the University of California, Arizona, and an M. Arch. From Harvard in 1924. He was mainly a

year, and the outlook is very favorable for attaching him permanently to our work. President Park has shown a very fine attitude toward our absorption of Duell, and I have a dream of turning him loose on the Mastabas of Sakkara for a complete edition in color – after he has had a season's experience at Medinet-Habu. This is still confidential, but the prospects for securing the funds are good.

Again, with all good wishes for the New Year to you and yours, I am | Very sincerely yours | JHB

P.S. – Since dictating the preceding letter, Miss Swindler's book has arrived, and I want to express to you again my appreciation of the sumptuous gift of the volume which you have so kindly sent me. I did not realize that Miss Swindler had attempted quite so comprehensive a task. It is an impressive achievement and I can understand that you must be very gratified that such a creditable piece of work should have been accomplished by one of your own students. I can readily understand that the dedication also is a source of real gratification to you. I shall, of course, be writing to Miss Swindler also.

I think she has done very well in handling the difficult and complicated matter of Oriental archaeology. It makes me regret the more that in the Philadelphia discussion last spring I spent so much time on the Prehistoric Survey that there was none left for proper presentation of the chronology of the historic age. I am still without the slightest doubt that the cultural development in the Nile Valley is much earlier than the Tigris-Euphrates Valley, and I have noticed with interest that in Gadd's new book on the Monuments of Ur he does not accept the early dates of Woolley, Hall and others.

Again thanking you for your beautiful gift, I remain | Very gratefully yours | JHB

---

classical archaeologist, and worked at the University of Cincinnati from 1925-26 and Bryn Mawr from 1927-29. He became the Field Director of the Chicago expedition at Saqqara in 1930-1936, then became a research fellow at the Fogg Art Museum at Harvard from 1936-1960.

22 February 1930                                              **0186**

La Solana Hotel | Pasadena,
California | February 22, 1930

CONFIDENTIAL

My dear Mrs. Williams:
You will recall the Palestine tomb treasure in our collections which we
purchased in New York. We are now informed that there was evidently
some illegality in their export from Palestine and I have been notified in
advance that a request is to be made to us by the Palestine Government
that we allow the dealer from whom we purchased it to repurchase the
treasure from us.

Apart from the lamentable loss to America of such valuable material,
the situation at once raises the question of publication. If the treasure
goes back to Jerusalem it is obvious that there is nobody there who will
be competent to publish this unique material. Even if there is, there is no
likelihood that there would be anybody who would be interested to do it or
the funds to subsidize the publication would be available. I am proposing,
therefore, to suggest to the Palestine Government that the treasure be
left in America to insure its adequate publication, and my son Charles
will carry this proposal to the High Commissioner's Office in Jerusalem.[212]
Charles is expecting to sail on the Ile France on March 7th and I supposed
will be leaving Chicago March 5th. I take it you will have discerned already
why I am troubling you with this letter. I am raising the question whether
you would not be able to undertake the publication of this unique treasure.
The practical arrangements would not be difficult. We could have our
preparatory build a small box with trays and compartments which would
contain the entire treasure, for it is not large. This box perhaps Mr. Williams
would be willing to safeguard in his business vault and this would enable
you to keep out one piece at a time for your work, which you could do at
home. The necessary photographing which you would want to have done
we could undertake at Chicago after you had indicated just what negatives
you would like to have made, and if you wanted a number of color plates for

---

[212] This would have been Sir John Chancellor.

the publication that could also be arranged.

Regarding financial arrangements in remuneration for your work, I have not the slightest idea what would be appropriate, for of course I do not know how much time the entire task would consume or, even assuming that you would be able to undertake the task, what proportion of your time you would be able to devote to the work from week to week. If the plan proves feasible, however, I would be grateful for your suggestions on this question and I should hope that our budget would be equal to any appropriate remuneration for the valuable labor you would be putting into this task.

Will you, therefore, kindly think the matter over bearing in mind especially the fact that this treasure is likely to return to the East to be in all probability about as fully lost to Science as if it had never been found, whereas, if you publish it we shall be able to rescue it from oblivion. It will be very useful to Charles at Jerusalem if he can have your reply before he leaves America, and as I said above I think you can reach him in Chicago any time before the 5th of March.

With kindest regards to you and Mr. Williams, and sincerely hoping that your present numerous obligations may not prevent you from assuming one more, I am | Very sincerely yours | JHB

P.S. Frances and I are trying to take a little vacation here in California, but so many Institute affairs are pressing me here that the vacation is rapidly becoming nominal. Please do not trouble to write two letters, I mean one to Charles and one to me. It will be quite sufficient if you send a little note of your decision to Charles only. Frances joins me in warmest greetings to you both. J. H. B.

**5 March 1930**                                                          **0187**

The Chesbrough Dwellings |
Toledo, Ohio | March 5, 1930

My dear Professor Breasted:-

I wish to thank you for the delightful opportunity tentatively and conditionally offered to me in your kind letter of February 22nd sent from Pasadena.

I wrote at once to Charles as you asked me to do and have received his acknowledgement of my reply. I intended to send you a copy of my letter, but, as Charles wrote that he was forwarding the letter to you, to do so would now be superfluous.

I do not know whether the best I could offer in time under present circumstances will seem to you adequate, in case it becomes possible to publish the jewelry in this country. In all other respects, there should be no difficulty.

I would suggest that in the event of the jewels coming here, the Institute rent a deposit box in its own name in one of the large downtown banks of Toledo, arranging that I have a key and free access to it. My husband would of course be hospitable to anything that you and I wished him to safeguard, but we regard it as a further precaution that the jewels should be by themselves in a deposit box which would never be opened except to gain access to them.

As to remuneration to me, I suppose I ought to charge what the Toledo Museum pays me, and likewise the Metropolitan Museum—even for work such as yours leading to publication—namely five hundred dollars a month, but if I were to undertake your jewelry, and the costs were mounting beyond what seemed to you reasonable, I would gladly throw in enough unsalaried time to make them what they should be. I wish I could say that I would make no charge, but the circumstances make it difficult for me to do this. My husband, who is seven years older than I am, wishes to retire as soon as he has provided adequately for our older years. Neither one of us has any pension to look forward to, and I must therefore make my work in Egyptology carry its own expenses, and I am even glad when I can contribute a bit to the family budget. I have never known a time when books on Egyptian subjects, to speak of only one of my items of expense, and the binding of books were so costly. Some things which I need among the older publications to make my working facilities first class cost individually a small fortune when at last one finds copies. But the greatest fun I have, aside from the pleasure of the work itself, is in improving my working library.[213] I have the collector's passion in trying to run down desirable things. I want to say that the salary paid me by the two institutions named was determined respectively by Mr. Godwin, Director of the local museum, and by Mr. Lythgoe, and is more than I had dared to hope for. While it would seem to me now perhaps unfair to them to undertake new work on a different basis, I recognize that remuneration cannot be judged solely by time, and at any time, for you or them, I should wish to bring the results for a given salary full up to expectations that you or they would have by unsalaried supplementary work rather than to have any piece of work of mine cost any institution an excessive amount. So practically the remuneration for this proposed possible task lies entirely with you to determine, which is as it should be.

I very much appreciated the long letter in which you told me some of the considerations entering into your employment of Dr. Frankfort in Mesopotamia. And I was delighted at your thought possibly to arrange later to send Herr Höllscher to Amarna. The place needs just such an experienced excavator with an architect's insight. I hate to see first one beginner and then another getting his training at the expense of Amarna. Thank you for your kind interest in my study of the Amarna material in the Metropolitan Museum. I have now completed two articles on it, one of which is already in galley proof; both are to appear in the <u>Metropolitan Museum Studies</u>, the first in the spring, the second next autumn.[214] Of course I shall send them to you. I have not failed to note that both your tentative suggestion about Amarna and your recent letter about the Palestinian jewelry are confidential.

At least you and Mrs. Breasted must be deriving some climatic benefits from the sojourn in California, if not all the rest you had hoped for. My love to Frances and kindest regards from us all to you both.

With much appreciation of your letters and the best of wishes |

---

[213] In the end, she had a wonderful library with over 700 volumes that she donated to the MMA in 1943.

[214] See note, above.

Egypt Dept

CAROLINE RANSOM
WILLIAMS

LIBRARY

OF

EGYPTOLOGY

PRESENTED
TO THE
METROPOLITAN
MUSEUM OF ART
MCMXLIII

141487

FIGURE 4: BOOKPLATE FROM A BOOK DONATED TO THE MMA'S
EGYPTIAN ART DEPARTMENT BY RANSOM WILLIAMS. COURTESY
CHARLES JONES, ANCIENT WORLD BLOGGERS GROUP.

Ever gratefully yours | Caroline Ransom Williams

One of my tasks for the M. M. A. is a new edition of the Menthu-weser
Stela, the first being exhausted. The proof of a colored frontispiece which it
is to have has just come from Max Jaffé of Vienna.

11 March 1930                                                    0188

408 S. Orange Grove Ave. | Pasadena,
California | March 11, 1930

My dear Mrs. Williams:

It has been a great pleasure to me to have your kind letter of March 5th preceded by your earlier letter to Charles, which he at once forwarded to me.

I wish that people like you and me, whose interest in any work on ancient human life is the supreme thing, never had to talk about finances and could always depend upon an inexhaustible bank account for buying books. Your suggestion of an arrangement for our work on the same basis as that which the Toledo Museum and the Metropolitan are paying is perfectly satisfactory and I would understand, then, that in order to put this arrangement through I would be adding one thousand dollars a year to our present salary budget for the support of this work on the Palestine jewelry.

The present arrangement is that Charles will confer with the British High Commissioner, Sir John Chancellor, and ascertain if any arrangement would be possible which would enable us to retain the jewelry long enough to have this work done. My only fear is that he would not want to extend the arrangement beyond this year, and that if you found two months insufficient for completing the work we might not be able to finish it. The Institute would be very glad to pay your travelling expenses if some time between now the next autumn you could visit Chicago and look over the materials and thus be able to make a more precise forecast of the amount of time the work would be likely to consume. It may, of course, meantime fall out that all our efforts in this direction are futile, for if the High Commissioner in Palestine were dangerous, we might not be able to keep it for the desired two months' work on your part, but we shall have this all settled within the next sixty days.

I am delighted to hear you are now about to issue two articles on the Amarna material in the Metropolitan Museum. There has been so little close and accurate work done on Amarna Art that your studies will be very welcome. It is fine that you are to give us a new edition of the Menth-weser-Stela with a colored frontispiece from Max Jaffé. I think we shall be obliged

time (pp. 256-7).[216]

I have been wishing for some time to write to you about other matters, but must defer doing so yet a few days. I wonder if you are enduring the general extreme heat in Chicago or in some more favorable place. We are inclined to think that home has certain advantages under such conditions. All July records in this city were broken by 102.4 degrees yesterday, and all records for the number of continuous days of abnormal temperature here have been exceeded this month. I have thought especially of Frances since she wrote me that she had not been quite well, and I do hope you and she have not found the torrid weather too trying.

Again my most deep-felt thanks for your valuable and welcome volumes which I shall treasure and profit by all the rest of my days.

Sincerely and always appreciatively yours | Caroline Ransom Williams

**30 July 1930**                                                    **0192**

July 30, 1930

My dear Mrs. Williams:

Acknowledgements of acknowledgements, if carried on indefinitely, might be embarrassing, but I cannot forbear thanking you for your most kind letter of July 21st, regarding the <u>Surgical Papyrus</u>. It is very gratifying to know that you are finding it useful.

If it has not already been sent, our University Press will be forwarding to you in a few days a copy of <u>Medinet Habu Volume I</u>, in which it gives us great pleasure to remember that you had a share. As one of the co-authors of the book, therefore, you need not write any letter of acknowledgement, which will relieve you of another letter in this hot summer weather! I am sure that you will take great pleasure in the appearance of the volume. We have already received some intimations of the effect on the Service des Antiquités in Cairo, who are now as actively engaged as possible in interpreting the word 'administration' to mean 'obstruction!'

I am so sorry to hear that you are suffering from the same kind of torrid weather which we have been having. We are planning to escape for

---

[216] Hermann Junker, *Gîza I. Band I: Die Mastabas der IV. Dynastie auf dem Westfriedhof* (Wien und Leipzig: Hölder-Pichler-Tempsky A.-G., 1929).

a month at Estes Park, and are leaving tomorrow. I wish that we might see you and Mr. Williams out there.

Again thanking you for your gracious letter, which has given me the deepest pleasure, and with kind greetings to your mother and Mr. Williams as well as yourself, believe me | Very sincerely yours | JHB

**31 July 1930**                                                              **0193**

The Chesbrough Dwellings |
Toledo, Ohio | July 31, 1930

Dear Professor Breasted:-

What a wonderful summer this is for the Oriental Institute, with the starting of its new building and the publication of two such important works as yours on the Edwin Smith papyrus and the first volume of Medinet Habu. You must feel that after the years of preliminary labor things are coming to pass, and be much gratified by these consummations of your far-seeing plans.

I do not know how to thank you enough for your generosity to me in sending me this second gift of a valuable volume. You can imagine possibly with what eagerness I turned its beautiful plates, and how well I understand what work has gone into them. I am most proud of my own modest connection with this first volume, and thank you for including me so kindly and generously—beyond my deserts, I feel—in your editorship of the volume.

I was disappointed not to see Mr. Nelson when he was in this country. I shall write my congratulations to him in the autumn when he is back at Chicago House.

The volume seems to me most satisfactory. It makes a very pleasant first impression in its combination of color plates, line plates, and photographic plates. That winter when I was in the counsels, it was still uncertain how many photographic details could be included, and I was agreeably surprised to find so many. I think the whole thing is just right to satisfy everybody's needs. The quality of the plates is superb, and I admire too the binding chosen for the Institute's publications. These fine volumes in press work and quality of plates and paper bear comparison with the best issued by any other institution, and that I doubt not is a matter of pride to you.

Please accept my heartiest congratulations on this successful beginning of the definitive Medinet Habu publications. I found your Foreword most interesting. I feel that Professor Hoelscher's contribution, too, is going to be one of great value. I read the preliminary account of his conclusions about the palace with much interest.

Again, Mr. Breasted, my warmest and most appreciative thanks for your great kindness in sending me this publication.

Ever sincerely yours | Caroline R. Williams


**9 October 1930**                                                   **0194**

The Chesbrough Dwellings |
Toledo, Ohio | October 9, 1930

Dear Professor Breasted:-

I have been delayed in sending you this Separate. First, the Separates were not issued to the contributors until a month after the journal appeared, then it was summer, and I heard that you were away on a motoring trip, next that you had gone to Estes Park. Further, I wished to send a letter with the Separate, and I spent much of September in New York. I am sending a second copy for the Oriental Institute's Department library.[217] The English forms used in my paper are due to Dr. Bull's editing.

I should so much like to know whether you still have in mind possibly to offer to cooperate with the Egypt Exploration Society in finishing the excavation of El 'Amarneh. Singularly enough, after my article appeared, Dr. Frankfort appealed to me to try to find American support for the excavations at El 'Amarneh. His estimate is that it would take seven years at the rate of £3000 a year to finish the site. Perhaps he may have said or written all this to you, but on the other hand he may not have felt at liberty to do so. I only hope you will not think my zeal for this cause excessive. As I understand it, next winter season is provided for in a small way, and I wish I did not feel so reluctant to see young Mr. Pendlebury on his own there. I

---

[217] CRW sent separates of the Amarna articles, see above note for citations.

ought perhaps to state that Mr. Frankfort was very careful to state that he could not speak officially for the Egypt Exploration Society, nevertheless he did not believe funds would be forthcoming from England without encouragement and aid from America for future work on the site.

I have been interested to hear from Mary Swindler that you have taken on Mr. Duell, and that he is to work at Sakkara. I hope he will settle all the problems of Old Kingdom technique which I have had to leave more or less in the air with no chance to work at Sakkara or return to Gīzeh. My 'Paper' on Per-neb's technique and color conventions will probably go to press in December. I am on the last lap with it. It has been much delayed by my working on 'Amarneh material. I can produce only about so much with the constant outside demands on me. Next week I must lecture at the Art Museum to try to help Toledoans appreciate the current exhibition of Davies copies of Theban wall paintings lent by the Metropolitan Museum.

I hear once in a while from the Ermans, the last time was by postcard from the Harz mountains where they were having fog and drizzle, but wrote: Es is doch schön da wir uns vor dem Wetter nicht scheuen.[218]

I think often of you and of Frances, always with admiration and the most earnest wishes for your good health and the success of all your enterprises so important to the future of Oriental studies.

Most sincerely yours | Caroline R. Williams

**14 October 1930**                                              **0195**

October 14, 1930

My dear Mrs. Williams:

It is so kind of you to have sent me a copy of your delightful essay on the Wall Decorations at El Amarneh. I appreciate also your goodness in sending another copy for the library, which we are cataloging with much satisfaction. I am very anxious to read the essay and want to thank you for your thoughtfulness in putting in the Photostats, which will be very handy for quick reference.

I am deeply interested in the question you raise regarding the

---

[218] 'It is nice because we are not afraid of the weather.'

completion of the excavation at Amarneh. I find both in my own experience and that of others that international cooperation in excavation is an experience not without its difficulties. The only such combination which the Institute is now carrying on is the publication of the Seti Temple at Abydos. In this task, however, the Institute is leaving the actual field work entirely to the E. E. S., and this arrangement has of course enabled us to avoid a good deal of complication. But even so you would be astonished at the difficulties which have arisen. I wish we might some time have a talk about it.

I feel, therefore, very hesitant about suggesting a combination at Amarneh. We have, as you know, the most cordial relations with our English colleagues, but I do not think they should have taken Amarneh away from the Germans unless they were very certain they had the funds to finish. The E. E. S. has now of course acquired priority rights in the site, although Alan Gardiner has told me repeatedly that he has urged the Society to pull out. There has been a tremendous struggle within the Society over the question of applying their funds – that is, as between excavation and the old Archaeological Survey work of copying. Gardiner of course favors the copying, and it was because he approached me in the matter that I finally brought up the question with Mr. Rockefeller on behalf of the Seti Temple.

I fear it sounds very chauvinistic, or perhaps selfish, if I say that nothing would suit me better than for the Institute to continue the job at Amarneh, of course using Hoelscher, who has done very brilliant work at Medinet Habu. But I shrink more and more from international combinations. The <u>excavation</u> work at Medinet Habu is absorbing all the available funds we have for this purpose at present, but we are likely to finish there in another season, or season and a half; and if the outlook improves it is barely possible that we might endeavor to make some arrangement with the E. E. S. for working at Amarneh.

With reference to Mr. Duell and our proposed edition of the Sakkara Mastaba scenes let me say that Mr. Rockefeller has pledged the funds for issuing a series of folios of the size of our <u>Medinet Habu</u> Volume I, to be done <u>in color</u>. You can imagine the pleasure with which I greeted this gift and the anticipation with which I have looked forward to seeing the work done. You can likewise perhaps picture the disgust with which I have received a letter from our former colleague, the illustrious Lacau, refusing us the concession!

As you of course know, practically every nation of Europe has done work in the Sakkara Cemetery, and the tombs have been copied and published with varying degrees of success or failure by Englishmen, Frenchmen, Belgians and Germans. Likewise, the photographers of Cairo have been given free access and have photographed them to their heart's content and hawked the photographs on the streets. Lacau's basis for refusing to allow an American expedition to make a definitive publication in color was based in his official letter on the statement that the Service would like to do it, using a corps of young Egyptians! Meantime, the Cairo Institut, now as you know, under Jouguet,[219] a most charming fellow, has long desired to copy and publish the Sakkara tombs. I have an amiable letter from Montet,[220] relinquishing any rights they may have had in copying in the Sakkara Cemetery, and urging us to leave out the Tomb of Ti, which he has already partially copied, and allow the French Institut to publish it. It might be said in conclusion that neither Lacau nor Montet knew that our proposed edition was to be in color. I think that a diplomatic handling of Lacau will result in our being allowed to go on. I think he would find it difficult to maintain his opposition to an American scientific expedition after the amount of work done by Europeans, not to add Cairo photographers.

I am delighted to hear that your paper on the technique and color conventions in the Perneb Tomb will be going to press in December. I have no doubt that it will be of the greatest value to us in our effort to publish the Sakkara tombs and I am very glad that we can put it into Duell's hands before he does any work there.

We have just been having a delightful visit from Carl Becker, the Berlin Arabist, who was, like myself, a student under Sachau, and now holds Sachau's chair at Berlin. Just before the German Revolution Becker's unusual administrative abilities carried him into the post of Kultus-Minister.

---

[219] Pierre Félix Amédée Jouguet (1869-1949) was a French Hellenist and Egyptologist who first went to Egypt to study Graeco-Roman sites in 1894. He lectured at the Sorbonne from 1919-28 then moved to the Institut at Cairo until 1940; he was Professor at the University of Cairo 1937-49.

[220] Jean Pierre Marie Montet (1885-1966) was a French Egyptologist who had studied under Loret at Lyons, then worked at the Institut in Cairo from 1910-14. His most important archaeological work was at Tanis, from 1929-40, 1945-51, 1955-56, where he found the greatest number of untouched royal burials in Egypt. He found four tombs and two princes, kings Psusennes, Osorkon II, and Sheshonk III, all of which are now in the Cairo Museum.

He held that post for fourteen years, and such was his skill and strength of character that he saved the German universities from destruction as a result of the absurd innovations which the Social Democrats would have put through. He also revolutionized the German schools. It seemed strange to have an Arabist lecture here on the general problems of education. We heard much of the inside of the present political situation in Germany, and I wish we might have a talk about it. You will be interested to know that he spoke with the greatest cordiality of Erman, and stated that Erman stood by him, thought all the older men regarded him (Becker) as an enemy of the universities.

Frances returned home yesterday from the hospital where she had her tonsils out. This was due to an effort to counteract an arthritis affection in the right hip. She is now on crutches, but within the next fortnight will be equipped with an appliance which she will have to wear day and night but which will supersede the crutches. She is in good spirits and otherwise in excellent health. She joins me in warmest greetings to you and your mother and Mr. Williams. I wish we might soon see you there.

Believe me | Very sincerely yours | JHB

P. S. Since dictating the above letter, I have had put into my hands a letter from Montet addressed to a Chicago woman of his acquaintance in the hope that she may be able to induce the hard-hearted Oriental Institute to desist from publishing the Tomb of Ti. The latter is amusingly infantile, but in it Montet makes an important statement, which I quote:

'La plupart de ces tombeaux ont été trouves par Mariette et d-autres Français, J[acques]. de Morgan et Loret, mais maintenant ils sont dans le domaine public et tout let monde a le droit de les reproduire.'[221]

---

[221] 'Most of these tombs were found by Mariette and other Frenchmen, J[acques]. de Morgan and Loret, but now they are in the public domain and everyone has the right to reproduce them.'

**13 November 1930**                                                  **0196**

November 13, 1930

My dear Mrs. Williams:

Referring again to your inquiry about Amarna, I fear that with a man's proverbial obtuseness I really did not grasp the full purport of your question. I wonder if you were tactfully inquiring about the intentions of the Institute in respect of Amarna in the hope that the place might be open for an expedition from the Toledo Museum. I trust that any hopes I expressed regarding the possibility of our doing work there may not in the least deter you if a Toledo Expedition might be in prospect.

There is only one further important point, however, to which I would like to refer in this connection. I fear our English friends do not yet realize how much it costs to run a really well-manned and well equipped expedition, and the $15,000 a year mentioned by Frankfort as the amount which he expected the E. E. S. to put into the Amarna work, is in my judgment far too little. The English are running all their expeditions, owing to financial stringency, without the needed architectural and photographic help, to say nothing of draftsmen and assistants in registering and carrying on the daily records.

In any case, I merely want to make it clear that I shall be delighted if you were contemplating an effort at Amarna on behalf of the Toledo Museum.

With kindest regards to you and your mother and Mr. Williams, in which Frances joins me, I am | Very sincerely yours | JHB

**14 November 1930**                                                  **0197**

The Chesbrough Dwellings | Toledo, Ohio | November 14, 1930

My dear Professor Breasted:-

Your most kind and welcome letter of October 14th ought to have been acknowledged immediately. I cannot tell you how much pleasure it gave me to come again somewhat in touch with your work. It seems ages since I have seen you and Frances, and now you have a new building under way and all sorts of changes in personnel and conditions of work at Chicago.

That I did not at once write again was due to pressure of trying to get some manuscript off to New York the first week of December. For reasons of budget, to have the publication costs come out of this year's appropriation, I am supposed to deliver my text before the Trustees' last meeting in mid-December, and I really need more time! The study of color-conventions has involved me in theories of color vision requiring knowledge outside of Egyptological training, and I have to seek help from busy people whom I do not like to bother. I feel the need of being most cautious where natural sciences are concerned. When I finished the jewelry book, I vowed I would never again attempt anything which took me outside of Egyptology proper, and now I am in a worse scrape than that book was!

One point in doubt I have settled, namely that Per-neb's blue pigment is not a cobalt blue as Mr. Maximilian Toch in New York proclaimed it to be, an opinion given much publicity by Mr. Lucas in his writings. On the contrary it is the 'Egyptian,' or 'Vestorian,' blue, the copper calcium silicate studied by Fouqué and Laurie and which has interested students of pigments since the beginning of the last century. Mr. Lucas (Materials) knows no example of it earlier than the XIth dynasty, but the German chemist, Dr. Eibner, identified it in samples from the Nuserre Sun temple and an Ann Arbor chemist has identified it for me in samples from Per-neb's tomb.

A curious situation exists about backgrounds. Mr. Lucas maintains that there was no burning of limestone for lime in Egypt until Roman times, that all mortar and plaster were gypsum and that when calcium carbonate occurs, it is there as an impurity. Herr Eibner (and Miss Swindler in her book on painting has followed him) talks constantly of lime and gypsum grounds, sometimes the one, sometimes the other, being used. Rählmann supposed gypsum to be characteristic of the Old Kingdom and lime to supersede it in the Empire, but Eibner, on the basis of forty unimpeachable samples sent him from Berlin, thinks both materials were used from the Old Kingdom on. I cannot deal with the general question, but even settling it for Per-neb's tomb is not wholly simple, due to paucity of samples at this late date. The mortar-plaster used in Per-neb's tomb before the sculptor began his work was certainly gypsum, the fine patching plaster used to make good defects in the carving, a plaster worked in a soft state as its smeared look proves, was probably a mixture of powdered limestone and gypsum, and

I have yet to find out—if I can—whether the fine film of glistening white which immediately underlay the colors was whiting or refined plaster of Paris. The test is simple enough, provided a sample can be isolated, but only a microchemical method will serve in this case. I am recopying my manuscript (which has been furnished once to the end) these days, taking up doubtful questions further as best I can.

About Amarna, my remarks really were only incidental to sending you a Separate of my article. I wish our Toledo Museum would do something so worth while for Egyptology, but I believe its funds are not available for excavations, and to seek funds in the city might seem to rival the Waterman excavations which I should not like to do. I believe I had a vague notion of trying to interest Mr. Winlock, if you did not hope to act in the matter. Amarna needs organized resources back of it, but I dare say a Museum would find it even more difficult than a University to enter on an international undertaking. If the English give up the concession, I wonder if it would be granted to Americans. The discovery of Amarna art at Assiout is a new interest. Both Professor Ranke and Dr. Keimer wrote me of the paper read at M. Capart's Egyptological week by Dr. Samy 'Gabra.[222]

Your Sakkara enterprise is even more important and thorough-going than I had supposed. When the proper time comes, if you want them, I should be glad to tell you of some questions which seem to me to need attention, but which I am not in a position to attack. And if you are to be in Chicago this winter (I am wondering if the new building will keep you there), may I go on some time for a day or two to use the library at a time when you would be free for some talk of evenings?

Who do you suppose will succeed Mr. H. R. Hall[223] in the British

---

[222] Sami 'Gabra (1892-1979) was an Egyptian archaeologist who began as a lawyer but soon shifted to study under Ahmad Kamal at the Ecole Normal in Cairo. He continued his studies at Liverpool from 1923-25 and at the Sorbonne from 1925-28. He was a curator at the Cairo Museum from 1928-30 and then Professor of Ancient Egyptian History at Cairo University from 1930-1952. Later on, he was a visiting professor at the Oriental Institute in 1952-53.

[223] Henry Reginald Holland Hall (1873-1930) was a British Egyptologist and historian. He studied classics at Oxford as well as Egyptian language and history under Griffith while there, getting his BA in 1895, MA in 1897, and his DLitt in 1920. He was an assistant to Budge at the British Museum in 1896; became Assistant Keeper in the Department of Egyptian and Assyrian Antiquities in 1919, then Keeper from 1924-1930. He excavated in Egypt and wrote a number of works on the history and archaeology of the Ancient Near East.

Museum? Has Mr. Glanville[224] the position and influence to be appointed to it? Eduard Meyer's[225] death must have come close to Professor Erman, for the two men were nearly the same age and life-long associates in the university. It rather shocks me to have Frau Erman write of always accompanying her husband when he goes to Academy meetings or to the University, but I suppose that is more because of his defective eyesight than general frailty.

I was much interested in what you wrote of former Cultusminister Becker's stay in Chicago. By the New York paper, I saw yesterday that he is sailing today on the Bremen, and that he has lectured too at Columbia.

Please believe me most appreciative of your two recent letters. With the kindest greetings from us all to you and Mrs. Breasted,

Most sincerely yours | Caroline Ransom Williams


**14 January 1931**                                                  **0198**


The Chesbrough Dwellings |
Toledo, Ohio | January 14, 1931

Dear Professor Breasted:-

Separates have just reached me of my second 'Amarneh article, and I am sending two herewith, one for you, the other from the Chicago library of the Oriental Institute.[226]

The two other 'Amarneh articles which I am expected to write for the Studies are temporarily shelved to enable me to get the monograph on color finished. These two articles have cost more time than you would

---

[224] Stephen Ranulph Kingdon Glanville (1900-1956) was a British Egyptologist. He was a Modern History Scholar at Oxford, receiving his BA in 1922 and MA in 1926. He studied under Griffith, and excavated at Amarna with the EES in 1923. He was appointed Assistant Keeper in the Department of Egyptian and Assyrian Antiquities in 1924 under Hall. He became Reader (1933-35) then Edwards Professor of Egyptology at University College, London (1935-46). He left UCL in 1946 to become Herbert Thompson Professor of Egyptology at Cambridge (1946-56).

[225] Eduard Meyer (1855-1930) was a German historian of the Near East. He was a leading historian of the period, often placed alongside JHB and Maspero in terms of expertise and impact.

[226] See citation, above.

suppose that they ought to take because the pieces that I handled are very numerous and desperately broken.

I have read in the papers with pleasure and interest of your election to the French Academy. I should think that would be the one among your many honors to give you the greatest satisfaction—at least I fancy I should value it even more than an Oxford degree.

My last letter from Frau Erman begged for news of you, and my last from Professor Erman, written New Year's Day, told of the advent of a new little grandson, Doris's child, at the moment in Dahlem to be baptized there, but to remain perforce yet a while in Heide, several members of the family, including his father, one sister, and grandmother, being ill in bed with the grippe.

I trust that all is well with you and Frances personally. We all appreciated your Christmas cards and unite in good wishes to you both for 1931. Miss Randolph is still with us but goes east on the 27th.

Ever with kindest regards | Sincerely yours | Caroline R. Williams

**22 January 1931**                                                 **0199**

January 22, 1931

Dear Mrs. Williams:

I am so glad to have the continuation of your work on the Amarna remains. You know how interested I am in the whole subject of Ikhnaton's revolution; and the studies you are now making, such as the one you have so kindly sent me, will be of the greatest assistance to me.

It was very thoughtful of you to send us a second copy for the Institute Library, which of course I am gratefully handing to our librarians. Many, many thanks.

I have about finished a new edition of <u>Ancient Times</u> and I am now hoping to begin at once a revision of my <u>History of Egypt</u>, and it is at this point that your new Amarna Studies will be exceedingly useful to me. I hope that the postponement of the final study, due to your monograph on color, may not defer it too long for me to use it in this history revision.

Many thanks for your kind references to my election to the French Academy. Morally it has done me a great deal of good. I fear that our treatment at the hands of Lacau has led me to unjustly harsh judgments about our French colleagues. I was very fond of Benedite[227] and I felt his loss very deeply. Moret, his successor in the Academy, is also a very charming fellow, and he wrote me a most delightful note. I am coming to feel, at least <u>want</u> to feel, that Lacau is an exception. His action in the case of Sakkara leaves a very bitter taste in one's mouth. He has come to his senses, and Charles has succeeded in getting our concession at Sakkara arranged. Duell is beginning work there now, in so far as I know the situation. But it took considerable building of back fires to bring Lacau around.

It seems that one of our letters to the Ermans miscarried, as did one of theirs to us. But we have now had charming Christmas letters from them.

Our new Institute building is gradually nearing completion, and is promised to us on the first of March. We are all quite excited about it. I wish you and Mr. Williams could run up here after we are settled and have a look around at our new work shop. There are many things that I would like to discuss with you, -problems of lighting sculpture and a thousand questions of installation, which no amount of museum experience ever seems satisfactorily to settle.

It was very pleasant to have your Christmas greetings. If our building were not in such a chaotic stage I might hope that you and Miss Randolph might see it before she goes east on the 27th.

With warmest greetings to you all, in which Frances joins me, I am | Ever sincerely yours | JHB

(Metropolitan Museum Studies; Separate Reprinted from Volume III, Part I – December, 1930. Two Egyptian Torsos from the Main Temple of the Sun at El Amarneh)

---

[227] Georges Aaron Bénédite (1857-1926) was a French Egyptologist who studied under Maspero from 1881-86, then copied Theban tombs from 1886-88. He became the Conservateur-Adjoint of the Egyptian Art department of the Louvre in 1895, and became Conservateur in 1907.

**30 January 1931**                         **0200**

The Chesbrough Dwellings |
Toledo, Ohio | January 30, 1931

Dear Professor Breasted:

Indeed I do know how interested you are in the whole subject of Ikhnaton's revolution. Was not the king's Sun-hymn the subject long ago of your doctor's dissertation! You were once good enough to give me a copy of it.

It is odd how divergent are the opinions about Ikhnaton. Last September I had a letter from Professor Newberry acknowledging the copy I had sent him of my first Amarna article, and in his letter he said: 'I hope soon to publish a paper on Ay and Ty with some new ideas. Akhenaten himself I dislike more and more as I study the period.'

For my part, I still subscribe to the conception of Ikhnaton which you set forth, and one of my most compelling reasons for doing so is the character of the portraits which he inspired. To me the Berlin head, inventory number 21348, is one of the very moving works of portraiture of all time. I wish we had the intact portrait of Petrie, <u>Tell el Amarna</u>, Pl. I, 15, now in the Metropolitan Museum, which surely represents the king, not the queen, and is of high quality. I am to take it up in my next Amarna article, but I do not know when that will be written. Having turned to the old Kingdom, I rather stay there now, for I am keen to study the fragments of royal reliefs reused at Lisht, which are to form a volume in the Museum's Excavations Series, in the format of the <u>Tomb of Senebtisi.</u>

How good that your work at Sakkara is to proceed.

I should indeed love to see your new building in the Spring.

With much appreciation of your welcome letter and kindest greetings from us all to you and Mrs. Breasted | Sincerely yours | Caroline R. Williams

**23 February 1931**                        **0201**

February 23, 1931

Dear Mrs. Williams:

It is a great pleasure to have your letter of January 30th and to know that you still feel some loyalty toward Ikhnaton. Of course Budge's disparaging remarks about anything or anybody would be merely amusing. Hall showed quite clearly that he was not envisaging the facts when he wrote of Ikhnaton. I feel that the same is true with my good friend Newberry. The known facts, in my judgment, still disclose the most powerfully individualistic mind that the Ancient World ever saw, until the rise of the Hebrew prophets.

We are hoping to see you in Chicago later this spring.

With kindest greetings to you all | Sincerely yours | JHB

**30 June 1931**                                                    0202

June 30, 1931

Dear Mrs. Williams:

You may be interested to know that in looking over some of Goodwin's papers for an article on Goodwin the Englishman, Warren R. Dawson,[228] has discovered three letters written to Goodwin by Edwin Smith. Dawson is going to edit these letters of Smith's and we shall publish them in facsimile form in the Oriental Institute Communications.

I find that as a matter of fact we are doing most of the editing for Dawson ourselves, but he writes us that he has no copy of your article on the early Egyptologists of America from the <u>Bulletin of the New York Historical Society</u> of April, 1920, and consequently he is not acquainted with the new facts which you have brought out on Edwin Smith. I am wondering if you still have an extra copy of the <u>Bulletin</u>, and whether you would kindly let us have one to forward to Dawson. I regret that we have only one copy here.

We are sailing from New York on July third, and leaving Chicago on Wednesday, July 1st. By 'we' I mean Frances and Astrid. I am being taken on a conducted tour by them to the fjords of Norway for nearly a month, and after that we are going down to Berlin where we shall arrive about the eighth of August.

I am inclined to think that yesterday morning you received a postcard very similar to one that I received, in dear old Erman's handwriting,

---

[228] Warren R. Dawson (1888-1968) got involved in Egyptology a little before World War I. He had some medical training and worked on mummies with Grafton Elliot Smith as well as publishing on a number of different subjects. He was Treasurer of the EES for 5 years, starting in 1917.

announcing the completion of the <u>Wörterbuch</u>! Mine was dated the 16th of June, but it bore pathetic evidence of the old man's failing eyesight, for in writing the top line of the postcard his pen ran off the upper edge twice.

I am sorry that we are not to see you or any of your family before we go. We shall not be returning until early October. With kindest regards and all good wishes for a pleasant vacation to you all, I am

Very sincerely yours | JHB

**30 June 1931**                                                **0203**

The Chesbrough Dwellings |
Toledo, Ohio | June 30, 1931

Dear Professor Breasted:-

I am sending you herewith copies for yourself and the Oriental Institute library of the limestone statue-head which you were so kind as to help me buy for the Toledo Museum, as now briefly published by the Museum.[229]

I trust that you and your family are having a good summer despite the present heat. After five months when it had been lying about editorial offices awaiting attention, I received back from New York the other day the typescript of my book on Per-nēb's decoration and am now hard at work going over it, as I hope, for the last time.

With the kindest greetings to you all from our family | Ever sincerely yours | Caroline R. Williams

**1 July 1931**                                                **0204**

The Chesbrough Dwellings |
Toledo, Ohio | July 1, 1931

Dear Professor Breasted:-

Your request for my April, 1920, article in the <u>N. Y. Hist. Soc. Bulletin</u> came in this morning, and I am sending you the only extra copy I have left. It could not be put to a better use. This will not reach you before you sail, but I

---

[229] CRW, 'An Egyptian Limestone Head,' *Toledo Museum of Art Museum News* 60 (June 1931), 2.

take it that someone in Chicago, perhaps Charles, will attend to forwarding the article.

It has been a pleasure to us to hear of your 'personally conducted' trip and intended visit to Berlin.

Sincerely yours | Caroline R. Williams

**5 December 1931**                                     0205

Toledo, Ohio | 1931 Dec 5 PM 2 07

Professor James H. Breasted
Director of Oriental Institute University of Chicago
Congratulations and best wishes to you and your scientific staff
        Caroline & Grant Williams

**11 December 1931**                                    0206

December 11, 1931

Dear Friends:

It was a great pleasure to have your kind telegram at the opening of our new Institute building, and it was a real encouragement to know that our friends are interested. I hope that you both will come up to Chicago some time in the near future so that I may have the great pleasure of taking you through the building.

Mrs. Breasted joins me in warmest good wishes to you both.

Very sincerely yours | JHB

**17 April 1932**                                                    **0207**

The Chesbrough Dwellings |
Toledo, Ohio | April 17, 1932

My dear Professor Breasted:-

The beautiful volume II of the Medinet Habu series presented to me with the compliments of the Oriental Institute came safely the other day and has afforded our whole family immense joy. I thought the first volume a great achievement, but this second volume is even finer in the sheer beauty and complete usefulness of its plates. You may be sure my copy will never have a chance to buckle by being placed upright. I have a good shelf for it made of rollers on ball bearings, and it can be taken in and out easily without strain to the volume.

I am very grateful for this valuable gift, and I think it was a great deal for you to do for me.

I am more than ever impatient for my own book on the technique of wall decorations and on color conventions to come out that I may make some slight and modest return to you and to the Institute by sending you copies of it, but alas, with six Egyptological books going simultaneously through the editorial offices, the Museum in New York will take many months yet, I fear, to bring out my volume.

In the meantime, I have here in Toledo mounted photographs of relief sculpture found at the North Pyramid, Lisht, and I have my summer's work cut out for me in the task of trying to cull out all those of the Old Kingdom. Yesterday I found a fragment of an inscription of the Third or early Fourth Dynasty with the rare titles:

1) ḥḳꜣ nśw.t
2) ḥry mdw
3) imy-rꜣ šnḏ.w nb.w n š rśy (or š.w rśy.w)[230]

---

[230] Hieroglyphs were included in the original letter, so they are included here.

3) 𓄿𓂋𓇳𓈖𓅱𓏏𓈖𓏏

The piece must be roughly contemporary with the tombs of Mtn and '3 iḫ.ty (Berlin and Paris, Weill, II et IIIe dyn. ég., pp. 262-273). Not only the titles, but the form and arrangement of the signs in successive short vertical columns without division lines between is favorable to an early dating of the fragment. Another piece bears the name of Pepy II, hence the range of date for reused Old Kingdom relief from Lisht seems to be III-VI dynasty.

The highly interesting and successful meeting of the American Oriental Society, for which your Institute did so much, lingers in memory giving me much to think about with profit. It also suggested to me getting from the public library some of the books of Sven Hedin, and my husband has taken to his 1925 book, 'My Life as an Explorer,' with avidity, reading it with an atlas spread out on his knees to locate every place mentioned. That for him, and Arthur Waley's Introduction to the Study of Chinese Painting (1923), which I am reading for the first time with exceeding pleasure, and now the new Medinet Habu volume, fill our evenings.

Again, my heartfelt thanks for your generous and most kind gift | Sincerely yours | Caroline Ransom Williams


**17 June 1932**                                                     0208

The Chesbrough Dwellings |
Toledo, Ohio | June 17, 1932

Dear Professor Breasted:-

This morning at the breakfast table I was surprised with letters about my doctor's dissertation published as a book by the University of Chicago Press in 1905.[231] As the book concerned chiefly classical material (a little

---

[231] Caroline L. Ransom, Studies in Ancient Furniture: Couches and Beds of the Greeks, Etruscans and Romans (Chicago: University of Chicago Press, 1905). She dedicated the book to her aunt, Louise Fitz Randolph.

Egyptian, however), you probably will not recall much about it, but I would nevertheless value your advice, if I may have it.

Through Professor Capps's kind interest, the Press gave me as favorable terms as it could, but our family paid the entire cost of publishing the book; through the years since, the Press has sold the book, retaining one-third of the sale price of each copy as its share for storing and marketing the book, and sending me each summer two-thirds of the sale price as my share as owner of the book.

Now suddenly, after an unintelligent effort to reach me, and without doing so, Mr. Hemens waves aside my contract with the Press, declares the book 'out of print,' proposes to give me 'without charge' so many copies of it as I want and to dispose of the rest. Will he sell what I do not take, keeping the sum realized for the Press, or destroy the remaining stock? His letters do not make clear.

My husband is inclined to stand up for the Press, saying that it has to be run as a business institution, and I am sure you know me to be not unreasonable. But are University Presses supposed to be quite so indifferent to all other considerations as are Presses which are purely business houses? I venture to think that my book, even though not a best seller, has not been a discredit to the University, and I do not think writing to the University's graduates in the way Mr. Hemens has to be will bind them in love for their institution. After all, it was something that my father did, to make financially possible the publication of the handsome volume by the University Press.

I certainly have no right to put you to any special trouble and the purpose of this letter is only to ask you whether you see any better way to handle the matter than that which Mr. Hemens proposes. I am naturally not indifferent in these times to the sudden withdrawal of the possibility of recovering in the next decade or so the $462 equity in the volume still remaining to me or at least some part of it. But if the press is not to go on selling the book, do you think that any plan could be reached to give away the copies instead of destroying them?

Because you were away from Chicago, I wrote also to Mr. Laing this morning, and to make the record about the book complete to date, I inclose a copy of my letter to him.

Every sincerely yours | Caroline R. Williams

P.S. I was delighted to receive a card from you and Mrs. Breasted mailed at Harrisburg

(five enclosures)[232]

**7 July 1932**                                                        **0209**

July 7, 1932

My dear Mrs. Williams:

I regret that my absence from home has delayed this reply to your letter of June 17 with accompanying correspondence regarding the treatment of your books by the University of Chicago Press. I must say I am exceedingly vexed at the way in which the whole transaction has been bungled by the Press. I am sending a letter to Mr. Laing, as Editor of the Press, regarding an obviously very much needed improvement in the treatment of such situations.

I have always valued the book so highly and referred to it with such appreciation that I was greatly surprised at the action taken by Press. I regard the action as totally unjustifiable, notwithstanding the fact that the sale of such a book is necessarily limited. If there is anything more than I can do in the matter please do not fail to let me know.

Believe me, with kindest greetings to you and your mother and Mr. Williams, | Always very sincerely yours | JHB

P. S. I am enclosing you herewith a copy of my letter of this date to Dr. Laing.[233]

---

[232] This issue is not strictly between CRW and JHB, so the included enclosures are available in the appendix.

[233] There is no copy of this letter in the correspondence, so it is also not present in the appendix.

8 July 1932                                          0210

The Chesbrough Dwellings |
Toledo, Ohio | July 8, 1932

Dear Professor Breasted:-

Thank you a thousand times for your most kind and understanding letter about my furniture book and for the supporting letter you wrote to Dr. Laing.

When I wrote to Dr. Laing the letter of which I sent you a copy, I was unaware that he stood in the relation of editor to the University of Chicago Press. I have since had a brief note from him dated June 21: 'I have just received your letter about your book on ancient furniture. I will take the matter up with our people here at once and report to you in a few days.' No second letter has come as yet, but I understand from Mr. Hemens's secretary that Mr. Hemens was not to be in his office again until about July 5. Further, the letter which he wrote me on June 20, of which I inclose a copy, takes care of the matter adequately for the time being.

I hate to take your attention further with the book, but I am inclosing the two copies that you may know what has transpired since I last wrote to you. It is not clear to me why, having its warehouses for storage and it organization for book-keeping, the Press should find the remnant of the edition of my book such a burden and expense to it, but I shall drop the matter now, and let the Press do as it likes under Dr. Laing's advice. I am sorry to have made such a to-do about it! And I certainly do not want you to be bothered about the book further.

You may be interested to know that I have just sent back to New York the second page proof of my monograph on Per-nēb's decoration together with galleys of the List of References Cited and the Indexes. There seems now some hope that the book may be out in the autumn.

Some day ere long I shall be writing to Mrs. Breasted whose card sent en route from Bedford, Pennsylvania, I much appreciated.

With kind greetings from all our family | Ever gratefully and sincerely yours | Caroline R. Williams

(two inclosures)[234]

---

[234] We can assume CRW means letters she wrote to Hemens after June 17th, when she wrote

**12 July 1932**                                          0211

July 12, 1932

My dear Mrs. Williams:-

I am very glad to receive copies of further correspondence between yourself and the University of Chicago Press regarding the future of your book. I have not yet heard from Laing but as soon as I do so, if there is anything of importance in connection with it, I will be sure to let you know. I think the attitude of the Press in this case is totally indefensible, not to say also regrettable.

I am delighted to hear that the second page proof of your monograph of Per-neb has already gone back to New York. This will fill a long felt want. Without doubt Duell will be very glad to have it also, to supplement his observations as Sakkara.

With kindest greetings to you all, in which Mrs. Breasted joins, I am always | Very cordially yours | James H. Breasted

**1 October 1932**                                          0212

The Chesbrough Dwellings |
Toledo, Ohio | October 1, 1932

Dear Professor Breasted:-

Just in these days I am in consultation with my friends in the M. M. A. about addresses to which I want copies of my book on Per-neb's decoration (now at last out) sent.

Your copy and one for the Institute's library ought to reach you ere long. The purpose of this letter is to ask you for Mr. Prentice Duell's address. I should like to send him a complimentary copy but do not know whether he is in this country at present or already gone to Egypt. In either case I need to have his precise address, since books are not forwarded the way letters are. Also will you be good enough to tell me whether Mr. William Edgerton and Mr. John Wilson are both in residence in Chicago this autumn, or are abroad, and in the latter case give me their addresses?

I should like to explain that one of the results of the depression is

---

the first letter about this issue. These are in the appendix.

that the Per-neb book had been issued only in paper covers. I have not had the option of getting bound copies for certain people, as I should certainly have done for you had it been possible.

I'm curious as to whether Mr. Glanville of the British Museum is lecturing for you on October 26th. He lectures in Toledo on October 27th and is coming to us via Winnipeg and Chicago. He is to lecture in Ann Arbor after being here and in the Metropolitan Museum on November 5th.

When Frances wrote to me last she asked if I had any recent word from the Ermans. After a long silence a letter came in this morning which makes me sad. Professor Erman's eyes are so bad that he can no longer read his own notes and is dependent on Frau Erman in trying to revise his handbook on Egyptian religion. His <u>Neuägyptische Grammatik</u> is done and will be published in November.[235] In order to remodel for renting a part of their house, he has had to give up his Arbeitszimmer.[236] To be sure, that is just what people, house-owners, all over our city are doing, converting houses formerly occupied in their entirety into 'duplexes,' but I wish such necessity need not have come to Professor Erman in his older years.

My warmest greetings to you and to Mrs. Breasted | Ever sincerely yours | Caroline Ransom Williams

**26 October 1932**                                                    **0213**

October 26, 1932

Dear Mrs. Williams:

It was indeed a very great pleasure on coming into my office recently to find lying on my table your delightful new volume on the <u>Tomb of Per-Neb</u>. Thus far I have been deprived of the privilege of doing anything more than looking through the plates, which are a real joy. For the first time we now have before us a body of materials from which we can learn the facts regarding the processes by which the wall paintings of the Old Kingdom were produced. I am eager for a little more leisure when I may sit down and study the book in detail. I congratulate you heartily on such a splendid piece of work.

---

[235] Adolf Erman, *Neuaegyptische Grammtik* 2 völlig (Leipzig: W. Englemann, 1933).
[236] Arbeitzimmer literally means 'work room' or 'study.'

Frances and I were deeply disappointed that we were unable to join you in the attractive program which you suggested for an outing together. The distressing financial situation has of course involved the Institute, and I was obliged to stay on in the vicinity of New York mending financial fences! When I finally did start west It was the tenth of October and Charles was in the hospital after an operation on his shoulder and arm, intended to remedy a purely physical and mechanical interference with both nerves and circulation caused by some unsolved pressure. When Frances and I reached Buffalo where we expected to take the steamer we found that the boats had stopped sailing on the 30th of September. We then thought at once that we might be able at least to spend a night in Toledo and enjoy an evening with you all. In passing through Cleveland, however, my brake lining being about worn out, I bumped into the back of a Ford on Euclid Avenue with disastrous results. We were delayed for a large part of the day in Cleveland and therefore failed to reach Toledo that evening as we had hoped, but were obliged to spend the night at Freemont which, I think, is about thirty-five or forty miles from Toledo. You can imagine our disgust! We could not stop because we felt anxious regarding Charles' condition, and it was well that we did not. I telephoned when within seventy miles of Chicago and found that Charles, after two days at home, had returned to the hospital very ill. The trouble proved to be a thrombosis which lodged in his left lung, and for three days we did not know what to expect. I am glad to say the accumulation is now absorbed, his fever has disappeared and he is on the road to recovery but it will be many weeks before he can return to his desk.

We wish that it might be possible sometime to undertake the delightful trip you suggested, provided the Breasted family can be counted upon to escape any mishaps.

Frances joins me in warmest greetings to you all | Very sincerely yours | JHB

**26 January 1933**                                    0214

The Chesbrough Dwellings |
Toledo, Ohio | January 26, 1933

Dear Professor Breasted:-
I have read in the <u>New York Times</u> with interest and delight of the splendid discoveries at Persepolis. Please accept my hearty congratulations.

I noted also that you are about to sail to visit the various branches of the work abroad. I trust this means that you are in better health again and keen to go, not that Charles has not fully recovered. I have wanted to inquire again about your son before this, but hated to trouble you with a letter to answer.

You may have noticed in the papers the death on December 29 of Miss Randolph, my mother's sister. It was a great shock to her and to me, for my aunt's illness did not take a serious turn until Christmas day. After she left us I had everything to do, as my Mother's frail strength had to be shielded as much as possible, and there was illness at the time among my cousins in Cambridge, none of them being able to come here. I needed to be about three people and hence am late in sending these notices to many persons who knew my aunt.

My mind turns back to a time in Berlin long ago when she got word of the Dwight gift, and that the Trustees had consented to its use for an Art Building. You were there then and were so kindly and sympathetically interested in her plans for the building. Lately I have been in South Hadley and this building with its spacious entrance hall and growing collections does seem to me worth the effort she put into it.

Soon, next week, we are to have the pleasure of seeing Professor and Mrs. Ranke. These rare visits of Egyptologists are a great boon to me and make me feel a little less out of everything than I should otherwise. I do not know whether I have written you that on November 14 last, Mr. Winlock sent me word to go ahead with another volume for the M. M. A., the one already begun, on reused fragments of Old Kingdom relief found at Lisht.

If you have already left Chicago, I hope your Secretary will forward this letter.

With best wishes for your journey and further successes from us all and love to Mrs. Breasted | Most sincerely yours | Caroline R. Williams

4 April 1934                                                            0215

The Chesbrough Dwellings |
Toledo, Ohio | April 4, 1934

Dear Professor Breasted:-

In the past weeks we have spoken very often of you and Mrs. Breasted and have wished we knew how she is progressing. I hesitated, and still do, to write directly to her, lest she ought not to be bothered with letters. But please give her my affectionate good wishes. Perhaps by now she is well enough to be at home again. I hope indeed so.

As an excuse for writing to you and introducing my inquiry, I am sending you the last letter that has come to me from Professor Erman. I had given him for Christmas Dana's Two Years Before the Mast, and you, who know so well about his father's visit to California before gold was discovered there, may be interested in our Professor Erman's response to the American classic.[237] And perhaps the letter will interest Frances, too, who is a Californian herself.

Has not Egyptology met with severe losses as of late? I refer especially to Mr. Peet's untimely death, as well as to Mr. Griffith's. Then I grieve over Mr. Lythgoe's passing more than I can say.

I have had a few letters from Egypt this winter—from Mr. Quibell, Mr. L. F. Hall, from Miss Byles of your Luxor work—you, of course, hear constantly. Mr. Quibell wrote that Dr. Resiner is hard at work at publications with the help of others to read and write for him and that some good finds have been made at Sakkāreh and Lisht.

We shall probably move sometime in the next few weeks or months, but except for that upset looming before me, I am at last ready to go back to the interrupted book and try to get it done, as Mr. Winlock wishes me to do. This address, however, will reach me for a long time to come, though I will give you the new address as soon as it is determined.

I mean to buy the new Abydos volume from the University of

---

[237] Richard Henry Dana, Two Years Before the Mast: A Personal Narrative of Life at Sea (Original edition: New York: Harper and Brothers, 1840). A story about Dana's time on a ship going from Boston to California, around Cape Horn, from 1834-36. In a second edition, published in 1869, Dana edited the volume to include narrative of his visit to California in 1859, which was after the Gold Rush. This is possibly the volume CRW sent to Erman.

Chicago Press as soon as I can include it in my budget. I refer to <u>The Temple of King Sethos I at Abydos</u>, Vol. I, edited by Dr. Gardiner and copied by Miss Calverley,[238] of which Kegan Paul, Trench, Trubner & Co., Ltd. have sent me a 'Now Ready' notice.[239] It will save me bother not to have to clear it through American customs myself.

With all kind regards from Grant and me to you both | Sincerely yours | Caroline R. Williams

**10 April 1934**                                                   0216

April 10, 1934

Dear Mrs. Williams:

It was very pleasant to have your kind letter of April 4 and I am sorry that I cannot give you better news about Frances. She is indeed at home again, but not because there is any improvement but merely because hospital diet did not agree with her. She is under the care of two nurses, day and night, but does not seem to make any progress. She will deeply appreciate your kind messages and inquiries and I know will greatly regret her inability to reply in her own hand.

It was very kind of you to send us the Erman letter, which I have read to Frances and which we both enjoyed very much especially in view of the personal allusions bearing on his father's visit in California so long ago. Almost in the next mail I had a similar lead-pencil letter from him, written in much the same spirit, and reminding one a good deal of the Erman of old days. He expressed himself with surprising freedom regarding the very discouraging situation of German science which I fear bids fair to decline very sadly if not to perish under the Nazi regime. One of the German scientists now lecturing temporarily here reported to me a few days ago

---

[238] Amice Mary Calverly (1896-1959) was an artist who worked for the EES and the Oriental Institute from 1933-1959.  Sir Leonard Woolley encouraged her to take up archaeological drawing in 1926 while she was in Oxford.  She went on to work with Myrtle Broome, copying the scenes at the Temple of Seti I at Abydos.

[239] Amice M. Calverley, Myrtle Broome, Alan H. Gardiner, *The Temple of King Sethos I at Abydos, Volume I: The Chapels of Osiris, Isis and Horus* (London: Egypt Exploration Society; Chicago: University of Chicago Press, 1933).

what looks like a very hopeless situation for science in Germany.

I have been much distressed, as I know you have been also, at the losses which Oriental studies have suffered in England. Poor Gardiner is very much discouraged. I have just received a card from Mrs. Griffith indicating that she is trying to keep up her husband's library with the idea of bequeathing it to Oxford University eventually.[240]

Before I forget it let me tell you that we shall be sending you a copy of Volume I of <u>The Temple of King Sethos I at Abydos</u>, and I hope you have not already ordered it. The book is by no means sent to you on condition that you write a review, but if you found it convenient to do so for one of the leading art journals with which you are much better acquainted than I am, we would deeply appreciate it. You have done so much work on Old Egyptian painting and there are so few Orientalists in America who would be competent to review such a work that we would greatly value a notice of it from your pen.

Like you, I have had few letters from Egypt this winter disclosing what is going on. I am very much gratified that the Sakkara Expedition working in the mastaba of Mereruka has now fallen into its stride. It is doing both good and rapid work. I was greatly surprised to find in a recent letter from Reisner a short paragraph reporting very favorably on the work done – indeed stating it was the best work done in Egypt.

Perhaps I have not told you that having last year very reluctantly accepted the Chairmanship of the Advisory Board of the American Council of Learned Societies, I was able to secure for Reisner a subvention enabling him to publish his latest volume on the <u>History of Early Egyptian Tomb Architecture</u>.[241] I have rarely had so tragic an experience as my call on him a year ago now, when I found him almost sightless and without the funds for publishing his last volume which was then nearly complete in manuscript. It did not require much magnanimity to forget his hostile attitude toward our museum project, and I am now very much please that his volume has gone to press.

Our Prehistoric Survey of the Nile Valley and the adjacent desert has now been completed for about a thousand miles. The results are to appear

---

[240] His library became the foundation for the Griffith Institute at Oxford in 1939.
[241] George A. Reisner, *The Development of the Egyptian Tomb Down to the Accession of Cheops* (Cambridge: Harvard University Press, 1936).

in six volumes, two of which are out; the third is on the press, and the remaining three are almost ready for the press.[242] I very much hope that in another year we can shift to Western Asia for similar work.

I take it that you would like to have Erman's letter returned and hence I am enclosing it herewith.

With cordial greetings to you and your husband in which Frances joins me, I am | Very sincerely yours | JHB

P. S. – Since dictating the above I have been looking up the art journals and it seems to me that the AMERICAN MAGAZINE OF ART would be a good place for reaching the art schools and other centers of interest in a book like our Abydos volume. On the other hand, you have done so much research work on Egyptian painting, especially in the Old Kingdom, that you might prefer to write something for the AMERICAN JOURNAL OF ARCHAEOLOGY, of which Miss Swindler is editor. I have not written her about it, but will do so if you approve.

I am enclosing herewith also my recent letter from Erman.

---

[242] These became the Prehistoric Survey of Egypt and Western Asia, which had 4 volumes: K. S. Sandford and W. J. Arkell, *Paleolithic Man and the Nile-Faiyum Divide: A Study of the Region During Pliocene and Pleistocene Times, Prehistoric Survey of Egypt and Western Asia*, Vol. I (Chicago: University of Chicago Press, 1929); K. S. Sandford and W. J. Arkell, *Paleolithic Man and the Nile-Faiyum Divide in Nubia and Upper Egypt: A Study of the Region during Pliocene and Pleistocene Times, Prehistoric Survey of Egypt and Western Asia*, Vol. II (Chicago: University of Chicago Press, 1933); K. S. Sandford, *Paleolithic Man and the Nile Valley in Upper and Middle Egypt: A Study of the Region during Pliocene and Pleistocene Times, Prehistoric Survey of Egypt and Western Asia*, Vol. III (Chicago: University of Chicago Press, 1934); K. S. Sandford and W. J. Arkell, *Paleolithic Man and the Nile Valley in Lower Egypt with Some Notes on a Part of the Red Sea Littoral: A Study of the Regions During Pliocene and Pleistocene Times, Prehistoric Survey of Egypt and Western Asia*, Vol. IV (Chicago: University of Chicago Press, 1939).

13 April 1934                                                    0217

The Chesbrough Dwellings |
Toledo, Ohio | April 13, 1934

Dear Professor Breasted:-

I am indeed much concerned to hear that my dear, good friend of so many years, Frances, is having such a suffering time.

I can sympathize with her about hospital-food. The one time I was ever in a hospital as a patient—when I underwent my thyroid operation, which she too has experienced—my recovery was made uncomfortable by the too highly seasoned food. It seemed to me a lamentable oversight, a careless slip, in an otherwise admirable and efficient institution to serve such meals as I had to the ill. And I never shall forget the evening my understanding nurse brought me creamed sweetbreads which she had prepared herself! I still relish them, and demand them occasionally, because they are so nourishing and easily digested—for me an easier food than chops or even poultry of any kind.

I can believe that Mrs. Breasted is happier at home where she sees you daily and where everything can be adjusted to her needs. I do trust this approaching Spring-time with its hopefulness and warmer weather will be just the further help she requires. I long to be able to do something for her but can only send her my affectionate good wishes.

Thank you very much for letting me see your recent letter from Professor Erman. How I agree with him that times were happier for us all 30 or 40 years ago! I spent three years and three months continuously abroad at the beginning of this century and travelled all over the face of Europe without fear or annoyance of any kind. I feel sorry for the young people of today, who, like your Jimmie, do not find it comfortable or profitable to study over there.

Do you suppose the Nazis have made way with Wreszinski?[243] The Orientalistische Literaturzeitung is still issued as under his editorship but that must be a mere mask. In January I had a letter from an old teacher

---

[243] Walter Wreszinski (1880-1935) was a German Egyptologist who studied with Erman in Berlin, getting his PhD in 1904. His *Atlas zur altaegyptischen Kulturgeschichte* came out in 5 volumes from 1913-36 and was his most important work. He was Professor at University of Königsberg on his death.

of mine, Geheimrat Professor Dr. Erich Pernice,[244] of Greifswald. He was in Berlin in my student days there, and I had a whole semester of lectures on Pompeii with him, and other courses as well, and used to be a good deal in his home. He is now 69, so he wrote me, and becomes emeritus in June, when he expects to devote himself to an enterprise inherited from the late Franz Winter, that of publishing the mosaics of Pompeii. He wrote as if he were heart and soul for the Nazi regime, that it would bring Germany up again to her former level in the respect of the nations. I wonder if he was sincere.

I feel that Professor Erman perhaps has always been somewhat more discerning, independent, and less easily regimented than many German scholars. The irrepressible spirit and humor of his letters, despite all difficulties, spur one to meet one's own troubles staunchly.

For your very generous thought to send me a complimentary copy of the great publication on the Sethos I temple at Abydos, I cannot be grateful enough. My working library is a kind of bottomless pit, yawning to absorb more funds than I have at command for it these days, and your kindness relieves me of one worry. Certainly I shall be very happy to review the book in whichever journal you wish. Please do not think that I would prefer A.J.A., if it would be more useful to you to have me try to make the work favorably known among the constituency of the American Magazine of Art. Whatever will best serve your purposes is what I should like to do. Indeed such a gift deserves two reviews, but I should think it would be to the interest of the book for you to enlist as many different reviewers as possible. So fit me in wherever you deem best.

I do not know that you are ready yet to have the book sent to me, but I would suggest not sending it until May 1 (or any time thereafter) and then directly to our address for the summer, 602 Tennyson Place, Toledo. We are removing sometime between the 16th and the end of this month. It is quite a chore to get my working material reorganized in a new place, and probably a temporary one at that, but I hope to spend the greater part of the summer at intensive Egyptological work.

---

[244] Erich Anton Pernice (1864-1945) was a German Classical Archaeologist who got his PhD in Bonn in 1888. He and CRW likely met when he worked at the Antiquarium in Berlin from 1897-1930.   See   https://www.deutsche-biographie.de/pnd116081929.html#ndbcontent_werke accessed 6 December 2016.

I do not need to tell you what a comfort the fine success of your Oriental Institute is to me. Whatever occasional set-backs and cares you have, you always come out on top in the end!

Fver gratefully and appreciatively yours | Caroline R. Williams

P.S. I was very glad to receive recently the catalogue of the publications of the Oriental Institute. I shall keep it filed where I can refer to it at any time, and it will be useful to me, as are constantly your two most recent books.

## 17 April 1934                                              0218

April 17, 1934

Dear Mrs. Williams:

It has been a great pleasure to have your kind letter of April 13 and I am exceedingly pleased that you are willing to review the Abydos volume. I have just been writing to Miss Swindler about a review for AJA, and perhaps she will write to you. I have also written to Frederick Whiting, Editor of the AMERICAN MAGAZINE OF ART. It occurred to me that with your detailed knowledge of Old Kingdom painting and Egyptian painting in general you might, in studying the Abydos plates, find a good many technical observations which you could throw quickly into a review for AJA, while a few paragraphs of more popular observations would undoubtedly serve for the AMERICAN MAGAZINE OF ART. I have, however, a very uncomfortable conscience in suggesting that you should assume the burden of the two reviews, and I have ventured the suggestion only because I know how interested you are in the technical problems and because I know what a valuable contribution you could make in the pages of AJA.

I am so sorry that your new address did not arrive in time for us to shift that shipment of the folio, as it has already gone off to your old address in Chesbrough Dwellings. I hope you can simply leave the package wrapped until you are moving and reserve examination until after you have made the change to your new quarters. You must find it a very heavy task to withdraw from the Chesbrough Dwellings with all your collections of books and materials after so many years of residence there.

I do not know whether I have told you that after long and wearisome negotiations with our esteemed colleague, Lacau, I was able last spring to secure one of the two statues of Tutenkhamon which Hölscher discovered in the neighboring mortuary temple of Eye and Harmhab. The statue has been in course of preparation all winter. It is a standing figure sixteen feet high. The top of the crown rises between the ceiling beams of our Egyptian Hall![245] We shall be unveiling it by June, I hope, and it would give us the greatest pleasure if you and your husband could come up to Chicago, perhaps also to visit the Exposition for a day or two, and incidentally you could pay homage to our old Egyptian sovereign.

Frances continues in about the same condition, with very little change either up or down. She has at last consented to let the nurses do everything and this is a gain because she has wearied herself with responsibilities which the nurses were perfectly capable of carrying on for her. She was greatly interested to hear from you and I am taking your letter of the 13th home to read to her.

With kindest greetings to you and your husband, I am | Always cordially yours | JHB

**18 April 1934**                                            **0219**

The Chesbrough Dwellings |
Toledo, Ohio | April 18, 1934

Dear Professor Breasted:-

The Abydos publication was at our living-room door when Grant and I came in after an evening ride last evening, and I hasten to let you know that I am safely in possession of it and to thank you again for this wonderful gift.

I could not resist opening the book, and we both gloated over the beautiful plates. I am glad to report that I possess the Blackman article on the Ritual mentioned by the Editor as published in too obscure a place, I also have the Capart volume, but not, to my regret, the old Marriette <u>Abydos</u>, the folios, though I have the Catalogue, nor did I even know about

---

[245] This is still a highlight of the Oriental Institute Collections. See: https://oi-idb-static. uchicago.edu/multimedia/61110/SOIMFO5.pdf for more information. Accessed 6 December 2016.

the recent German publication.[246] The Blackman discussion seems to me the most important thing to have, and I trust I can do a decent review without referring to the things I haven't got, especially as you wish me to comment especially on the painting as represented in the colored plates.

I was very glad to hear, as you wrote me in an earlier letter, that the Griffith library is likely to be kept together for Oxford University. It would be a thousand pities, if it were to be dispersed. In a very small way in comparison, I have been trying through the years to build up a good working collection for Egyptology. I derive from doing so a kind of collector's fun, and of course it has been necessary, if I am to operate effectively at all here in Toledo, where there is no other technical library for Egyptology. I am beginning, however, to wonder what is to become of my books after I am through with them; at present they are willed to Mount Holyoke College, but as the institution is a college, not giving higher degrees except the master's, I may be planning to give them what they could not so well utilize.[247]

This hotel is now in the control of a bondholders' protective committee and is not being run to our liking. The only other which is a good going concern has no porches, and we are now going where we shall have an outdoor living porch, one screened and private, which we expect greatly to enjoy for the summer. What we shall do afterwards is still a good deal in the air. This address will reach us for a long time to come, but I repeat for your convenience the new one, 602 Tennyson Place, where we shall be by May 1st.

I am so very glad that Frances is getting on a little easier; please give her my love.

Thank you for your kind suggestions, should we be visiting the Exposition. At least we have the memory of your valuable new acquisition—the Tutenkhamon statue—as we saw it with you, still in process of being installed.

---

[246] Aylward M. Blackman, 'The Sequence of the Episodes in the Egyptian Daily Temple Liturgy,' *Journal of the Manchester Egyptian and Oriental Society* 8 (1918-19): 27-53; Jean Capart, *Abydos. Le Temple de Séti Ier* (Brussels: Rossignol & Van den Bril, 1912); Auguste Mariette, *Abydos, Description des Fouilles, Exécutées sur l'Emplacement de Cette Ville, Tome Premier* (Paris: Librairie A. Franck, 1869).

[247] See note 213.

Grant joins me in very warm greetings to you and to Mrs. Breasted.

I shall await word from the editors of the two magazines and do my best for this latest fine achievement of the Oriental Institute.

Sincerely yours | Caroline R. Williams

**23 April 1934**                                                   **0220**

April 23, 1934

Dear Mrs. Williams:

This note is merely to confirm to you the fact that I have heard from Mr. F. A. Whiting, Jr., Assistant Editor of THE AMERICAN MAGAZINE OF ART (801 Barr Building, Washington, D. C.), and also from Miss Swindler, and both will be very much pleased to receive the review. Indeed, Mr. Whiting suggests the possibility of a short article, but I hope you will not feel in the least obligated to write this article. I enclose a copy of his letter of April 19 so that you can decide what it may seem best to you to do.

I take it that Miss Swindler is writing you direct.

With kindest greetings to you both | Ever yours | JHB

Enclosure[248]

P. S. – This is not an acknowledgment of your kind letter of April 18 in which I was very much interested. I am glad you are going to have an attractive home for the summer, with outdoor responsibilities.

I regret to report that Frances is about the same.

Very sincerely yours | JHB

---

[248] There were no enclosures in the archives.

14 May 1934                                                    0221

602 Tennyson Place |
Toledo, Ohio | May 14, 1934
Dear Professor Breasted:-
Two days ago I received another delightful surprise-gift, the third volume
of the Medinet Habu publication. I feel especially interested in this one
because of the welcome text of the calendar from the exterior of the south
wall.

When I was in Luxor, Mr. Nelson by his own enthusiasm aroused my
interest in it, and of late Dr. Robbins of the University of Michigan consulted
with me about Egyptian calendars of Unlucky Days. He is to publish a
papyrus of Roman date acquired in Egypt on which such a calendar is given
in connection with a Roman and an 'Egyptian calendar,' the last-mentioned,
I presume, one of feast days.[249] It interested me that the purely superstitious
document should be given standing, as it were, by association with what
represented in calendars the science of the time. The only ancient Egyptian
calendars of lucky and unlucky days of which I have knowledge are the
three in the British Museum (the one from Kahun, the Sallier IV, and the
one on the same papyrus with the Wisdom of Amenemope), and these
are all separate documents in nowise linked with calendars of the type at
Medinet Habu. I wonder if the two ever were associated before the end of
the dynasties.[250]

---

[249] The University of Michigan has a papyrus collection. Frank E. Robbins published two
articles based on Michigan Papyrus number 1, which was astrological in focus. See Frank
Egleston Robbins, 'A New Astrological Treatise: Michigan Papyrus No. 1,' *Classical Philology*
22:1 (January 1927): 1-45; Frank Egleston Robbins, 'P. Michigan 149, *Astrological Treatise*,' in
*Papyri in the University of Michigan Collection III: Miscellaneous Papyri, Volume III*, ed. J. G. Winter
(Ann Arbor: University of Michigan Press, 1936), 62-117. See also: http://www.lib.umich.
edu/files/collections/papyrus/exhibits/MPC/Religion/Astrology_Frameset.html (accessed
8 December 2016).
[250] Calendars of Lucky and Unlucky Days appear in Egypt from the Twelfth to the Twentieth
Dynasties. They tend to focus on relationships between Egyptian gods and how their
interactions can affect life on earth. For more on these see Ronald A. Wells, 'Horoscopes,' in
*Oxford Encyclopedia of Ancient Egypt, Vol. 2: G-O* (Oxford: Oxford University Press, 2001), 117-
19. This entry cites a classic article about the calendars with which CRW and JHB were no
doubt familiar: F. J. Chabas, 'Le Calendrier de jours fastes et néfastes de l'année égyptienne,'
*Bibliothèque Égyptologique* 12 (1905): 127-235. For information on the papyri in the British

I thank you most heartily for this generous and kind gift, too. I shall write to Dr. Nelson, also, of my pleasure in receiving it.

I have been very slow in acknowledging your last letter, that of April 25—as you will have guessed, I trust, because of the demands in moving and settling. I have heard from Miss Swindler and have written her that I will do the review for the American Journal of Archaeology, and a letter is now on the way to Washington to set me in direct connection with Mr. F. A. Whiting, Jr., and I purpose doing the review for the American Magazine of Art first, certainly delivering it before July 1st. Then I will take up the one for A.J.A. a little later in the year, when I can approach it freshly, with quite different wording and, I hope, point of view, but I will surely do it before the expiration of 1934. I hope this will be right with you.

I shall be glad to have at her convenience the list of such loose plates as you have (mentioned by Miss Roberts in a note added to your letter) and consider suitable for reproduction in the American Magazine of Art.

Please tell Frances she must try to get well fast and come along alone, or better still with you, to see how we are living now. We are much enamored of housekeeping; I have such a competent German maid (the one who cared for my mother during the last five years of her life) that I shall be about as free for Egyptological pursuits as when we lived in a hotel and with much more congenial conditions. We have had only four meals indoors since we arrived here May 1st.

With kindest regards to you and Mrs. Breasted from us both and my renewed thanks for Medinet Habu, volume III | Sincerely yours | Caroline R. Williams

---

Museum, see the Papyrus Sallier, here: http://www.britishmuseum.org/research/collection_online/collection_object_details.aspx?objectId=110337&partId=1 (accessed 8 December 2016) and Sebastian Porceddu, Lauri Jetsu, Tapio Markkanen, and Jaana Toivari-Viitala, 'Evidence of Periodicity in Ancient Egyptian Calendars of Luck and Unlucky Days,' *Cambridge Archaeological Journal* 18:3 (2008): 327-339.

**23 May 1934**                                                     **0222**

May 23, 1934

Dear Mrs. Williams:

I am very glad to have your kind letter of May 14 and I wish we might discuss the interesting questions you bring up about the calendar.

I hope that we have not been overburdening you with the labor of these two reviews, and I am glad to know that the arrangements have all been made with both editors. Since writing you last I have had a note from Miss Swindler in which she stated she had heard from you. I believe I have neglected to let you know that a copy of <u>The Temple of King Sethos I at Abydos</u> has also been sent to THE AMERICAN JOURNAL OF ARCHAEOLOGY.

Miss Roberts reports that our loose plates are almost entirely of subjects which have not yet appeared and which are probably coming in the next volume, although three collotype plates and one color plate are available. These are plate numbers 15 (colored), and 21, 29, and 34 (collotype), and I do not know that they are really suitable for reproduction in the AMERICAN MAGAZINE OF ART. I am taking it for granted that the line drawings, for technical and mechanical reasons, would not make a successful reproduction.

Frances and I are very much interested to hear of your new housekeeping venture, and we should be very much interested if we might look in upon you. I am sorry to say that Frances continues very weak, with no immediate prospect of improvement.

With kindest greetings to you both, in which Frances joins me, I am | Very sincerely yours | JHB


**25 May 1934**                                                     **0223**

602 Tennyson Place |
Toledo, Ohio | May 25, 1934

Dear Professor Breasted:-

I have your kind letter of May 23rd.

Do not be concerned about the two reviews. I can manage them very nicely, and there really does seem to be a dearth of reviewers for Egyptian books, as Mrs. Dohan has just made clear to me.[251] I do not myself care to do many until I have finished that book, already too long delayed, for the M. M. A., but this is a special case.

On the whole I should think plate 29 better than 21 for reproduction; perhaps the upper part, (a), of plate 34 could be used. If you feel disposed to have these two collotypes sent at once to Mr. Whiting, Jr., I could then learn from him whether or not he considers them desirable for reproduction and write my review accordingly. He would like to have the copy for it June 18th, and so I expect to take it up promptly on the first of June.

I am taking for granted that the Magazine probably would not wish to go to the expense of reproducing colored plate 15 or do you wish to risk the quality of such reproduction, but if you think differently, perhaps you will arrange with Mr. Whiting. Naturally, if successful, such a colored reproduction would be very usable and attractive in connection with a review.

I had already judged from Miss Swindler's letter that you had sent a copy of the volume to the American Journal of Archaeology. Inasmuch as you had so kindly sent me a copy, I told her I would not claim that one. She is always hard put to it to secure books for the Bryn Mawr College Library, and probably you are not losing a purchase there, if, as I deem likely, she and Mrs. Dohan agree that Bryn Mawr may have that copy; there, the book will reach many potential archaeologists. I hope you do not have to give another copy to the American Magazine of Art. I mentioned in my first letter to Mr. Whiting Jr. that I have a copy of the book.

I wish there were something I could do for Francis. Please tell her I think of her every day with affection and concern.

Most sincerely yours | Caroline R. Williams

---

[251] Edith Hayward Hall Dohan (1877-1943) was an American classical archaeologist who was the first to receive a PhD in the subject at Bryn Mawr in 1906. She studied at the American School of Classical Studies at Athens. She went to Mount Holyoke in 1906, which is likely where she and CRW met. She excavated in Crete in 1910 and 1912, then moved to the University of Pennsylvania Museum to do curatorial work. She married in 1915 and temporarily suspended her career to care for her two young children, returning to the University Museum in 1931 as associate curator of the Mediterranean section. She published extensively and died suddenly at her desk in 1943. See more about her here: http://www.brynmawr.edu/library/exhibits/BreakingGround/dohan.html (accessed 8 December 2016).

**28 May 1934**                                    **0224**

May 28, 1934

Dear Mrs. Williams:

Replying to your kind letter of May 25, I am having Plates 29 and 34 of THE TEMPLE OF KING SETHOS I AT ABYDOS sent to Mr. Whiting, Jr., and we are raising with him the query as to whether he could undertake the expense of reproducing a colored plate.

With kindest greetings to you and Mr. Williams | As ever yours | JHB

**9 October 1934**                                 **0225**

602 Tennyson Place |
Toledo, Ohio | October 9, 1934

Dear Professor Breasted:-

Not many days ago I was made very happy by the gift of The Excavation of Medinet Habu, vol. I.[252] This splendid folio was accompanied by a printed slip 'With the Compliments of the Author,' and I have already acknowledged the book to Professor Hölscher. But I know full well to whom ultimately I am indebted for it, and I think you may like to know of its safe arrival here and the pleasure and help it gives me.

I had known only in a general way of this by-product of your Epigraphic Survey at Medinet Habu. With so competent an architect in charge, and Dr. Anthes[253] to look after linguistic and archaeological details of the incidental objects, the Excavation-Series will be a much-valued addition to your growing lists of publications already out and projected. I spent the whole morning reading your Foreword and Professor Hölscher's

---

[252] Uvo Hölscher, *The Excavation of Medinet Habu, Volume 1: General Plans and Views* (Chicago, University of Chicago Press, 1934).

[253] Rudolf Richard Georg Philipp Gottfried Anthes (1896-1985) was a German Egyptologist. He studied in Berlin, under Erman and had the dubious honor of being Erman's final graduate student when he earned his PhD in 1923. He worked in museums in Germany and Egypt, excavating with Hölscher from 1931-33. After the Second World War he had the monumental task of rebuilding the museum at the University of Halle and reopening the Humboldt University in Berlin. From 1950-1963 he was professor of Egyptology at the University of Pennsylvania, and the curator of the Egyptian Section at the University Museum.

Introduction and in looking carefully at the plates, with which I am delighted, and I shall look forward to studying the text volumes as they appear. Please believe me very appreciative of this most generous gift.

If you have already returned to Chicago and had time as yet to look at the summer's accumulations, you will have found my review of Abydos I which appeared in the August issue of Art in America.[254] Miss Roberts acknowledged it very courteously and said that it would be kept for you. I mention it only to explain that I deferred the review for the American Journal of Archaeology until autumn, wishing if possible to get some of the older publications on the temple, and I had the good fortune to secure the rare Mariette, Abydos, and am using it now in connection with the Zippert dissertation, in which the references to Mariette's old work are numerous. I had long been familiar with Blackman's discussion of the ritual. I shall concentrate on this second review now and send the copy for it to Mrs. Dohan within a few weeks.

You and Astrid have been often in our thoughts since we learned from Miss Roberts of your journey to Alaska. I hope you have returned, or will return to Chicago much rested. You will both miss Mrs. Breasted and the readjustment will not be easy. In this you have my sympathy, for I understand what it means to have the accustomed background of one's life changed. I, too, shall miss the occasional letters from, and visits with, Frances, who was always a most loyal and kind friend to me.[255]

We expect to be at 602 Tennyson Place until the Spring of 1935, the owners of this apartment having decided to winter in California.

With kindest regards from us both to you and your family | Caroline R. Williams

---

[254] CRW, 'Reviewed Work: The Temple of King Sethos I at Abydos (Volume I, The Chapels of Osiris, Isis, and Horus.) by Amice M. Calverley, Myrtle F. Broome, Alan Gardiner,' The American Magazine of Art 27:8 (August 1934): 444-46.
[255] Frances Breasted died in mid-July of bacterial endocarditis, an infection of the heart tissue that can now be treated with antibiotics and, occasionally, surgery.

**11 October 1934**                                                  **0226**

October 11, 1934

Dear Mrs. Williams:

This is to let you know that in beginning to dig through the summer's accumulations on my desk since my return from the Northwest, I have now found your very kind review of ABYDOS I, for which I want to thank you most appreciatively.

Astrid and I are just endeavoring to settle ourselves in the new apartment at the Cloisters, 5811 Dorchester Avenue (Apartment 6-G), and we hope you may soon be in Chicago and will allow us to put you up.

We have a large accumulation of associations which I wish we might talk about, and not least among them are our old friends the Ermans, whose present sad situation is pathetic indeed, especially since the death of Sethe last summer.

Believe me, with kindest greetings to you and Mr. Williams | Very sincerely yours | JHB


**23 October 1934**                                                  **0227**

602 Tennyson Place |
Toledo, Ohio | October 23, 1934

Dear Professor Breasted:-

You were most kind to suggest in your last letter that you and Astrid would like to put me up if I were going to Chicago in the near future.

I would almost make the trip to have a talk with you about our German friends. I have been greatly troubled about them from what I could read between the lines of Professor Erman's letters, and I was beginning to think that no formal notice was to be taken of his 80th birthday, when along came a request yesterday from Professor Steindorff that I join in a project of his that does not seem to me, so far as I understand it, to include any practical help or to have much dignity of conception but which may well make some gayety and cheer for him. The letter practically asks me to do more than my pro rata share because many contributors of necessity must do less, accordingly I am sending in the next days two and a half times as much as the pro rata amount. You must know all about this, far more probably than I do. I had already written such a letter as I could for the birthday and sent a book that I thought they could enjoy together, Frau Erman reading. About the worst result of the famous depression is that one cannot do as much for friends like the Ermans as formerly. But enough of that, if I may possibly have the great advantage of talking with you instead.

I could go to Chicago almost any week, preferably avoiding week-ends and also not being away from Toledo on November 5 and 6. Our local election is of extra-ordinary importance this year, inasmuch as we are to vote on a City-Manager government on the model of Cincinnati's and all right-minded citizens are striving against heavy odds to put this reform across. Toledo is now wretchedly misgoverned and in debt, teachers in the public schools have had their salaries cut 50 per cent and are not sure of getting them at that, while judges in the lowest courts who 'don't know enough to pound sand,' as Grant puts it, draw liberal salaries which they could not earn as private citizens.

I have had in mind to apply at International House to be put up there for a couple of days while I looked up a few things in the Oriental Institute's library, inasmuch as the Windermere is so far away. But if, instead, I am to go to you, I shall wait for you to say when you would find it convenient to have me. Just tentatively I had thought of some time between election and Thanksgiving, but there is no reason why I might not go earlier or wait until after Thanksgiving, if that suited you better. And as your time is so valuable and your engagements so numerous, if it should not be expedient after all for you and Astrid to have me, I shall one day carry out my original intention and see if I can be taken care of at International House.

With much appreciation of your recent letter and kindest regards from us both | Sincerely yours | Caroline R. Williams

**25 October 1934**                                                   **0228**

October 25, 1934

Dear Mrs. Williams:

I am very glad to have your letter of October 23 and to learn of the probability that we shall soon see you in Chicago. With the exception of curtain hangings we are almost entirely settled in our new apartment and should be delighted to see you any time after this week. I note that you prefer the middle of the week, and we would be very glad to have you select any of the weeks beginning Monday, October 29 until Friday, November 23. If it were convenient for you to select the week of Monday, November 5 to Friday, November 9, it would be a great pleasure if I might take you down to the Woman's Club to see a presentation of our motion picture THE HUMAN ADVENTURE on Wednesday, November 7.[256] But if this does not meet your convenience or would be taking too much of your time while you are here, do not by any means inconvenience yourself.

I note with interest your references to the coming local election in Toledo. I suppose there is nothing which so conclusively demonstrates the futility of Democracy as our local governments. Though I must confess that I never felt so hopeless about Democracy even in our national government as I do at present. If this highly idealistic N. R. A. program would only secure a few people who do know how to 'pound sand' as your husband might say, we might have some hope for the future.[257]

Astrid joins me in kindest greetings to you and in the hope that we shall see you soon at our new apartment.

Sincerely yours | JHB

---

[256] 'The Human Adventure' was the title of a boxed-set of books by a number of historians, published by Harper and Brothers, which included JHB's book *The Conquest of Civilization* (New York: Harper and Brothers, 1926). The Human Adventure film that he mentioned in this letter was a film produced by the Oriental Institute, under the direction of Charles Breasted. For more on the filming and production, see Abt, *American Egyptologist*, 382-387. Watch the film, in its entirety, on the Oriental Institute's YouTube Channel: https://www.youtube.com/watch?v=yysHJk0v5XA (accessed 8 December 2016).

[257] National Recovery Administration was part of the New Deal, and had to do with fair labor practices and more.

**27 October 1934**                                    0229

602 Tennyson Place |
Toledo, Ohio | October 27, 1934

Dear Professor Breasted:-

Your very kind letter of October 25th awaited me when I returned last evening from a day spent in the University library at Ann Arbor.

I should be very glad to go to Chicago by day train on Tuesday, November 6, reaching Englewood at 2.45 P.M., Central Standard time, as I can vote in the morning here before boarding the train, No. 19. I would then take a taxi from the Englewood station, and reach your address, The Cloisters, 5811 Dorchester Avenue, (Ap. 6 G) shortly after three o'clock, I should suppose. If convenient for you and Astrid to keep me two nights, I would return by some one of the day trains on Thursday, November 8th. Should anything in the meantime come up on your side to render any shifting of these dates better for you or your daughter, I shall count on your telling me, for my plans can be entirely flexible.

I should indeed delight to see the motion picture 'The Human Adventure,' the more so that I was so unfortunate as to miss an opportunity to see a private showing here. I knew nothing about it in advance and had already gone down town on fatiguing business and shopping when the Erpi Consultants representative telephone to our house. By afternoon when I returned and got the message, I was at the end of my strength for the day! I do trust Toledo is to have a showing of the picture; I believe the Art Museum has it under consideration.

With much appreciation of your generous courtesy to me and pleasant anticipations of seeing you and Astrid | Very sincerely yours | Caroline R. Williams

**30 October 1934**                                    0230

October 30, 1934

My dear Mrs. Williams:

Astrid and I are very glad to have your letter of October 27 and to learn that we may expect you in the early afternoon of November sixth. We both hope you will stay longer than the two suggested nights.

I am greatly pleased to know that you will be able to go down to see THE HUMAN ADVENTURE, which I am glad to say is now receiving a very wide distribution. Jayne, of the University Museum at Philadelphia, reports that he has sold out his afternoon showing in the Academy of Music holding over thirty-two hundred people, and he always sells out his evening showing, which means that nearly sixty-five hundred people will see the film in Philadelphia on its first day there.

With kindest greetings to Mr. Williams and pleasant anticipations, I am | Very sincerely yours | JHB

**25 November 1934**                                        **0231**

602 Tennyson Place
Toledo, Ohio | November 25, 1934

Dear Professor Breasted:-

Here is the curious 'freak' letter again. The writer is unknown to us and our friends, but the following items may interest you in connection with the impertinent communication. The name Bucklew occurs in the Toledo telephone book but once, and that telephone owner lives at a different address and has a different first name. My husband looked in the latest Toledo City Directory and did not find the name Bruce V. Bucklew, but he did find listed as living at Bruce's address, 3178 Glenwood Avenue, two men of other first names with Bucklew as last name, one of them a taxicab driver, the second a tool-maker. The north end of Glenwood Avenue where this number occurs is a factory neighborhood near the Overland's big idle plant. We drove past the house numbered 3178 early this afternoon; it is a decent, but shabby, small, two-storied building which Grant said would rent for $16 to $20 a month. What puzzles me is that this person Bruce should have your former private address. Do you suppose he could once have been a cab driver in your part of Chicago?

You will be interested to know that I invited the President and Vice-President of the Toledo Branch of A.A.U.W. to tea with me one day last week and presented to them the question of bringing the moving picture, 'The Human Adventure,' here, both the President of the Toledo University and the Director of the Art Museum having declined to take any financial share in bringing it, or even to aid by advice and a show of interest in the undertaking. I am hopeful that the college club will swing it alone. Their executive committee meets tomorrow when the question will be decided. If they do take hold of the picture, I think the other institutions will in the end come to it and help about publicity and sale of tickets. And if they do not, I have other possibilities in mind. The college women agreed with me that we better to try to afford Western Electric Sound Equipment and thus put the whole responsibility for the technical excellence of the showing up to Erpi Picture Consultants, Incorporated. We are in correspondence about it all with Mr. Shields.

No doubt you have received Professor Erman's rewritten book on Egyptian religion. My copy arrived two days ago.[258] I am glad of his remarks about your 'Religion and Thought in Ancient Egypt.'[259] I never shall forget hearing those lectures on the Morse foundation in New York. They opened me to such a new world of ideas that they excited me emotionally as fine music does.

We have been invited to Ann Arbor to eat Thanksgiving dinner with the Worrells. It is such a little distance by motor car we go often, as a week ago today when we took two Toledo friends with us and dined at the Michigan Union.

I am pleased that you enjoy Mrs. Chanler's Roman Spring.[260] We are reading just now with equal interest Mrs. Wharton's A Backward Glance, also a 1934 book.[261] I have long been familiar with delightful writings about the Boston literary coterie of the days of Longfellow and Lowell, but I needed Mrs. Wharton to picture the contemporary New York and the time of her own young years there.

I am still working through the texts of 'The Temple of Sethos I,' vol. I, as best I can. I have a notion about the sšpt of episode 24 (Mariette 15), which Capart mentions as a 'bandelette' and Blackman as 'an object called sšpt, which is conventionally represented [Figure 7] (really, as Blackman

---

[258] Adolf Erman, Die Religion der Ägypter, ihr Werden und Vergehen in vier Jahrtausenden (Berlin: De Gruyter, 1934)

[259] JHB, Development of Religion and Thought in Ancient Egypt: Lectures Delivered on the Morse Foundation at Union Theological Seminary (New York: Charles Scribner's Sons, 1912).

[260] Margaret Chanler, Roman Spring: Memoirs (Boston: Little, Brown, and Company, 1934).

[261] Edith Wharton, A Backward Glance (New York: D. Appleton-Century Company, 1934).

FIGURE 7          FIGURE 8          FIGURE 9

should have given, [Figure 8]) and probably has some connection with the collar,' that it may well be an example of the so-called 'braces' which in the XXI-XXII dynasties were made of red leather with embossed ends of undyed leather. With such actual specimens the m'nḫt has occasionally been found. The coloring at Abydos is favorable to the view that the 'braces' worn by gods in the various scenes were also of red leather, though not as yet with embossed ends but sometimes bound in undyed leather. (Calverley I, pls. 5, 15). I wish I knew the coloring of the sšpt offered by the king in the Osiris sanctuary (Calverley, I, pls. 10 lower extreme left). If also red, and the way it appears photographically in Capart, Temple de Séti Ier, pl. XX, suggests this, then I should feel that it might be reasonable to propose the possibility that the [Figure 9] offered is the object of similar shape on yet worn by Osiris in episode 24, but on his person in the adjacent episode 26 of Blackman's numbering, together with the m'nḫt, also not worn in episode 24. And if it be said that the 'braces' are won only by gods whose forms approach that of a mummy, one may recall that all the gods in the temple service in theory are Osiris before whom his son Horus is officiant, and that therefore anything appropriate to Osiris may be ceremonially offered to any one of them. I hope this chat about an archaeological detail won't bore you.

    With kindest regards from us both | Sincerely yours | Caroline R. Williams

**28 November 1934**                                            **0232**

November 28, 1934
Dear Mrs. Williams:
I have been greatly interested in your kind letter of November 25. I did not realize that I had been involving you and your husband in any Sherlock Holmes operations when I enclosed you in the 'freak' letter which you have been kind enough to return. Both in England and in America there are a great many ignorant people whom emotional evangelists enlist in the distribution of tracts, and my Toledo correspondent is evidently one of these.

I do hope that you will not consider yourself in the least obligated to push the showing of THE HUMAN ADVENTURE in Toledo. I am sorry to hear that the President of the University and the Director of the Art Museum are not willing to aid you in the matter. Last evening I attended a showing of the film in my boyhood village of Downers Grove, twenty miles west of Chicago. The largest auditorium in the town, which was a Methodist Church of unusual size, was packed to the doors and scores of people were turned away, much to my regret. If we can do anything to be of assistance to you, please let me know.

I am glad to hear that you have received a copy of Erman's new edition of his Die Religion der Agypter. In view of your notice of his reference to my Religion and Thought in his Preface, it may be of interest to you to know that after the appearance of the first edition of Erman's book he sent me a very kind letter, evidently written in some distress of mind at the fact that he had totally overlooked my book and had only later discovered that there were some new and original facts in it. Of course I had not the slightest feeling in the matter. It is a habit of mind of European friends and colleagues just to take it for granted that very little good can come out of Nazareth – that is, their natural attitude is that America does not produce their kind of thing. In dear old Erman's case I am astonished that, in view of his blindness, he ever was able to find out what was in the book. It was of course the loyal and indefatigable Käthe who read it to him, as I have often found her doing when I visited them. I went through his notes in the back of the volume and I find that he has actually used the <u>Religion and Thought</u>, but religion as developing out of social processes and social experience is almost unknown to our German colleagues. Some of the theologians are acquainted with it in Hebrew history. But the only European Orientalist who grasped at once what I was driving at in the Religion and Thought was Georges Benedite of the Louvre. He came to me about it at once in Egypt and told me he had immediately put my name before the committee of the Academie des Inscriptions for foreign membership. He died, poor fellow, before he could ever bring it to a vote. He was a very lovable and attractive Frenchman, with the same kind of spirit which Pottier displays in the beautiful letter which you let me read.

Excuse me for running on so much about myself. I am glad you and your husband are going to have a pleasant Thanksgiving dinner with the Worrells. I wish Toledo were not so far away and that we might have had the pleasure of seeing you both here.

Reverting again to Mrs. Chanler's Roman Spring, you may be interested to know that by a curious coincidence I received from her two or three days ago a copy of her latest book called, 'Cleopatra's Daughter,' containing her card.[262] It seems to be an attempt at a more or less romantic picture of the whole Roman-Egyptian situation in the Eastern Mediterranean.

I can see that you are having a good time with the Temple of Sethos I, and I hope you are finding the investigation of the volume, preliminary to your review, is fully worth the time and trouble. I should think you were on the right track regarding the SSPT. I think you have probably put your finger on the weak point of the publication – somebody of archaeological experience ought to spend months in the temple studying in the originals just such questions as those which you are bringing up. You are likely to know far more about it than the editors when you shall have finished your review!

With kindest regards to you both, I am | Very sincerely yours | JHB

---

[262] Beatrice Chanler, *Cleopatra's Daughter: The Queen of Mauretania* (New York: Liveright Publishing, 1934)

**22 January 1935**                                                        **0233**

January 22, 1935
CONFIDENTIAL
Dear Mrs. Williams:
I want to thank you for your kindness in remembering me with a copy of the Toledo Museum of Art Catalogue, containing an illustration of a slab of relief from Persepolis, about which I am very glad to know. It is another example of the terrible vandalism that ran riot at Persepolis before we gained the concession. There is a whole series of these reliefs still on sale in Paris, some in London, and a few in New York – which were stolen by the local population, probably, and could in all probability be replaced in their original positions. What makes it particularly vexatious is the fact that at our first division at Persepolis the Persian government did not allow us even a single piece of such relief sculpture, although we discovered for them thousands of square feet of such reliefs.

I take it that the Toledo Museum authorities understand that the figure is that of a palace guard and <u>not</u> a 'royal personage.'

Thanking you very much for your kindness in sending me the catalogue, and with all good wishes of the season to you and Mr. Williams, I am | Very sincerely yours | JHB


**26 January 1935**                                                        **0234**

602 Tennyson Place |
Toledo, Ohio | January 26, 1935
Dear Professor Breasted:-
Thank you for your confidential letter of January 22nd. What you say about Persepolis reliefs will not be mentioned to anyone by me.

I had occasion to write to Mr. Blake More Godwin about something else on January 17 and referred at the close of my letter to the ancient Persian relief fragment here saying 'it quite certainly, in my opinion, represents one of the Palace Guards, one of the "Ten Thousand Immortals".' So the Director of the Museum has had his attention called to the mistake in the Museum's catalogue, but it will not trouble him!

The Persian exhibition was got together by Mr. McLean and his assistant Miss Blair. It is not a travelling exhibition. I have not heard who wrote its catalogue. Mr. Godwin told me a day or two ago that Dr. Richard Ettinghausen[263] was not invited here by the Toledo Museum of Art nor is he being paid anything by this Museum. He was sent here, Mr. Godwin said, by the Institute of Persian Art in New York in recognition of the fine loan exhibition Mr. McLean had collected. The Toledo Museum has made him welcome and sponsored his lectures in connection with the exhibit of Persian art.

He is still here with his bride of a few weeks, but is leaving, I believe, tomorrow. Mrs. Ettinghausen was, perhaps intends still to be, an assistant of Mr. Arthur Upham Pope.[264] She is an energetic young American woman, a graduate of the University of Wisconsin.

I heard it said in Detroit where I have been recently to see the delightful Franz Hals exhibition that Mr. Pope has made himself persona non grata in Persia, and that his writings on Persian art are quite vulnerable. I do not know how just this statement is.

We had the Ettinghausens at dinner, and Dr. E. said that he was formerly on the staff of the Kaiser Friedrich Museum in Berlin, and I believe he said he had lived in or near Dahlem. At any rate he was entirely familiar with the names of all the people in Germany whom I know or have corresponded with. Dr. E. made a pleasant impression on me. He is modest, also young-looking. I have no means of judging his competence, knowing nothing of his field, the Persian art of the Mohammedan period, but his

---

[263] Richard Ettinghausen (1906-1979) was a German historian of Islamic Art. He moved to the US in 1934 and went to work for Arthur Pope (see below) at the Institute of Persian Art and Archaeology in New York. He taught at the Institute of Fine Art at New York University and then at Michigan from 1938-1944. He then went to the Freer Gallery, the Department of Near Eastern Art which is part of the Smithsonian Institution. In 1966 he went back to the Institute of Fine Art at NYU as the Hagop Kevorkian Professor of Islamic Art, and remained so until he died of cancer in 1979 (https://dictionaryofarthistorians.org/ettinghausenr. htm, accessed 11 December 2016).

[264] Arthur Upham Pope (1881-1969) was an American archaeologist and historian of Persian Art. He held a number of museum positions and founded the American Institute for Persian Art and Archaeology, ultimately the Asia Institute, in New York. He was central to the development of the study of art in Iran, and is buried there, in Isfahan, and there is a mausoleum for him.

lectures inspired a certain degree of confidence, though he has much still to learn of the technique of lecturing. He has a brother active in Oxford, England, as a teacher of German, who is giving instruction to Mr. Gunn's American student who followed him from Philadelphia to Oxford.

With kind regards from us both | Caroline R. Williams

**30 January 1935**                                                                     **0235**

January 30, 1935

CONFIDENTIAL

Dear Mrs. Williams:

Your kind letter of January 26 finds me just leaving for a meeting of the American Council of Learned Societies in Boston, but I want to send you a word of acknowledgment. I found your letter very interesting, and the information it conveys is valuable.

We are just now in the process of adjusting our personnel question in Persia, and your reference to Mr. Pope is in full accord with official information now in our hands. His presence in Persia is to us a real problem, and one which we have not yet very successfully resolved.

Thanking you for the additional light which you have given us, and with kindest greetings to you and Mr. Williams, I am | Very sincerely yours | JHB

**3 May 1935**                                                                         **0236**

602 Tennyson Place |
Toledo, Ohio | May 3, 1935

Dear Professor Breasted:-

I am very happy to know through your kindness about the new edition of Ancient Times. It was very good of you to send me a copy and to inscribe it in such a friendly way.[265] I am in process of reading the pre-Greek pages

---

[265] JHB, *Ancient Times: A History of the Early World*, Second Edition (New York: Ginn and Company, 1935).

and take much interest in the alterations of text and new illustrations you have introduced.

From the time when you were writing the first edition, then still living in your Lexington Avenue home and somewhat begrudging the time it took away from what you felt was your real work, I have always thought that the writing of this school history was one of your biggest services to your own and younger generations. One intellectual woman of my acquaintance, now in older years, who holds a high place in the esteem of Toledoans, told me the other day that she is just rereading <u>Ancient Times</u> with much pleasure. And many parents of young people of school age hear of the book through its use as a text book. The first evening after the new edition came my husband monopolized it!

Astrid may be interested to know that I have met her German teacher's mother, Mrs. Sasse, since I was in Chicago, and that I went to a luncheon last Saturday at the home Mrs. Walter Eversman, Betty Eversman's mother. My husband is friendly with Mr. Eversman, and I have always felt drawn to Mrs. Eversman, though I see her far too seldom.

I hear occasionally from the Ermans, but they write only of their family life, and I am completely in the dark as to what has happened in Egyptological circles in Berlin—whether Professor Junker, despite his Roman Catholicism and the excesses of the Nazi government, was wanted for, and cared to accept, the Berlin professorship, whether Professor Schäfer retired at Easter and who has been appointed in his place, why Professor Ranke lost his professorship in Heidelberg and what provision, if any, had been made for him elsewhere. I heard that he was in Egypt last winter. My last direct word from the Rankes was a Christmas greeting by Frau Ranke's hand dwelling sadly on the loss of their older son, who I suppose was either murdered or took his own life. It has been a shattering blow to them, and especially to the mother. At Christmas they were in Heidelberg. Steindorff's successor in Leipzig has sent me Heft I of Leipziger Ägyptologische Studien[266] which sounds like an obvious attempt to suit himself to the times in Germany; I refer especially to the words: Sie (die neuen Studien) rechnen auf das Interesse nicht nur des engen Fachkreises der Agyptologie, sondern aller derer, die aus der Betrachtung der grossen

---

[266] Walther Wolf, *Individuum und Gemeinschaft in der Agyptischen Kultur* (Leipzig: Glückstädter Verlag Augustin, 1935).

Kulturen der Weltgeschichte eine Klärung unseres geschichtlichen Bewusstseins und eine Vertiefung der Erkenntnis unseres eigenen Wesens erhoffen.[267]

Dr. Gardiner was good enough to send me his second publication of Beatty papyri (I already had the first), and I fell with avidity on text No. IX which concerns the temple service in its final stage of a ceremonial meal for the god.[268] I had long and unheeded on my shelves the Golenischeff publication of the Cairo copy of the same text. I noted with interest that Gardiner thinks a thorough-going study of the older temple ritual will have to take into consideration data preserved in texts of the Graeco-Roman period. (Those texts are a closed book to me!) About the time I was reading that remark, Dr. Bull wrote me that apropos of a task Mr. Winlock set him of dealing with late inscriptions from the Dakhleh Oasis—copied by Mr. Winlock before 1909-10 and still unpublished—he is working on 'Materials for a Sign-List for the Ptolemaic Roman Period.'[269]

At present my modest efforts are concentrated at the opposite extremity of Egypt's long history. I am endeavoring to digest Junker's <u>Giza II.</u> and finding myself much interested in his discussion of the evidence on the funerary beliefs and practices before Sun-worship became the state religion and Osiris began to invade the realm of the dead.[270] The difference of opinion among those who, like Junker and Reisner, know Old Kingdom material best, as to the dating of early reliefs and Old Kingdom tombs is appalling. It is disappointing too that Porter and Moss are erratic and unreliable on dates.[271] Of course that does not affect the high value of their

---

[267] They (the new studies) count on the interest not only of the narrow professional circle of Egyptology, but all those who, from the consideration of the great cultures of the world's history, hope for a clarification of our historical consciousness and a deepening of the knowledge of our own being.

[268] Alan H. Gardiner, The Library of A. Chester Beatty: Description of a Hieratic Papyrus with a Mythological Story, Love-songs and Other Miscellaneous Texts, The Chester Beatty Papyri, No. I (Oxford: Oxford University Press, 1931). The Chester Beatty Papyri is a collection of papyri originally purchased in Cairo in the early twentieth century. The whole collection is now in the Chester Beatty Library in Dublin, Ireland, although some related papyri are in Michigan.

[269] Ludlow Bull, 'Appendix: Inscriptions at Deir el Hagar,' in Ed Dākhleh Oasis: Journal of a Camel Trip made in 1908, H. E. Winlock (New York: Metropolitan Museum of Art, 1936), 65-77.

[270] Hermann Junker, Giza II: Die Mastabas der beginnenden V. Dynastie auf dem Westfriedhof (Vienna and Leipzig: Hölder-Pichler-Tempsky, 1934).

[271] Bertha Porter (1852-1941) and Rosalind Moss (1890-1990) were the authors of the essential

volumes for handy reference, but such an error as in vol. III, p. 110, of assigning to the IV Dynasty the tomb of a Prophet of the Sun-Temples of Neferirkere and Nuserre ought to be avoidable by them.[272]

Professor Erman's <u>Religion</u> in its new guise, the first part of <u>Mélanges Maspero</u> with Engelbach's clever settling of Capart's loose comments on the portraiture exhibited in the statues of Ranofer and much of interest besides, the first Lieferung of references for the <u>Wb.</u>, Mr. Davies's colored plates of Rekhmire are among the new things that I fine stimulating, despite my isolation here.[273] I am beginning to plan to try to get out to Egypt once more, if only to take the cures off the book I must finish for the M. M. A., and before long I hope to get my affairs and studies in shape for a few needed periods of work in New York.[274]

We are to stay in our present apartment until the last of September and do not yet know what we shall do next. You must be very proud of your grandson and take much delight in him. Again my sincere appreciation of your kind gift of a copy of the second edition of <u>Ancient Times</u>. With warm regards from us both | Sincerely yours | Caroline R. Williams

P.S. Grant has something to attend to in Mount Pleasant, Michigan, and made a sudden decision to go there this weekend. We are spending the

---

*Topographical Bibliography of Ancient Egyptian Hieroglyphic Texts* that went to six volumes and were published between 1927 and 1939. There have been more editions of volumes I-III in the mid-1970s and early 1980s. Porter was a professional bibliographer for the *Dictionary of National Bibliography* and was hired by Francis Griffith to build the volumes. Moss, a professional anthropologist, joined the project by 1924, and continued the project after Porter's retirement in 1929. See more about the women in Barbara Lesko 'Bertha Porter (1852-1941) and Rosalind Moss (1890-1990),' *Breaking Ground: Women in Old World Archaeology*, http://www.brown.edu/Research/Breaking_Ground/bios/Porter_Bertha.pdf (accessed 12 December 2016).

[272] Bertha Porter and Rosalind Moss, *Topographical Bibliography of Ancient Egyptian Hieroglyphic Texts, Reliefs, and Paintings. Volume III: Memphis (Abu Rawash to Dahshur)* (Oxford: Oxford University Press, 1931). The volumes are available online here: http://topbib.griffith.ox.ac.uk//index.html (accessed 12 December 2016).

[273] Erman's volume cited above; *Melanges Maspero: Volume I: Orient Ancien* (Le Caire: Imprimerie de l'Institut Français d'Archéologie Oriental, 1934); the 'Wb.' is Worterbuch, or Erman's Dictionary, she had gotten her first 'Lieferung' or delivery of references; Norman de Garis Davies, *Paintings from the Tomb of Rekh-mi-Re' at Thebes* (New York: Metropolitan Museum of Art, 1935).

[274] CRW went to Egypt one more time, for the 1935-36 season with the MMA's Egyptian Expedition.

night comfortably in the state's capital and I mail this letter here. The fruit trees are so lovely, it is a pleasure to get out of town.

**27 May 1935**                                                    **0237**

May 27, 1935

My dear Mrs. Williams:

Absence from home on scientific meetings in the East and a lecture at New York University have delayed this reply to your very interesting letter of May 3.

I have been greatly interested by your news from Germany. I have just had a delightful letter from Erman written in his usual half-facetious omitting any details such as we would be so glad to have. I do not yet know whether Junker has been called to Berlin or would accept if he were called. I suppose Schäfer has retired, for he wrote me in January that he was looking forward to this not altogether disagreeable event. I was much shocked to hear your news that Ranke had lost his professorship at Heidelberg. He has just forwarded me his article on the origin of the Egyptian tomb statues in the <u>Harvard Theological Review</u> and wrote on it a pleasant message in quite his old spirit.[275] He wrote me before his departure for Egypt but made no reference to his University situation, merely stating that he and his wife were to take a long needed rest on a voyage up the Nile. I suppose you are correct that Ranke's son without doubt took his own life. I had a letter from Wreszinski asking for certain Institute publications for review in OLZ, and I sent an inquiry to the publisher Hinrichs in Leipzig regarding Wreszinski's address.[276] I now have a letter from Hinrichs stating that Wreszinski is now dead.[277] I should say it was practically certain that he took his own life. The situation is simply appalling. Erman, too, in his recent letter refers to Wreszinski's death but does not in any way intimate how he died.

I was greatly interested in your quotation from the publication of Steindorff's successor in Leipzig. I should say that it displays exactly the

---

[275] Hermann Ranke, 'The Origin of the Egyptian Tomb Statue,' *The Harvard Theological Review* 28:1 (January 1935): 45-53. He did not leave Heidelberg until 1937.
[276] Orientalistische Literaturzeitung.
[277] 9 April 1935.

Nazi spirit. I wonder if you have heard that the student body at Berlin has been reduced to one third of its former numbers. The rector in the University, which the names of von Humboldt, Virchow, Helmholtz and Mommsen have made illustrious, all of whom, like Erman himself, served as rector magnificus—this University now has as its rector an unsuccessful German immigrant horse doctor, thirty-five years old, formerly of New York, who returned to Berlin and entered the political arena. He wears his gold chain of office (which for three generations has adorned the shoulders of men like those I have mentioned), over his brown shirt displaying his Nazi affiliations! I do not wonder that poor Erman never makes any reference to such conditions.

I am noting your account of your studies, and I quite envy you. I find so little time for scientific work myself. The burden of Institute administration becomes heavier and heavier.

I hope you will stick to your purpose of going out to Egypt once more, and I wish you might persuade Mr. Williams to go with you. We should be delighted to see you at Sakkara and Luxor.

I wish Chicago had been a little nearer to your route on your way to Mount Pleasant, Michigan.

Believe me, with kindest greetings to you both, and many thanks for your most interesting letter | Very sincerely yours | JHB


**29 July 1935**                                                    **0238**

July 29, 1935

My dear Mrs. Williams:

I want to thank you for your admirable review of the first Abydos volume in the current number of AJA.[278] You put far more work into this discussion than I had anticipated, and I hope that it has not taken too much of your time and strength. Your review is really a highly specialized contribution to the subject which I am sure all Orientalists will appreciate, and I am very grateful indeed.

I am wondering whether you and Mr. Williams are expecting to

---

[278] CRW 'Review: *The Temple of King Sethos I at Abydos, Vol. I: The Chapels of Osiris, Isis, and Horus* by Alan H. Gardiner,' *American Journal of Archaeology*, 39:2 (Apr.-Jun. 1935): 273-278.

attend the Congress in Rome. Perhaps I have already written you that Astrid is in France attending courses on the history of art at the University of Paris. She and her traveling chum, another Vassar girl, are expected to finish the courses in Paris on August 10, then go on down into Italy where we are arranging to meet them toward the end of August, and after touring a little in northern Italy we expect to settle down in Florence until about September 15, when we shall arrive in Rome a week before the beginning of the Congress on September 23.

I have never yet visited Ravenna, where I am exceedingly anxious to see the Byzantine mosaics in the church of San Vitale which first led me to my conclusion that the mosaics of this age are directly descended in spirit and style from the paintings which we find at Dura (Salihiyah) on the Euphrates.

It would be a very great pleasure if we might look forward to seeing you and Mr. Williams in Rome. Besides some reduction in ocean steamship rates, the Italian railways are granting a reduction of 70% on all railway fares between the frontier and Rome, and 50% on all fares for casual touring until the end of October. You have perhaps noticed that the lira has slumped substantially, and this from our point of view is also all to the good.

With kindest greetings to you and Mr. Williams, I remain | Very sincerely yours | JHB

**9 August 1935**                                                    0239

602 Tennyson Place |
Toledo, Ohio | August 9, 1935

My dear Professor Breasted:-

You were most kind to write to me on seeing my review in the last A. J. A. I am more gratified than I can say that you liked the review and think it will be useful. The editors of A. J. A. had had sixty separates struck off for me like the two I am sending you under separate cover, and I am getting them off to such friends as I have among scholars who might care to see the review. A. J. A. comes oftener to the attention of Classical Archaeologists than of Orientalists, but it is the one journal in this country that still prints long reviews and is hospitable to those on Egyptian subjects.

We had of course learned with much sympathetic interest of your marriage recently—first through the New York Times and then by your own and Mrs. Richmond's announcement.[279] I feel as if I knew Frances's younger sister, for Frances used to talk much of her and once, I recall, in 1923 or thereabouts, we did meet in the old Hotel Beresford in New York. I was there making a prolonged stay while working for the New York Historical Society, you were abroad with Charles, and Astrid and Jimmie were with their mother.

Your 'at home' date being December 1st, and the paper having said you were going to Italy, I had not written to you, thinking you were already abroad. And I should have responded more quickly to your recent letter, had it not waited here a few days before my return from Montreal, where I spent some five weeks at McGill's French Summer School, trying to recover something of my one-time conversational use of French, German, which I learned to talk later than French, having driven the latter largely out of my head.

It was great fun going to school once more, and I was much interested in the academic routine of teaching French, never having studied a foreign language except with private teachers in the countries where the respective languages are spoken. I had never been in Montreal before, and altogether the experience gave me just the change of scene and thought I needed. There were Americans and Canadians there from states and provinces stretching from the Pacific to the Atlantic, and from New Orleans in the south to Edmonton, Alberta, and Keenville, N. S. in the north. One mother and her daughter were among the students, also a number of negroes, among them a man refused at Middlebury, Vermont, because of his race, whose pronunciation and knowledge of French are remarkably good. The instruction and variety of helps seemed to me admirable, and although I went alone from here, I soon met people who knew friends of mine and had a general satisfactory time.

Nothing could be so ideal as going to Italy for the Congress, about

---

[279] JHB married Frances' younger sister Imogen Hart Richmond (1885-1961) in early June. Imogen had been married to a New York stock broker and had two children. The two divorced and she had been raising her children alone. It is not clear when she and JHB started courting, but they got married less than a year after starting their courtship (Abt, *American Egyptologist*, 389-90).

which I have heard only through you, no invitation to go having reached me. My husband and I much appreciate the information you conveyed to us and your kind suggestion. Unfortunately Grant is tied to his business and will be, I fear, until he closes it for good and all. Just now he is doing some work for the Government, nothing of his own seeking but something that was fairly thrust upon him by people in this city who considered him the best person to secure options for two large slum-clearance projects. I can scarcely look at him in business hours, his office being filled with the numerous property owners whose ninety-day options he is getting, with proper consideration of values fair to them but without letting them put over any extravagant demands on the Government. It is a delicate job, and one to which he brings qualifying experience in dealing with all kinds of property owners. Whether in the end the Government will take up the options is more than Grant knows. He is no friend of New Deal policies, but in this case is doing a service to the community. There won't be any graft or injustice in the part in which he is concerned.

How delightful for Astrid to be using her French in studying Art and Art History in Paris. Please give her my affectionate greetings.

I do not know whether this letter will catch you before you sail, but if it finds you both still in Chicago, I wish it might be possible that you could spare the time to stop in Toledo on your way east. You may come as incognito as you like, and there is a residence hotel in our quarter of the city where we should be delighted to entertain you; the Lindsley Halls[280] of the M. M. A. were comfortable there in a ninth story apartment with a fine view of the city. The hotel is one in which I am expecting us to land some day when our pleasant experiments in housekeeping are over. The trouble with our present apartment, which we resign to its owners the last of September, is that it is too small to afford comfort to guests. You would be most welcome, now, or at any time, and I do trust that Mrs. Breasted will take me for a friend since I knew and loved her sister so well.

Ever with kindest greetings from Grant and me | Sincerely yours | Caroline R. Williams

---

[280] Lindsley Hall (1883-1969) was an American draughtsman who worked for the Metropolitan Museum of Art's Egyptian Expedition from 1913-1949. He worked closely with Winlock and in 1922 worked on Tutankhamun's tomb, drawing plans of the main chamber for that expedition.

P.S. I have a very happy memory of Ravenna having visited it with my aunt, Miss Randolph, when I was an eighteen-year old girl. I have never been able to return, much as I should like to do so.

**10 August 1935**                                                   **0240**

August 10, 1935

My dear Mrs. Williams:

It has been a great pleasure this morning to find in the mails your kind letter of August 9. I am very grateful to you for your generosity in sending me two copies of your review in AJA. I do not know whether you are sending one to Alan Gardiner or not so I think I will forward one of these to him as he will, of course, be greatly interested. I was glad that you touched on some matters of rigid exactness in the epigraphy. Gardiner has never provided for the careful collation of the finished drawings such as we insist upon at Medinet Habu and Karnak. I think there can be no doubt about the very high quality of these Abydos plates but without the rigorous collation which we always make I hardly think we can expect the same accuracy which our Luxor group has attained.

I was much interested to hear of your going back to school for renovation of your French in Montreal. I wish Mrs. Breasted and I could have accompanied you.

I was greatly interested to hear of the task in which Mr. Williams is now engaged. He will be doing a very real public service if he can save our government any money in these days of such appalling waste and reckless extravagance. You will be interested to know that the teacher of dramatics at Vassar has been handed 14 million dollars with which to open the theaters all over the country and give our unemployed actors and actresses some occupation for a time. Imagine a woman without any business training and obliged to build upon her own organization where none now exists, launching upon an enterprise such as this! I am glad to see that at Toledo at least the New Deal knew where to go for the right kind of guidance.

I do not recall whether I told you in my last letter that my son James, Jr., is to be married on the fourteenth of this month, that is, next week

Wednesday, to a charming girl in Lake Forest. We are therefore inevitably tied down here every minute until we leave for our ship on the fifteenth. Mrs. Breasted is at the moment in the East but returns tomorrow. I am sure that with circumstances different we would be delighted to stop off in Toledo for a visit with you and Mr. Williams.

With many thanks for the kind invitation and warmest greetings to you and your husband, I am | Very sincerely yours | JHB

**3 December 1935**                                              **0241**

1935 Dec 3 AM 9 49

LC CHARLES BREASTED (ORIENTAL INSTITUTE OF THE UNIVERSITY OF CHGO)=ORINST CHICAGO=

DEEPEST SYMPATHY WITH YOU ALL=
CAROLINE WILLIAMS.

**4 December 1935**                                              **0242**

Memphis – Sakkara, Egypt |
December 4, 1935

My dear Mr. Breasted:-

I am grieving with you and all the members of Dr. Breasted's family.[281]

To me, too, the loss is irreparable and I feel it keenly. I never had a truer, kinder, more helpful friend than your father had always been to me from the time in 1898 when I first became his pupil. The younger

---

[281] JHB caught a cold on board the ship home from his trip, which turned into strep throat made worse by a 'latent malarial condition.' Upon his arrival in New York, he was rushed to the hospital where he was treated for five days, which got rid of the malaria but not the strep infection. He died on 2 December 1935. 'In a twist he would have enjoyed, his five attending physicians issued 'a signed statement' on the precise cause of his death. ... 'to eliminate any possibility that Dr. Breasted's death might be attributed to the oft-discredited story of 'King Tut's curse.'" (Abt, *American Egyptologist*, 390). Letters poured into the Oriental Institute and to Charles Breasted from around the world.

generation who could not have him as a teacher do not know how much they have missed. Truly your father's great versatility is one of the outstanding characteristics of his life as I knew him. I cannot think of any activity in which he did not excel, --first and foremost as a scholar, but also as a lecturer, teacher, after-dinner speaker, executive, financier, and in those warm human qualities which made him such a delightful companion and friend. Oh, I feel so unreconciled that he should not have had another decade or more of life.

Is it not a curious circumstance that news of his passing should have come to me here where I am enjoying the friendly hospitality and the opportunities of one of the centers of study which his initiative and vision created? We were all working yesterday in the tomb of Mereruka when in the middle of the morning word came that Mr. Duell wished us to return to the house; we were a subdued company riding down in the car, each one feeling sure there must be some grave reason for the summons. There was no speculation audibly, I thought perhaps war had broken out between England and Italy and truly had that been so, it could hardly have seemed to me a greater calamity! Of the sad truth I had not the slightest premonition.

Many of this household have told me in what fine form he seemed when here only a few weeks ago, how merry he was, how much he enjoyed seeing old friends and acquaintances. Mr. Duell showed me a photograph of him sitting with Reisner, Junker and Borchardt. I am glad that Mrs. Breasted and Astrid will have the memory of the happy time together here.

My heart goes out to you all. I know how you, the eldest child, adored your father; and to your brother and sister, too, the world will never seem quite the same with that loving, loyal, wise and companionable father gone beyond their ken.

The only comfort I have known under like circumstances is the thought that nothing can rob one of what one has had. The past is secure in tender and inspiring recollections.

My husband would wish me to add his condolences to mine. I am glad for him that he had the privilege of knowing Dr. Breasted a little.

Will you please share this letter with your family so far as they would care to see it? I do not even know where to address Jimmie and Astrid.

Ever sincerely yours | Caroline R. Williams

# Epilogue

The last letter in the archives from Ransom Williams is the one of condolences she sent to Charles Breasted after her friend and mentor had died unexpectedly. From 1935 until her own death in 1952, there is a handful of extant documents that give a glimpse into her work, but there are a few things we know. It is clear that she continued working in Egyptology. In fact, she was in Egypt in 1935-36 to work with the Metropolitan Museum of Art in their Egyptian Expedition and had been working with the Coffin Texts project when she heard about Breasted's death. Upon her return to the United States in 1936, she probably did not go to the field again. By this time, she was in her mid-sixties and, with her husband's failing health, she stayed close to Toledo.[1] Many letters between 1935 and 1952 appear in the archives at the Egyptian Art Department at the MMA. I have not included any of them here, but some of the information contained in them helps to round out her life story.

Ransom Williams continued working with the MMA from 1935, intermittently until her shortly after her husband's death. In 1937 she received an honorary degree from the University of Toledo for her work in the field of Egyptology and archaeology. She continued to publish book reviews and articles until Grant died on Christmas Eve, 1942 from an extended illness.[2] From this point on, her friend Katharine Reusch became

---

[1] Lesko, 'Caroline Ransom Williams,' 6.

[2] 'A Relief from Lisht Representing Wep-wawet in Therianthropic form,' *Melanges Maspero, I* (Cairo: 1935), 525-527; 'Review of Harold H. Nelson and Üvo Hölscher, *Work in Western Thebes 1931-33*,' *AJA* 39:4 (Oct-Dec 1935): 621; 'News Items from Egypt; The Season of 1935 to 36,' *AJA* 40:4 (Oct-Dec 1936): 551-56; 'Review of Nina M. Davies and Alan H. Gardiner, *Ancient Egyptian Paintings*,' *AJA* 41:4 (Oct-Dec 1937): 638-42; 'Review of William C. Hayes, *Glazed Tiles from a Palace of Ramses II at Kantir*,' *AJA* 42:3 (Jul-Sep 1938): 425; 'Review of George Andrew Reisner, *The Development of the Egyptian Tomb down to the Accession of Cheops*,' *AJA* 44:3 (Jul-Sep 1940): 398-99; 'Review of H. E. Winlock, *Materials Used at the Embalming of King Tut-'Ankh-Amun, Metropolitan Museum of Art Papers, 10*,' *AJA* 46:3 (Jul-Sep 1942), 441. 'Grant Williams Taken By

a steady companion.[3] In 1943 Ransom Williams gave her 'small collection of Egyptian antiquities' to her alma mater, Mount Holyoke College.[4] According to the acquisition records at the Mount Holyoke Art Museum, the 1943 donation consisted of approximately 16 small scarabs that were from the collection of Professor Louise Fitz-Randolph.[5] In 1944, she gave a sixteenth-century print of the Pantheon in Rome to the museum, as well. Fitz-Randolph had been donating objects to Mount Holyoke since 1902 and her estate has continued to gift the museum as late as 2013. Because Mount Holyoke holds some of Fitz-Randolph's papers, it is possible that some of Ransom Williams' papers went to her alma mater as well, but as I write neither I nor the archivists at Mount Holyoke have been able to find any substantial collection.[6] Her library, which she mentioned frequently to Breasted throughout their letters, was the subject of a newspaper article in 1933.[7] She had detailed to Breasted how she had been growing the collection one acquisition at a time. It was useful to her in her work, and it seems that most, if not all, of her library went to the library of the Egyptian Art department at the MMA in 1943 and later.[8]

Ransom Williams died February 1, 1952 from myocarditis, after a very short illness. She was remembered in the Toledo *Blade* as 'Dr. Williams, Woman Distinguished as Egyptologist.'[9] As I write, I have not found any other obituaries, eloges, or memoriams of Ransom Williams around the time of her death or in the years after it. Barbara Grace Spayd, a friend of Ransom Williams, wrote to Ambrose Lansing, then Curator of the Egyptian Art department at the MMA, of her passing. She asked for some bibliographic

Death,' *Toledo Blade* 25 December 1942: 18.

[3] Barbara Grace Spayd to Ambrose Lansing, 9 February 1952, Egyptian Art Department Archives, Folder: Williams, Carolyn [sic] Ransom 1937-1952, MMA, New York.

[4] Lesko, 'Caroline Ransom Williams,' 6.

[5] See, for example the collections database search: http://museums.fivecolleges.edu/info.php?s=ransom+williams&type=all&museum=mh&t=objects (accessed 18 December 2016).

[6] Personal communication, 29 October 2015.

[7] Ethel Lewis, 'Library on Egyptology Bares Secrets of Ancient Pharaohs in Toledo Home: Mrs. Grant Williams Has Noted Collection for Her Study,' [Chicago] *Times*, 21 May 1933, cited in Lesko, 'Caroline Ransom Williams.'

[8] Charles Jones, 'Bookplates of Scholars in Ancient Studies,' 4 April 2013, Ancient World Bloggers: http://ancientworldbloggers.blogspot.com/2008/08/bookplates-of-scholars-in-ancient.html (accessed 29 December 2016).

[9] 'Dr. Williams, Woman Distinguished as Egyptologist,' *Toledo Blade* 3 February 1952.

notes on Ransom Williams, and Lansing must have sent them.[10]   Ransom Williams' name did not appear in any of the journals she wrote diligently for, remembrances did not materialize from any of the institutions she gave her time and expertise to, or from any of the colleagues she left behind. She did pass away after many of her contemporaries were already gone, but it seems that memories of her life and work went with the passing of those who knew her.

Ransom Williams' story, in and of itself, is an important one in the history of science. Her contributions and impact on the fields of Egyptology, museum curation, and language study were critical and the esteem to which men like Breasted, Lythgoe, and others held her demonstrated that. But her life also fits into the large group of women professional scientists who lost (and continue to lose) their careers because of the difficulties of balancing the physical and emotional burdens of home with the pressures and deadlines of academic work. Professional academic work largely lacked the infrastructure for understanding that scientists sometimes must be able to care for families as well as participate in a professional capacity. Ransom Williams' colleagues continued to include her in their pursuits and plans because of her expertise, but these were too far afield for her to commit to them. Despite her hard work, she was one of many women who had followed the same path her male colleagues took, but who did not receive credit for her accomplishments.

This volume is meant to introduce Ransom Williams' life and work. But we must do more than point to her to show she was here; there is clearly more to be done. Through these letters we begin to glimpse the work she did, but we must now analyze the impact of her achievements. Further, throughout her lifetime she collected objects and a full library, all of which were donated to institutions after her husband's death. Those collections deserve further study. Finally, she had nieces and nephews who are hard to trace, but no children, so it is not clear where the bulk of her papers and personal items went. It is not clear if she kept a diary, so her correspondence is crucial. There are more existing letters of hers in the MMA Egyptian Art department archives, in the Bryn Mawr special collections (she corresponded with M. Carey Thomas, former president of

---

[10] Barbara Grace Spayd to Ambrose Lansing, 9 February 1952, Egyptian Art Department Archives, Folder: Williams, Carolyn [sic] Ransom 1937-1952, MMA, New York.

the College), possibly at Mount Holyoke, and in the other museums of art she worked for. In order to trace the rest of her life and get more details into her personal and professional activities, it is important to read these letters and construct the story of her life around them. She may have been temporarily buried in the dust of the archive, but we must use these sources to shed more light on her life and career.

# Appendix

These letters pertain to the issue in letter 0208, between CRW and the University of Chicago Press.

**5 February 1932**                                                    A01

COPY | The University of Chicago Press |
February 5, 1932

Dear Miss Ransom:-
The copyright on your book, 'Studies in Ancient Furniture,' expires in the next few weeks. It is our opinion that the purpose for which it has been taken out has been served and, therefore, we plan to let it expire and to declare it out of print.

There are still a few copies in our stock and I am wondering if you would like to have some of these for your personal files. If you will let us know promptly how many you want, we will be glad to send them to you without charge up to the limit of our supply.

Very truly yours | THE UNIVERSITY OF CHICAGO PRESS | Rollin D. Hemens


**7 June 1932**                                                        A02

COPY | The University of Chicago Press | 5750 Ellis Avenue |
Chicago, Illinois | June 7, 1932

Dear Miss Ransom:
Since we have not heard from you with reference to our letter of February 5, we assume that it has gone astray and are inclosing a copy of it.

Obviously, the copyright on your book, 'Studies in Ancient Furniture,' expired quite some time ago and the book was consequently declared out of print. The remaining stock has not been destroyed, however, inasmuch as we supposed that you might want some copies for your personal files. If you do, will you please let us know how many you want so that the rest can be disposed of?

Very truly yours | THE UNIVERSITY OF CHICAGO PRESS | Rollin D. Hemens

**15 June 1932**                                                    **A03**

COPY | The University of Chicago Press | 5750 Ellis Avenue | Chicago, Illinois | June 15, 1932

Dear Mrs. Williams:
I am inclosing two letters which were addressed to your former residence and which have been returned to us. They are dated February 5 and June 7, 1932 and concern your book, 'Studies in Ancient Furniture.'

My we hear from you at your earliest convenience?

Very truly yours | THE UNIVERSITY OF CHICAGO PRESS | A. N. | Secretary to Mr. Hemens

**17 June 1932**                                                    **A04**

COPY | June 17, 1932

Dear Sir:-
I am in receipt this morning of your two letters of February 5, 1932, and June 7, 1932, and your secretary's letter of June 15th.

It seems to me a very high-handed, not to say stupid, proceeding, to write to me as 'Miss Ransom' at 2112 Jefferson Avenue, and, without getting into communication with me at all, to declare my book 'out of print' and to propose to withdraw from sale the remaining one hundred and fifty-four copies and dump them (or part of them) on me, as a favor to me, disposing of the rest in your own way.

In the first place, since 1916 my name and address have been: Mrs. Grant Williams, The Chesbrough Dwellings, 1505 Jefferson Avenue, Toledo, Ohio. And every year the University press has sent me a royalty on the book addressing me correctly. This change of name and address, now of long standing, is therefore a matter of record with the University of Chicago Press, besides being ascertainable in the alumni office, in the published directory of alumni, etc.

My contract with the University of Chicago Press, dated November 1, 1904, lies before me as I write. It contains no time limit, and it does not say that the expiration of the copyright will cancel the contract. My equity in the remaining copies amounts to $462, no slight sum these days. But even more important from my point of view is the killing of the book, which ought not to go 'out of print.' Nobody will want to reprint it, so the lapse of the copyright is of no consequence, but the book's contents have never been superseded, and from time to time persons or libraries will want to obtain copies. Four were sold last year, as the Press's report of June 30, 1931, indicates.

You will please do nothing further about this book until I have had an opportunity to get advice in the matter.

Very truly yours, | (Mrs. Grant Williams)


**17 June 1932**                                                    **A05**

COPY | The Chesbrough Dwellings |
Toledo, Ohio | June 17, 1932

Dear Professor Laing:-

I do not know whether you will still recall me as a one-time pupil of yours who once took your course in Roman life and talked in your class on Roman furniture.

In the absences from Chicago of Professor Breasted, to whom I would naturally write, the matter being rather peremptory, I am venturing to send you copies of letters which came to me only this morning and of my reply to them.

Mr. Williams read them at the breakfast table and remarked: 'If all books were as slow in their turn-over as this one has been, the Press would soon go out of business.' That is one side of the matter, and I do not wish to be unreasonable, but I am wondering whether something could be done to salvage the remainder of the edition. The book is a cheap book today at $.50, with its nine-color lithograph as frontispiece, its XXIX good half-tone plates at the back, and its fifty-three interesting text illustrations. Miss Richter's book on ancient furniture, if I mistake not, costs $35.00. I do not think the usefulness of my book is past. Within three months, two young graduate students, one of Chicago, one at the University of Michigan, have spoken to me of having consulted it. Personally, I feel that if the University Press had handled my book a little differently in these last years, the edition would have been sold out long ago. And we all know what a nuisance it is to want to buy a book and to find that it is out of print.

I should be grateful to you if you are in a position to do so and would be so kind as to restrain Mr. Hemens from any further drastic action as to my book until I have had a chance to see what can be done. If times were different it might be possible to dispose of the remaining copies at a discount to some dealer in second-hand books. And if you should yourself feel any interest in the matter, the subject of the book being more classical than Egyptian, I should be very grateful for your advice.

Most sincerely yours | (Mrs. Grant Williams)


**17 June 1932**                                                          **A06**

COPY | June 17, 1932

Dear Sir:-
Earlier in the day I wrote to you in reply to letters of yours received in the morning mail. This evening I have shown to Mr. Williams my contract with the University of Chicago Press with reference to the sale of the book.

My husband suggests that I send you a copy of the contract, as he thinks that in the years since it was drawn and under various managements, the Press's copy may have been lost or mislaid and that you may be unaware of its provisions.

As we read it there is no provision in it for the cancelation of the contract at your option and you seem to us to be under obligation to go on with its terms until the one hundred and fifty-four copies still remaining of the edition at the time of your last report, June 30, 1931, are sold out.

The showing was poor in 1931, but in 1929 nine copies were sold, and in 1930 the number was eight.

Very truly yours | signed Mrs. Grant Williams

Dear Mr. Breasted:-

This letter will be mailed in the morning. There may be some general law of time limits for such contracts, of which I have no knowledge. In any case, I am disinclined to insist on the Press continuing to carry my old book if after reading the contract the University authorities think I ought to allow it to lapse.

C.R.W

**20 June 1932**                                                       A07

COPY | The University of Chicago Press | 5750 Ellis Avenue | Chicago, Illinois | June 20, 1932

Dear Mrs. Williams:-

The letters which you received from us relative to declaring out of print your book, 'Studies in Ancient Furniture—Couches and Beds of the Greeks, Etruscans and Romans,' were not intended to be high-handed in any way.

As a title of such outstanding merit and as your book has been on our list a great many years, it is not without considerable hesitation and regret that we reach a decision to declare it out of print. We find, however, that with the new studies being completed and submitted for publication each year, it is necessary to drop from our list the earlier publications which have already had a good distribution and which, therefore are no longer in great demand.

No copies of your book have been disposed of as remaindered stock and we have every one of them in the warehouse.

We are going to continue the title on our list for one more year. If there is any indication during that time of enough increased demand for the book so that we may continue it on our list even longer but without absolute financial loss, we shall be glad to carry it. On the other hand if sales continue at approximately their present rate, I am afraid we shall be forced to declare the title out of print. In that case, we can send to you such copies as you want and forward for your attention all orders which come to us.

Very truly yours | THE UNIVERSITY OF CHICAGO PRESS | Rollin D. Hemens

**22 June 1932**                                                                                   **A08**

COPY | The Chesbrough Dwellings |
Toledo, Ohio | June 22, 1932

Dear Mr. Hemens:-

Commenting on your letter of June 20, 1932, I am glad that you will defer for at least another year declaring my book, 'Studies in Ancient Furniture— Couches and Beds of the Greeks, Etruscans, and Romans,' out of print, although it seems to me hardly fair to make a test year of its marketability one which is a year of deepest depression. The very fact that at such a time I have a potential several hundred dollars locked up in these copies naturally makes me desirous to have them sold out in time. There has been no year since the book was issued that some copies have not been sold (that is, unless the present year ending June 30, 1932 has seen no sales), bringing me each summer a welcome, even though small, check.

Since you are so reluctant to continue the book on your lists, I must rest such claims as I make on the original contract of which I have already sent you a copy. Clause 3 of that contract gives as an agreement of 'Party of the First Part': 'To announce said book in its catalogue, to see that it is listed in trade papers, and to keep it in stock with its agents in the principal book centers.' I am in no position to judge whether the University Press has carried out through the years the first two of these items, as I do not see the Press's catalogues or trade papers, but from such yearly reports as I have on file, I do not see that the third item has been carried out, except in the first decade after the book's publication. From 1905-1914 inclusive, copies varying from 22 to 4 in number were reported as 'on sale.' After 1915, only in 1920 and again in 1921 was a single copy on sale, in the reports of other years a zero stands under that captions. As I judge the matter, if the book had been given the chance from 1915 on of being in the hands of your agents, or at least of some of them, the edition might have been sold out by now.

I would suggest, too, that today books of the size, quality of paper, quality and number of illustrations (colored lithograph as frontispiece, XXIX half-tone plates, 52 text illustrations, some of them full page), all well bound in a buckram, cannot be published to sell for $4.50. So classicists who purchase the book get a good deal—regarded as a piece of book-making—for their money.

Very truly yours | (Mrs. Grant Williams)


**30 June 1932**                                                     A09

RE: MRS GRANT WILLIAMS VS U OF C PRESS

I telephoned Mr. Hemens' office to-day regarding the above, and find that Mr. Hemens is away – returning Tuesday, 5 July.

Before he left, however, he arranged to continue Mrs. Williams' book on the lists for another year. He also wrote to Mr. Moore about the matter of copyright, etc., but has not yet had a reply.

I presume this is all that can be done until Mr. Hemens gets back.

(He has written Mrs. Williams, his secretary says, about continuing the book on the list, and has tried to placate her in every way.)

I have not yet shown this file to Dr. Breasted.

JMR

Thanx! –Please show this file to JHB
CB

# Bibliography

All of the letters transcribed here are from the Oriental Institute Archives. I have not notated which folders they came from in the text, but the archives are organized chronologically in boxes and then alphabetically by either institution or last name. For this volume, the organization is as follows:

Letters 0001-0003, written in 1898, were filed under 'L' because Ransom was writing from Lake Erie Seminary.

Letters 0004-0005, written in 1899 and 1900, were filed under 'R' for Caroline L. Ransom.

Letters 0006-0010, written from 1908 to May of 1910, were filed under 'B' for Bryn Mawr College.

Letters 0011-0064, written from May of 1910 to May of 1916 were filed under 'M' for Metropolitan Museum of Art.

Letters 0065-0241, written from September of 1916 to December of 1935, were filed under 'W' for Mrs. Grant Williams.

Letter 0242, from Ransom Williams to Charles Breasted in December of 1935, was in the Condolences file.

A few letters from the MMA's Egyptian Art Department Archives have been cited in footnotes for biographical purposes only.

Source Abbreviations
AJA: *American Journal of Archaeology*
JEA: *The Journal of Egyptian Archaeology*
MMAB: *Metropolitan Museum of Art Bulletin*
NYHSQB: *New York Historical Society Quarterly Bulletin*
NYT: *The New York Times*

*Annual Report of the President of Bryn Mawr College.* Philadelphia: John C. Winston, Co., 1908-11.

*The Assyrian Dictionary of the Oriental Institute of the University of Chicago*, Vols 1-21, eds. Martha T. Roth, et al. (Chicago: Oriental Institute Publications,

1956-2010). Available for download: https://oi.uchicago.edu/research/publications/assyrian-dictionary-oriental-institute-university-chicago-cad Accessed 22 December 2016.

'Backmatter.' *MMAB* 15:10 (1920): 239.

'Dr. Williams, Woman Distinguished as Egyptologist,' *Toledo Blade*, 3 February 1952.

*The Egyptian Coffin Texts*, Vols 1-8 (Chicago: Oriental Institute Publications, 1935-2006). Available for download: http://oi.uchicago.edu/research/publications/oriental-institute-publications-oip Accessed 22 December 2016.

'Grant Williams Taken by Death.' *Toledo Blade*, 25 December 1942, p. 18.

*The Human Adventure*. Directed by Charles Breasted. Chicago: The Oriental Institute of the University of Chicago, 1935.

'James Breasted Jr., Art Historian, Dies; Led Coast Museum.' *NYT: Obituaries*, 6 May 1983.

'Notes: The Abbott Collection of Egyptian Antiquities.' *NYHSQB* 1:1 (April 1917): 14.

*Recueil d'études égyptologiques dédiées à la mémoire de Jean-François Champollion à l'occasion du centenaire de la lettre à M. Dacier relative à l'alphabet des hiéroglyphes phonétiques, lue à l'Académie des inscriptions et belles-lettres le 27 septembre 1822* (Paris: E. Champion, 1922).

*The University of Chicago Magazine*, 14:1 (November 1921): 54.

Abt, Jeffrey. 'The Breasted-Rockefeller Egyptian Museum Project: Philanthropy, Cultural Imperialism and National Resistance.' *Art History* 19:4 (December 1996): 551-572.

------. *American Egyptologist: The Life of James Henry Breasted and The Creation of His Oriental Institute*. Chicago: University of Chicago Press, 2012.

Adams, John M. *The Millionaire and the Mummies: Theodore Davis's Gilded Age in the Valley of the Kings*. New York: St. Martin's Press, 2013.

Adler, Cyrus. 'Paul Haupt.' *Journal of the American Oriental Society* 47 (1927): 1-2.

Blackman, Aylward M. 'The Sequence of the Episodes in the Egyptian Daily Temple Liturgy.' *Journal of the Manchester Egyptian and Oriental Society* 8 (1918-19): 27-53.

Bierbrier, Morris L. *Who Was Who in Egyptology*, 4th Revised Edition. London: The Egypt Exploration Society, 2012.

Breasted, Charles. *Pioneer to the Past: The Story of James Henry Breasted, Archaeologist, Told by His Son Charles Breasted*. New York: Charles Scribner's Sons, 1943; Reprint edition, Chicago: University of Chicago Press, 2009.

Breasted, James H. *Ancient Records of Egypt: Historical Documents from the Earliest Times to the Persian Conquest, Collected, Edited, and Translated with Commentary*, 5 vol. Chicago: University of Chicago Press, 1906.

------. *Development in Religion and Thought in Ancient Egypt: Lectures Delivered on the Morse Foundation at Union Theological Seminary*. New York: Charles Scribner's Sons, 1912.

------. *Ancient Times: A History of the Early World*. Boston, Mass.: Ginn and Company, 1916.

------. 'The Edwin Smith Papyrus: An Egyptian Medical Treatise of the Seventeenth Century Before Christ.' *NYHSQB* 6:1 (April 1922): 5-31.

------. 'The Oriental Institute of the University of Chicago: A Beginning and Program.' *The American Journal of Semitic Languages and Literatures* 38:4 (July 1922): 233-328.

------. 'Book Review: 'The Art of the Ancient Craftsman in Gold, Silver, and Semi-Precious Stones: *Gold and Silver Jewelry and Related Objects (The New York Historical Society Catalogue of Egyptian Antiquities, Numbers 1-160).* Caroline Ransom Williams." *The American Journal of Semitic Languages and Literatures* 41:3 (April 1925): 200-202.

------. *The Conquest of Civilization.* New York: Harper and Brothers, 1926.

------. 'Annual address of the president of the American Historical Association, delivered at Indianapolis, December 28, 1928.' *American Historical Review* 34: 2 (January 1929): 215-36.

------. *The Edwin Smith Surgical Papyrus: Published in Facsimile and Hieroglyphic Transliteration with Translation and Commentary in Two Volumes*, Vols 1-2. Chicago: University of Chicago Press 1930.

------. *Ancient Times: A History of the Early World, Second Edition*. New York: Ginn and Company, 1935.

Binion, Samuel Augustus. *Ancient Egypt or Mizraïm. Profusely illustrated with fine engravings and colored plates by the best artists, from the works of L'Expedition de l'Egypte, Lepsius, Prisse d'Avennes, &c., &c.* New York: Henry G. Allen, 1887.

Bull, Ludlow. 'Appendix: Inscriptions at Deir el Hagar.' In *Ed Dākhleh Oasis: Journal of a Camel Trip made in 1908*, H. E. Winlock, 65-77. New York: Metropolitan Museum of Art, 1936.

Calverley, Amice M., Myrtle Broome, and Alan H. Gardiner. *The Temple of King Sethos I at Abydos, Volume I: The Chapels of Osiris, Isis and Horus*. London: Egypt Exploration Society; Chicago: University of Chicago Press, 1933.

Cantor, Geoffrey and Gowan Dawson, eds. *The Correspondence of John Tyndall, Volume I: Correspondence 1840-3*. Pittsburgh: The University of Pittsburgh Press, 2016.

Capart, Jean. *Abydos. Le Temple de Séti Ier*. Brussels: Rossignol & Van den Bril, 1912.

Cartland, Bernice M. 'Balls of Thread Wound on Pieces of Pottery,' *JFA* 5:2 (April 1918): 139 and Pl XXII.

Chabas, F. J, 'Le Calondrier de jours fastes et néfastes de l'année égyptienne.' *Bibliothèque Égyptologique* 12 (1905): 127-235.

Chanler, Beatrice. *Cleopatra's Daughter: The Queen of Mauretania*. New York: Liveright Publishing, 1934.

Chanler, Margaret. *Roman Spring: Memoirs*. Boston: Little, Brown, and Company, 1934.

Chauveau, Michel. *Egypt in the Age of Cleopatra: History and Society under the Ptolemies*. Ithaca: Cornell University Press, 2000.

Cohen, Getzel M. and Martha Sharp Joukowsky, eds. *Breaking Ground: Pioneering Women Archaeologists*. Ann Arbor: University of Michigan Press, 2004.

Coletta, Lisa, ed. *The Legacy of the Grand Tour: New Essays on Travel, Literature, and Culture*. Lanham, Md.: Rowman & Littlefield: 2015.

Dana, Richard Henry. *Two Years Before the Mast: A Personal Narrative of Life at Sea*. Original edition: New York: Harper and Brothers, 1840.

Davies, Norman de Garis. *Paintings from the Tomb of Rekh-mi-Re' at Thebes*. New York: Metropolitan Museum of Art, 1935.

Deutsches Archäologisches Institut, ed. *Antike Denkmäler, Band II*. Berlin: Verlag Georg Reimer, 1908.

Drower, Margaret. *Flinders Petrie: A Life in Archaeology*. Madison, Wisc: University of Wisconsin Press, 1985.

Ebers, George. *Papyros Ebers: Das hermetische Buch über die Arzeneimittel der alten Ägypter in hieratischer Schrift, herausgegeben mit Inhaltsangabe und Einleitung versehen von Georg Ebers, mit Hieroglyphisch-Lateinischem Glossar von Ludwig Stern, mit Unterstützung des Königlich Sächsischen Cultusministerium*. Leipzig: W. Englemann, 1875.

Elwick, James, Bernard Lightman, and Michael S. Reidy, eds. *The Correspondence of John Tyndall*. London: Pickering & Chatto, 2014; Pittsburgh: University of Pittsburgh Press, forthcoming volumes.

Emberling, Geoff, ed. *Pioneers to the Past: American Archaeologists in the Middle East, 1919-1920*, Oriental Institute Museum Publications, 30. Chicago: The Oriental Institute, 2010.

The Epigraphic Survey. *Medinet Habu, Volume I, Earlier Historical Records of Ramses III*. Chicago: University of Chicago Press, 1930.

Erman, Adolf. *Ägyptische Grammatik mit Schrifttafel, Litterature, Lesestücken un Wörterverzeichnis*, 4th ed. Berlin: Verlag Von Reuther & Reichard, 1894.

------. *Aegyptisches Glossar: Die Häufigeren Worte der Aegyptischen Sprache.* Berlin: Verlag von Reuther & Reichard, 1904.

------. *Die Hieroglyphen.* Berlin un Leipzig: G.J. Göschn'sche Verlagshandlung, 1912.

------. *Neuaegyptische Grammtik,* 2 völlig. Leipzig: W. Englemann, 1933.

------. *Die Religion der Ägypter, ihr Werden und Vergehen in vier Jahrtausenden.* Berlin: De Gruyter, 1934.

Erman, Adolf and Hermann Grapow, eds. *Wörterbuch der ägyptischen Sprache.* Berlin: Akademie-Verlag, 1926-1961.

Fitz-Randolph, Louise. 'History of the Department.' *Mount Holyoke Alumnae Quarterly* (January 1918): 197-202.

Fowler, Harold North and James Rignall Wheeler. *A Handbook of Greek Archaeology.* New York: American Book Company, 1909.

Gardiner, Alan H. and Arthur Weigall. *A Topographical Catalogue of the Private Tombs of Thebes.* London: Bernard Quaritch, 1913.

Gardiner, Alan H. *Egyptian Grammar: Being an Introduction to the Study of Hieroglyphs.* Oxford: Clarendon Press, 1927.

------. *The Library of A. Chester Beatty: Description of a Hieratic Papyrus with a Mythological Story, Love-songs and Other Miscellaneous Texts, The Chester Beatty Papyri, No. I.* Oxford: Oxford University Press, 1931.

Gray, Christopher. 'Streetscapes: The Beresford, the San Remo, the Majestic, the El Dorado, the Century; Namesake Precursors of Central Park West's Towers.' *NYT* 14 September 1997.

Goodspeed, Edgar J. 'Greek Documents in the Museum of the New York Historical Society.' In *Mélanges Nicole: recueil de mémoires de philology classique et d'archéologie offerts à Jules Nicole à l'occasion de 30e anniversaire de son professorat,* 177-91. Geneva: Imprimerie W. Kündig & Fils, 1905.

Higley, Mary C. J., ed. *One Hundred Year Biographical Dictionary of Mount Holyoke College, 1837-1937. Bulletin Series 30, No. 5.* South Hadley, Mass.: Alumnae Association of Mount Holyoke College, 1937.

Hölscher, Uvo. *The Excavation of Medinet Habu, Volume 1: General Plans and Views.* Chicago, University of Chicago Press, 1934.

Hussey, Mary I. 'Babylonian Tablets.' *Mount Holyoke Alumnae Quarterly* (January 1918): 211-16.

Junker, Hermann. *Grammatik der Denderatexte.* Leipzig: J. C. Hinrichs'sche Buchhandlung, 1906.

------. *Gîza I. Band I: Die Mastabas der IV. Dynastie auf dem Westfriedhof.* Wien und Leipzig: Hölder-Pichler-Tempsky A.-G., 1929.

------. *Giza II: Die Mastabas der beginnenden V. Dynastie auf dem Westfriedhof.* Vienna and Leipzig: Hölder-Pichler-Tempsky, 1934.

Kemp, Martin, ed. *The Oxford History of Western Art*. Oxford: Oxford University Press, 2000.

Klebs, Luise. *Die Reliefs des alten Reiches*. Heidelberg: Carl Winters Universitätsbuchhandlung, 1915.

------. „Die Tiefendimension in der Zeichnung des alten Reiches.' *Zeitschrift für Ägyptische Sprache und Altertumskude* 52:1 (December 1915): 19-34.

------. *Reliefs und Malereien des Mittleren Reiches*. Heidelberg: Carl Winters Universitätsbuchhandlung, 1921.

------. *Die Reliefs und Malereien des neuen Reiches*. Heidelberg: Carl Winters Universitätsbuchhandlung, 1934.

Larson, John. 'Joseph Smith and Egyptology: An Early Episode in the History of American Speculation about Ancient Egypt, 1835-1844.' In *For His Ka: Essays Offered in Memory of Klaus Baer*, ed. David Silverman, 159-78. Chicago: Oriental Institute, 1994.

Leach, Eleanor Winsor. 'Mary Hamilton Swindler.' In *Breaking Ground: Women in Old World Archaeology*, http://www.brown.edu/Research/Breaking_Ground/bios/Swindler_Mary%20Hamilton.pdf

Lepsius, Richard. *Das Todtenbuch der Ägypter nach dem Hieroglyphischen Papyrus in Turin*. Leipzig: bei Georg Wigand, 1842.

Lesko, Barbara S. 'Caroline Louis Ransom Williams, 1872-1952.' In *Breaking Ground: Women in Old World Archaeology*, http://www.brown.edu/Research/Breaking_Ground/bios/Ransom%20Williams_Caroline%20Louise.pdf

Lesko, Barbara S. 'Bertha Porter (1852-1941) and Rosalind Moss (1890-1990).' In *Breaking Ground: Women in Old World Archaeology*, http://www.brown.edu/Research/Breaking_Ground/bios/Porter_Bertha.pdf

Lewis, Ethel. 'Library on Egyptology Bares Secrets of Ancient Pharaohs in Toledo Home: Mrs. Grant Williams Has Noted Collection for Her Study.' [Chicago] *Times*, 21 May 1933.

Lloyd, Alan B. 'The Late Period.' In *Ancient Egypt: A Social History*, ed. B. G. Trigger, B. J. Kemp, D. O'Connor and A. B. Lloyd, 279-348. Cambridge: Cambridge University Press, 1999.

Lythgoe, Albert M. 'Recent Egyptian Acquisitions.' *MMAB* 2:12 (December 1907): 193-94.

Mariette, Auguste. *Abydos, Description des Fouilles, Exécutées sur l'Emplacement de Cette Ville, Tome Premier*. Paris: Librairie A. Franck, 1869.

Marino, Elisabetta. 'Three British Women Travelers in Egypt: Sophia Lane Poole, Lucie Duff Gordon, and Emmeline Lott.' In *The Legacy of the Grand Tour: New Essays on Travel, Literature, and Culture*, ed. Lisa Coletta, 51-70. Lanham, Md.: Rowman & Littlefield: 2015.

Maspero, Gaston. *Manual of Egyptian Archaeology: Guide to the Study of Antiquities in Egypt. For the Use of Students and Travellers*, New Edition. Transl. Amelia Edwards. New York: G. P. Putnam, 1895.

Maspero, Gaston. *Art in Egypt* New York: Charles Scribner's Sons, 1912.

Maynard, John A. 'In Memoriam: A Bibliography of D. D. Luckenbill.' *The American Journal of Semitic Languages and Literatures* 45:2 (January 1929): 90-93.

Mellink, Machteld J. 'Mary Hamilton Swindler, January 1, 1884-January 16, 1967.' *Expedition: The Bulletin of the University Museum of the University of Pennsylvania* (Spring 1967): 19.

Ministère de l'éducation nationale. *Melanges Maspero: Volume I: Orient Ancien.* Le Caire: Imprimerie de l'Institut Français d'Archéologie Oriental, 1934.

Moret, Alesandre. *Histoire de l'Orient.* G. Glotz: 1929-1930.

Patrick, Mary Mills. *Under Five Sultans.* New York: The Century Co., 1929.

Pratt, Ida A. 'Ancient Egypt: A List of References to Material in the New York Public Library.' Foreword by Richard Gottheil. *Bulletin of the New York Public Library* 27:9 (September 1923): 723-66.

Porceddu, Sebastian, Lauri Jetsu, Tapio Markkanen, and Jaana Toivari-Viitala. 'Evidence of Periodicity in Ancient Egyptian Calendars of Luck and Unlucky Days.' *Cambridge Archaeological Journal* 18:3 (2008): 327-39.

Porter, Bertha and Rosalind Moss. *Topographical Bibliography of Ancient Egyptian Hieroglyphic Texts*, 6 Vols. Oxford: Clarendon Press, 1927-1939.

Ranke, Hermann. 'The Origin of the Egyptian Tomb Statue.' *The Harvard Theological Review* 28:1 (January 1935): 45-53.

Ransom, Caroline L. *Studies in Ancient Furniture: Couches and Beds of the Greeks, Etruscans and Romans.* Chicago: University of Chicago Press, 1905.

------. *A Handbook of the Egyptian Rooms, Metropolitan Museum of Art.* New York: MMA, 1911.

------. 'The Value of Photographs and Transparencies as Adjuncts to Museum Exhibits.' *MMAB* 7:7 (July 1912): 132-34.

------. 'Egyptian Furniture and Musical Instruments.' *MMAB* 8:4 (April 1913): 72-79.

------. 'A Model of the Mastaba-Tomb of Userkaf-Ankh.' *MMAB* 8:6 (June 1913): 125-130.

------. 'Nubian Objects Acquired by the Egyptian Department.' *MMAB* 8:9 (September 1913): 200-208.

------. 'The Stela of Menthu-Weser' *MMAB* 8:10 (October 1913): 213, 216-18.

------. *The Stela of Menthu-Weser.* New York: MMA, 1913.

------. 'A Late Egyptian Sarcophagus.' *MMAB* 9:5 (May 1914): 112-120.

------. 'Pots with Hieratic Inscriptions.' *MMAB* 9:11 (November 1914): 236-243.

------. 'A Commemorative Scarab of Thutmose III.' *MMAB* 10:3 (March 1915): 46-47.

------, 'Heart Scarab of Queen Amenardis.' *MMAB* 10:6 (June 1915): 116-117.

------. *The Tomb of Perneb: With Illustrations*. New York: MMA, 1916.

Ransom Williams, Caroline. 'The Abbott Collection.' *NYHSQB* 1:2 (July 1917): 34-37.

------. 'The Egyptian Ushebtis Belonging to the New-York Historical Society.' *NYHSQB* 1:4 (January 1918): 91-102.

------. 'Some Bronze Statuettes in the Abbott Collection,' *NYHSQB* 2 (July 1918): 43-53.

------. 'The Egyptian Collection in the Museum of Art at Cleveland Ohio.' *JEA* 5:3 (1918): 166-178.

------. 'The Egyptian Collection in the Museum of Art at Cleveland Ohio (Continued).' *JEA* 5:4 (1918): 272-85.

------. 'Wooden Statuettes of Gods in the Abbott Collection.' *NYHSQB* 2:3 (October 1918): 75-88.

------. 'Stela of a High-Priest of Memphis.' *Bulletin of the Cleveland Museum of Art* 5:8-9 (October-November 1918): 67-69.

------. 'The Place of the New York Historical Society in the Growth of American Interest in Egyptology.' *NYHSQB* 4:1 (April 1920): 3-20.

------. *The New York Historical Society Catalogue of Egyptian Antiquities, Numbers 1-160: Gold and Silver Jewelry and Related Objects*. New York: NYHS, 1924.

------. 'A Plea for Tell el-'Amarna.' *Egypt Exploration Society American Branch*, 1927.

------. 'Wall Decorations of the Main Temple of the Sun at El-Amarneh.' *Metropolitan Museum Studies* 2:2 (May 1930): 135-51.

------. 'Two Egyptian Torsos from the Main Temple of the Sun at El 'Amarneh,' *Metropolitan Museum Studies* 3:1 (December 1930): 81-99.

------. 'An Egyptian Limestone Head.' *Toledo Museum of Art Museum News* 60 (June 1931): 2.

------. *The Decoration of the Tomb of Per-Neb: The Technique and the Color Conventions*. New York: MMA, 1932.

------. 'Reviewed Work: *The Temple of King Sethos I at Abydos (Volume I, The Chapels of Osiris, Isis, and Horus.)* by Amice M. Calverley, Myrtle F. Broome, Alan Gardiner.' *The American Magazine of Art* 27:8 (August 1934): 444-46.

------. 'Review: *The Temple of King Sethos I at Abydos, Vol. I: The Chapels of Osiris, Isis, and Horus* by Alan H. Gardiner.' *AJA*, 39:2 (Apr.-Jun. 1935): 273-78.

Wosk, Julie. *Women and the Machine: Representations from the Spinning Wheel to the Electronic Age.* Baltimore: Johns Hopkins University Press, 2001.

# Character index

There are a number of characters mentioned in the letters between Ransom Williams and Breasted. Except for the two of them, Frances Breasted who is mentioned in almost every letter, and Grant Williams who is mentioned in almost every letter from 1916 on, here is a reference to the letters in which the people are mentioned by name. For further biographical information, there are footnotes after the first appearance of each person's name in the main text, respectively.

# Index